Michael Norman

Haunted Heartland

Second Edition

The University of Wisconsin Press

The University of Wisconsin Press
1930 Monroe Street, 3rd Floor
Madison, Wisconsin 53711-2059
uwpress.wisc.edu

3 Henrietta Street, Covent Garden
London WC2E 8LU, United Kingdom
eurospanbookstore.com

Haunted Heartland was first published in 1985 in a hardcover edition by Stanton and Lee, and then in a 1986 mass-market paperback edition by Warner Books. Barnes and Noble Books reprinted the book in hardcover in 1992.

Printed in the United States of America

This book may be available in a digital edition.

Library of Congress Cataloging-in-Publication Data

Names: Norman, Michael, 1947 June 29- author.
Title: Haunted heartland / Michael Norman.
Description: Second edition. | Madison, Wisconsin: The University of Wisconsin Press, [2017]
| Original edition published in 1985 by Beth Scott and Michael Norman.
| Includes bibliographical references.
Identifiers: LCCN 2017010433 | ISBN 9780299315146 (pbk.: alk. paper)
Subjects: LCSH: Ghosts—Middle West. | Parapsychology—Middle West.
Classification: LCC BF1472.U6 S36 2017 | DDC 133.10977—dc23
LC record available at https://lccn.loc.gov/2017010433

Some stories in this book were previously published, in different form, in *Haunted America, Historic Haunted America, Haunted Heritage, Haunted Homeland,* and *The Nearly Departed: Minnesota Ghost Stories and Legends.*

In some stories, names and locations were changed to protect the identities of those involved. Some scenes have been added for continuity or dramatic interest. These *are ghost stories*, after all. And ghosts are notorious for not leaving behind traces of their comings and goings.

Haunted Heartland

To the memory of

Beth Scott,

my coauthor for the first edition.

Contents

Illinois

Indiana

Contents

Iowa

Kansas

Michigan

Contents

Minnesota

Missouri

Nebraska

Contents

Ohio

Wisconsin

Preface to the Second Edition

Incomprehensible? But because you cannot understand a thing, it does not cease to exist.

Blaise Pascal (1670)

The oldest and strongest emotion of mankind is fear, and the oldest kind of fear is fear of the unknown.

H. P. Lovecraft

We—or our primitive forefathers—once believed that the return of the dead, unseen forces, and secret injurious powers were realities, and were convinced that they actually happened. Nowadays we no longer believe in them. We have surmounted those modes of thought; but we do not feel quite sure of our new beliefs, and the old ones still exist within us ready to seize upon any confirmation.

Sigmund Freud

With those quotations from a seventeenth-century scientist/philosopher, a notable author of fantasy and science fiction, and a pioneering psychiatrist, my late coauthor Beth Scott and I began the preface to the original 1985 edition of *Haunted Heartland*. Now, more than thirty years later, I find myself revisiting those ideas and more as I prepare this second, revised edition. (Note: My friend and colleague Beth Scott passed away in 1994.)

Haunted Heartland was a follow-up of sorts to our *Haunted Wisconsin*, the first book devoted solely to ghost stories from that state. After its publication, we expanded our research into ghost stories and legends in the rest of the Midwest. *Haunted Heartland* brought together stories from Illinois, Indiana, Iowa, Kansas, Michigan, Minnesota, Missouri, Nebraska, Ohio, and Wisconsin. It, too, was a first-time collection of regionally based stories of the supernatural that had arisen not from an author's imagination but rather from purportedly "true" events involving ghosts and hauntings, possessions and exorcisms, bobbing mystery lights, and more. Some of the stories fit within the parameters of folklore while others involved experiences from contemporary individuals who said they had seen a ghost or had another kind of paranormal encounter. But whether called folklore, "psychic experiences," or something else, we wanted to find out just how prevalent ghost stories might be. Over five years of research and writing went into the original *Haunted Heartland*.

Many of the people and episodes within these pages appear out of step with the world around them, with what we believe to be reality. From a haunted mansion in Ohio to a college office in Nebraska lost in time, and from a peculiar incident at a highway intersection in Minnesota to ancient specters that wander the Ozark hills, incidents of the supernatural in the Midwest might occur anywhere—urban or rural, based on what I have found over the years. This book explores a world unknown to most of us, yet quite obvious to others. Those were the people willing to share their contemporary experiences. Sometimes the ghost or haunted place has become at least locally famous, embedded in local lore. The ghost of Resurrection Mary roaming Archer Avenue in southwest suburban Chicago is an example of that, a fleeting figure in a white party dress who is so well known she has had a song written about her.

The line between legend and reality in these stories is imprecise at times. Many are more clearly rooted in the storytelling traditions of a particular community or locale. In the Ozarks, for example, many "true" ghost stories have been told and retold so many times—each recitation adding its own twists and turns—that it is hard to know for certain where, when, or how each story originated. Other stories in this book fit within the sometimes controversial study of parapsychology, dealing as they do with people who say they have experienced perplexing encounters that are supernatural in origin.

Are these stories "true" then in the strictest sense of the word? How does one prove the existence of ghosts? I do not think it can be done so that skeptic and believer alike are satisfied. And besides, that is not the ultimate intention of *Haunted Heartland*. This is neither an academic text nor a how-to manual for ghost hunting. What matters most is that these ghost stories are *told* as true. Even if they occur within a region's folklore traditions, they seem to have originated with some sort of supportable event: a death, for instance, that leads to the sighting of a ghost believed to be the deceased, as in "The Girl on Sheridan Road" from Illinois. Most often for a contemporary story to be included in this collection there was an individual (or individuals) who either personally experienced the event or learned of the facts through some other direct means. Sometimes material developed by other writers and researchers has been incorporated into the narratives. The bibliography and acknowledgments cite those sources.

The stories in this book include most of the original material from the first edition. I have included new or updated information where it was available and relevant. Be aware, however, that circumstances involving a particular site or story may have changed after this book's publication date. Nearly all of the stories have been revised, and there are stories new to this edition. All come from remote and diverse sources. Many leads originated in archival and on-site research for the original edition, while other, primarily contemporary accounts were collected through interviews with the subjects involved, witnesses, or other knowledgeable people, along with written archival documentation that bear on the particular story.

However, in compiling the original edition of *Haunted Heartland*— and in my revisions for this 2017 edition—we (or I in this edition) did not include every potential ghost story. There were several reasons for this.

First is the sheer number of Midwest/Heartland ghost stories out there. I do not know of any methodology for counting ghosts (a census might be awkward) or for declaring this state or that is the most haunted, but I can verify that the Midwest as a region seems filled with spectral beings of one type or another, if one is to believe even a fraction of the tales and experiences that served as source material. I have found hundreds of stories, tales, or instances of ghosts all around the Midwest, enough to fill stacks of archival boxes. I found that amazing, given the region's tranquil reputation. One does not need to visit an abandoned Southern plantation or decrepit inn along Maine's foggy coast to find ghosts and ghost stories. One need only look around communities from one end of the Midwest to another. It is the rare newspaper indeed that does not dig into a community's haunted history for a Halloween feature. Internet sites are devoted to ghostly sightings and haunted places, thousands of them, in every state of the Union. There are even smartphone apps that provide interactive directions to haunted locations.

Yet at the same time, it seems to me, good old-fashioned ghost story-*telling*, the kind found around a summertime campfire late at night, seems to be dying out. What we have instead are film and television programs and websites with lots of spooky effects but varying degrees of authenticity. Resurrection Mary herself might have a lonely stroll indeed with all her potential prey safely tucked away inside their homes watching as her story unfolds in high definition.

A story might not have been included for other reasons: not enough could be found about the original event or it was too thinly vetted to use or suspect in some other way, perhaps even an outright fabrication, though that was unusual.

Finally, I wanted to avoid too much duplication, to include only those tales that were unique in some way, that did not replicate another story. For instance, there are mysterious female phantoms in black or white dresses that roam American roadways of towns large and small long after dark only to suddenly appear in a driver's headlight beam or accost an innocent pedestrian. Many continued their rounds into the twenty-first century; others seem confined to decades past. One Missouri tale arises from shortly after the Civil War. Their behavior is oddly repetitious despite their broad geographical distribution. I have included just a few of the most interesting ones here.

These were not hard and fast rules but generally guided how material was selected for inclusion in both the first and second editions.

Haunted Heartland is not an encyclopedia of Midwestern ghost lore—that would take a lifetime to complete—but rather represents a selection of what I think are intriguing stories that fairly typify the ghost stories found in the ten states represented here. I included stories from other Midwest states in my books *Haunted America, Historic Haunted America,* and others.

Finally, let me be clear: I do not profess to be a parapsychologist or a ghost hunter (I hunt ghost *stories*); nor, as I wrote earlier, does this purport to be a how-to manual on finding a ghost in your own home, or purging it from, say, your attic. All these stories are told from a distance. I am an author dealing with what I believe to be an interesting subject. I hope you find the topic interesting as well. These "true tales of the supernatural" imaginatively told are offered for what they are, a bit of entertainment, a slight detour, if you will, as you speed your way through the "real" world.

Both editions of *Haunted Heartland* could not have been written without the assistance and contributions of many people. Foremost I want to express my limitless gratitude to my colleague Mark Lefebvre, who shepherded the original *Haunted Heartland* into print three decades ago and has continued to be my professional mentor, advisor, and treasured friend. Without him I would not be here. Also, my deep gratitude to Elizabeth Lefebvre, a computer and design genius, who unlocked the secrets of all the software I had to use to prepare this new edition. I am deeply appreciative to Raphael Kadushin, executive editor of the University of Wisconsin Press, for his priceless support and to the press staff as the second edition moved, sometimes haltingly, from idea to publication. Every staff member at the UW Press has been kind and helpful, but I am especially grateful to the support and helpfulness of senior editor Sheila McMahon and my exceptional copyeditor Michelle Wing. Also thanks to our original Stanton & Lee editors Doug Bradley, Meg Saart, and Betty Durbin.

In addition to the bibliographic citations you will find at the end of the book, I want to express my gratitude to the following individuals and institutions that provided support and information or who answered my many questions: *Firehouse Magazine*; the late Mary Margaret Fuller, *Fate Magazine*; Laurel G. Bowen, Illinois State Historical Society, Springfield; Fiora Fuhrmann, Lake Zurich, Illinois; the Chicago Historical Society; the late Edith T. Piercy, *Rockford Register Star*, Rockford, Illinois; E. G. Brady Jr., *Commercial Appeal*, Memphis, Tennessee; Cathy Hess, *Indianapolis Star News*; Patricia A. Harris, Michigan City Historical Society, Indiana; the Old Lighthouse Museum, Michigan City, Indiana; Dorothy Rowley and staff, LaPorte County Historical Society, Indiana; Tina Bucuvalas, formerly with the Folklore Institute, Indiana University, Bloomington, and staff; Eric Pumroy, Director of Library Collections, Bryn Mawr College, formerly Indiana Historical Society Library, Indianapolis; Robert K. O'Neill, Boston

College; Ronald L. Baker, Indiana State University, Terre Haute; Deborah Griesinger, Mathias Ham House Historic Site, Dubuque County Historical Society, Dubuque, Iowa; the late Lowell R. Wilbur, Iowa Department of History and Archives, Des Moines; Jane Norman, Washington, DC; the late William E. Koch, Kansas State University, Manhattan; Jane Abernathy, Topeka, Kansas; the late Kay Tice, Greeley County Library, Tribune, Kansas; the late John Cumming, Clarke Historical Library, Central Michigan University, Mount Pleasant; Philip LaRonge, Wayne State University, Detroit; the late Paul Sporn, Wayne State University; Janet L. Langlois, the Folklore Archive, Wayne State University; the late Elizabeth Bright, Iron Range Research Center, Chisholm, Minnesota; Dorothy M. Murke, Minneapolis History Collection, Minneapolis Public Library and Information Center; Hazel H. Wahlberg, Roseau County Historical Society and Museum, Minnesota; Sandra Peddie, formerly of the *St. Paul Pioneer Press*; Nancy Bagshaw-Reasoner, St. Paul; Stan Sauder, Pine Island, Minnesota; Jude Martin, Tom Campbell, Richard Rewey, and staff, the Fitzgerald Theater, St. Paul; the late Jack LaZebnik, Stephens College, Columbia, Missouri; Mrs. Ellis (Hester) Jackson, Webster County Historical Society, Marshfield, Missouri; Dr. Thomas P. Sweeney, Springfield, Missouri; the late Si Colborn, *Monroe County Appeal*, Paris, Missouri; Janet C. Lu, Roger Cognard, and the late David Mickey and Karen Cook, all of Nebraska Wesleyan University, Lincoln; Anne P. Diffendal, Nebraska State Historical Society, Lincoln; Robert B. Smith, *Ohio Magazine*, Columbus; Jannette K. Hemsworth, Alumni Office, Denison University, Granville, Ohio; James L. Murphy, the Ohio Historical Society, Columbus; the family of David K. Webb; the late Nancy Steen, Bowling Green State University, Ohio; Great Lakes Historical Society, Vermillion, Ohio; Cleveland Public Library; Richard W. Heiden, Milwaukee, Wisconsin; Michael Kluever, Wausau, Wisconsin; Sue Kurth, former reporter, *Beloit Daily News*, Wisconsin; staff, Big Foot Beach State Park, Lake Geneva, Wisconsin; the late Tom Hollatz, *Lakeland Times*, Minocqua, Wisconsin; Tim Ericson, retired professor and archivist, University of Wisconsin–Milwaukee; the late Mary Abdoo, Mineral Point, Wisconsin; and Linda Sterling.

Many of these individuals provided assistance during the writing of the first edition of *Haunted Heartland* and thus their current affiliations may have changed. Any error or omission in the names and institutions is unintended and accidental and will be corrected in future editions if it is brought to the author's attention. I extend my deepest gratitude for the assistance all have provided with both editions of *Haunted Heartland*.

MICHAEL NORMAN

May 2017

Haunted Heartland

Illinois

The Girl on Sheridan Road

Lake Forest

Sensational so-called trials of the century probably began in 1901 with the trial and conviction of Leon Czolgosz for the assassination of President William McKinley. Since then, there have been many other American trials that have captured the imagination of millions of readers all over the world, but none of them have the startling legacy that a century-old Lake County, Illinois, murder trial might have: most certainly the trial attracted intense and sensational newspaper coverage from coast to coast, but there is something else that makes it stand out from all others—the young female victim may haunt a section of Sheridan Road in Lake Forest not far from where she died.

The 1916 trial of William Orpet in Waukegan on charges of first-degree, capital murder had all the lurid details the sensationalist press of the period loved to splash across its front pages: A handsome defendant in young William, a University of Wisconsin college student from Lake Forest. A young and lovely victim, Marion Lambert, a high school senior also from Lake Forest and William's former girlfriend. And most horrific of all, death came by cyanide poisoning either ingested by the victim or forcibly meted out by the killer. When her body was found, her lips and mouth were black and blistered as if from acid burns. Her death spasms would have been horrifyingly painful to endure.

All the crime details were wrapped in the surprising location: the quiet, wealthy community of Lake Forest along the Lake Michigan shoreline north of Chicago. Murders of any sort rarely, if ever, took place there, and certainly none in memory connected to the multimillion-dollar estates of the influential families who lived in the area. The fathers of both William and Marion worked for two of them. His father's employer, Cyrus McCormick Jr., son of the founder of International Harvester, hired William's elite team of defense attorneys. Chicago clothing magnate Jonas Kuppenheimer employed Marion's father.

The young man's life was on the line. The capital murder charge meant a guilty verdict would send him to the gallows. The Lake County prosecutor promised that the sentence would be carried out.

Newspapers from coast to coast ran lurid stories with all the juicy details unfolding in the Waukegan courtroom along the shore of Lake Michigan. Readers loved stories about the sins and foibles of the rich and famous.

But the contemporary twist of this tragic tale is unique. The story of the phantom girl on Sheridan Road has been told now for some time. Witnesses have reported a sudden, disturbing appearance by a diaphanous, barefoot specter with short, brown, curly hair dressed in a long, blue dress along Sheridan Road, not far from where Marion Lambert's body was found a century ago. That area was known then as Helms Woods, south of the former Barat College, now part of the Villa Turicum subdivision.

The details of the sightings are similar, including one from a woman who spoke to a Chicago newspaper reporter. Her car's headlights picked out the woman's figure along the side of the roadway; she slowed down, thinking perhaps it was an accident victim, someone in distress. She picked up her cell phone to call for help. Yet something was wrong here. The driver could see right through the woman. Her dress was muddy along the hem. Most disturbingly of all, perhaps, was that the specter smiled, revealing a mouth rimmed by burned and blackened lips and rotting teeth.

The tragic story of young William Orpet and Marion Lambert begins on those wealthy Lake Forest estates. William's father, Edward, worked for the McCormicks as chief caretaker and groundsman, while Marion's father, Frank, was head gardener for the Kuppenheimers. Both families lived in homes on the estates and would likely have known one another; one source notes both fathers were members of the North Shore Horticultural Society.

Marion's parents doted on her as an only child. Growing up, she was described as an outgoing and vivacious girl with lots of friends and an active social life. Her minister said she was the happiest member of his congregation. Contemporary photographs depict a strikingly attractive young woman with short, dark, curly hair gazing pensively and slightly away from the camera, though in another photograph her broad smile reveals a more mischievous side.

William was three years older than Marion. Both attended Deerfield-Shields High School. Although the two may have known each other growing up, it seems they did not begin a serious relationship until sometime later in high school, probably during the spring of her junior year, when William was already attending the University of Wisconsin in Madison as a journalism major.

Having William Orpet as her beau would certainly have made Marion the envy of her girlfriends. He was, to use the parlance of the time, a "dreamboat." A photograph taken of him during the trial depicts a handsome, serious young man sitting comfortably in front of a shelf of law books. He has on a smart, three-piece wool suit (Kuppenheimer's?) with cuff-linked sleeves. He has a smooth face, an aquiline nose, penetrating brown eyes, and dark, stylishly cut hair with a slightly off-center part.

William wrote to Marion often from college. Witty and light in the beginning, his words soon took a more intense, romantic tone. In one that was used as evidence at trial and quoted often, he wrote: "I want to see you, dearest, and want you badly. If I could only get my arm around you now, and get up close to you and kiss the life out of you, I would be happy." She was still a junior in high school.

All through the spring and summer, William kept after her, even going so far as to press his romantic intentions on her in public during parties. This was still a time when young women were expected to behave "properly." That expectation no doubt conflicted with her desire not to lose him. Give in or continue to play hard to get?

Sometime in late September 1915, William was home from college and asked Marion to go for a drive with him. They ended up at Helms Woods, near the Sacred Heart Convent. He asked her if she would like to go for a walk. Yes, she said. Their stroll ended and they made love in a small clearing where three oaks grew quite close together.

No one knows of course what exact words were exchanged between the young lovers, but it is apparent by the couple's later behavior that Marion thought their lovemaking meant she could look forward to a wedding in the near future. William did not see it that way. It was all about his sexual gratification; she was a fling that he had been angling for since they started dating.

William returned to Madison and his college studies. His letters became infrequent and perfunctory, and he claimed he could not visit her again anytime soon because his college work kept him on campus. What he did not tell her is that he had started dating other women, including a high school chemistry teacher he thought he might want to marry.

He tried to break it off with Marion, thinking, perhaps rightly, that she was trying to snare him into marriage. She resisted his entreaties.

In November 1915 she upped the ante. She wrote William that she might be pregnant. He did not believe her. They had sex only that once and he used a condom. But just in case, he got a pharmacist friend to concoct a potion that would terminate a pregnancy and sent it to her. It is not known if she drank it or if, by this time, she knew that she was not pregnant. Her autopsy confirmed she was not.

Marion Lambert turned eighteen on February 6, 1916, with a big celebration. Two days later, while her best friend Josephine Davis was visiting, she got a telephone call from William. They spoke for only a few minutes out of earshot of Josephine. At the trial her testimony was that Marion appeared troubled when she came back in the room. Josephine later admitted that Marion confided in her, "If Will throws me over and marries that other girl, I'll kill myself."

That is quite an emotional distance from the cheerful high school senior looking forward to college that her friends, family, and minister described.

On the very cold morning of Wednesday, February 9, 1916, Marion, wearing her favorite green coat, walked as usual with her friend Josephine to the Sacred Heart station of the North Shore interurban line, where they would catch the train to their high school in Highland Park. But oddly, at the last minute, Marion begged off. She had forgotten she had to mail a letter. She would catch the next train.

Only one person may have ever seen her again—whoever was with her when she died.

Frank Lambert showed up at the Sacred Heart station a little before eight that night to pick up his daughter. She had told her parents there was a party she would like to attend after school and they gave their permission. The 8:05 train arrived and disgorged a few passengers, but not Marion. Other trains arrived, stopped for a few minutes, and left over the next hour, but none with Marion. At last Frank went to Highland Park, where he discovered that his daughter had not been at the party; neither had she been at school that day.

Distraught and feeling helpless, Frank Lambert went home, where he told his wife that Marion was missing. The couple put a lamp in the window, hoping that in some way it would help light her way home.

The couple spent a sleepless night. When there was still no sign of Marion as dawn approached, her father raced back to the Sacred Heart train station. He would start a search from the last place he was certain Marion had been. Striking stick matches to illuminate his way, he was able to see two sets of footprints leading from the station off into Helms Woods. He decided to wait until the sun was up to continue the search and left for a friend's house not far away. The men returned in full light and set off to follow the footprints, noticing immediately that one set was significantly larger than the other.

The pair of footprints meandered through the woods until they neared a small clearing. Frank Lambert noticed a splash of green on the snow beneath three bare oak trees. He broke into a run and found what he had dreaded he might—the lifeless, frozen body of his daughter, Marion. Her left arm lay frozen at an angle, her schoolbooks still held in the crook. The palm of her bare right hand held what appeared to be a trace of a white, powdery substance. Her face was a dreadful sight. Her mouth was blistered and charred black as if burned by acid.

The coroner's office wasted little time in performing the autopsy, which was completed by midnight. Marion's death came as a result of consuming a cyanide and acid mixture, accounting for her burmed, blistered lips and the powdery residue on her hand.

The Lake County state's attorney, Ralph Dady, a man one reporter later said had a Lincolnesque bearing, spoke to the growing crowd of reporters in the early morning hours of February 11, 1916. He said that while they were confident Marion was poisoned, they did not know if she committed suicide or if a person or persons unknown forced it on her. However, Dady was certain a man was with her, and when they found that person, they believed the motive would be explained.

William Orpet promptly became the focus of the authorities' attention following interviews with Marion's family and friends. Josephine told them about his call on February 8.

He was at school in Madison when first a reporter and then the police tracked him down. He expressed surprise and sorrow at the news of Marion's death. Yes, he confirmed, they had dated, but it was not serious; he had not even seen her recently. But yes he had sent her a letter wishing her luck on her exams.

William's story quickly unraveled. True, he had mailed her a letter (which police found still at the post office), but searches of Marion's bedroom found other letters from him, making it abundantly clear that their affair had been a serious one and that she feared she was pregnant.

In one letter, he had written: "I'll try to get down to see you, probably the ninth of February, and will call you up the evening of the eighth. Remember the dates. If everything is not all right by the time I see you, it will be, leave it to me."

What else could he have been alluding to except the unwanted pregnancy that somehow he would make "all right" if it was still an issue when he came down to see her? That was enough for the prosecutor. William had been lying about his whereabouts and about his relationship with Marion Lambert, of that he was certain.

William Opet was arrested in Madison and questioned. Later, he was brought back to Lake Forest, where he was made to walk the route from the train platform to the clearing where Marion's body was found.

His answers were a series of falsehoods; in the end he admitted that he had been with Marion the morning of her death but he denied all else. Yes, they had dated, but not any longer; he had been trying to break up with her, thus his letter setting up the rendezvous. He had called her when he got to the train station on February 8, but she could not get away. They agreed to meet the next morning. He spent that night in a greenhouse on the McCormick estate. He had agreed to see her because she was threatening to kill herself if he did not come down. He kept the trip secret and his whereabouts hidden because he did not want his parents to know.

William said he and Marion had met at the station and gone for a walk. He told her he planned to marry someone else. She pleaded with him, but he was steadfast in refusing her entreaties. He left her in that clearing beneath the oak trees. He heard her sobs but did not turn back, even when she called out to him. The next thing he heard was a scream. He saw her in the snow, her body writhing and wracked with spasms. She died within seconds. He went back to the train station and returned to Madison.

Prosecutor Ralph Dady did not believe a word of it.

William had gone to great lengths to hide his trip—he did not make his bed when he left Madison to make it look like he had slept in it; he asked a friend to post some letters from him; he even wore a friend's overcoat to disguise his appearance.

Worst of all for William was that a police search of the McCormick estate, where his father worked, uncovered lumps of cyanide. Dady described the haul as enough cyanide to "kill a whole high school of girls."

William was arrested and put in a small cell of the central Waukegan jail. Three weeks later he was indicted by a grand jury on charges of first-degree murder. A guilty verdict meant the noose.

The case had received such frenzied coverage by the Chicago and national press right from the moment Marion's body was discovered that it became clear early on that the trial itself would attract enormous attention. Both the prosecution and the defense boasted well-known attorneys.

Over twelve-hundred men (no women served on juries at that time) were questioned over twenty-three days before a panel of jurors was seated. The lengthy jury selection process was an indication that most county residents thought William guilty. The trial began on May 15, Judge Charles Donnelly presiding. It would last nearly two months.

Dady thought his case was strong, especially with the discovery of cyanide where William Orpet could have had access to it. But his solid wall of evidence soon started showing cracks. Josephine Davis changed her story, probably so she would not have to lie under oath. She tried to describe her friend as happy and optimistic but eventually confessed that Marion had been depressed that William might leave her and spoke of suicide.

The defense found a classmate who said he had seen Marion alone in a chemistry lab not long before, a lab in which cyanide was stored.

Although Marion's parents and other friends testified to her positive frame of mind, Dady knew he had to get William on the stand and under oath to save the prosecution's argument. He put the defendant on the stand for hours upon hours over four days in that sweltering hot courtroom.

In the end all he could get was a young man who admitted to all sorts of rotten character traits—coward, liar, seducer, modern-day Lothario—but steadfastly claimed he was not a murderer. Marion Lambert committed suicide, he said. He was there; he heard her screams of agony as he walked away but did nothing about it. He was a coward as well, leaving her body in the cold, winter woods without the common decency to call for help.

But what clinched it for the defense was the testimony of several chemists that the cyanide Marion had ingested was potassium cyanide, the type found in her high school chemistry lab, and not sodium cyanide, the type for killing rodents found on the McCormick estate.

On July 16, 1916, the jury took just five hours to acquit William Orpet of killing Marion Lambert. They concluded there was enough evidence to suggest she had committed suicide.

Despite William Orpet's declaration that he wanted to "start in where I left off and make good," most Lake County residents considered him a pariah. The University of Wisconsin booted him out; ministers called him immoral. The DeKalb chemistry teacher he hoped to marry dumped him.

Within months of the trial, the Orpet family moved to Santa Barbara, California, where his father took a job as the superintendent of parks. Some reports say William became a gardener like his father. He served in World War I and may have been a cowboy in Wyoming. He took the pseudonym W. H. Dawson and moved to San Francisco for a time. He purportedly jilted a young Detroit woman he had promised to marry. He died at the age of fifty-three in 1948 and was buried in a Los Angeles military cemetery. Newspaper obituaries made note of the infamous murder case.

Marion Lambert is buried next to her parents in Lake Forest Cemetery.

And so we come back to the ghost on Sheridan Road, the girl who might be Marion Lambert.

No one is quite sure when the first sightings of the specter took place or by whom, but they seem to go back at least a couple of decades. They center on a portion of Sheridan Road in Lake Forest, not far from the old train station and the location where Marion's body was found. A haunting there might make sense. A reporter covering the trial for the *Los Angeles Herald* wrote that defense testimony and photographs showed "what a conspicuous spot . . . three oaks is, especially in winter when the leaves are off the trees . . . *any one standing at the foot of the trees could be seen easily from Sheridan Road and from the electric train cars*" (emphasis added).

The defense team used that argument to suggest that no one would choose such a public space to commit a premeditated murder. But one could use the proximity of Marion Lambert's last breath to the site of the alleged appearance of her ghost as something more than happenstance.

Then there are those descriptions of the ghost: she is translucent and barefoot, wearing a mud-splattered blue dress; like Marion, she has short, curly, brown hair that frames a soft, gentle face; and she has that horrific burned mouth and blackened, crumbling teeth.

Ghost hunters and historical societies sometimes organize forays to find evidence of Marion Lambert's spirit but so far as is known, none have been successful.

Perhaps a *Chicago Tribune* reporter summed it up best when he wrote of one such unsuccessful attempt to find a ghost: "Nothing remains but the mystery, haunting us like a shadowy girl in the middle of the road."

Resurrection Mary

Chicago

Nearly as elusive as the ghost of Marion Lambert along Lake Forest's Sheridan Road is a captivating, blue-eyed, flaxen-haired girl in her late teens who loves to dance. She wears the same long, off-white ball gown in which she died in the 1930s.

She is known simply as Resurrection Mary, after the cemetery in which she is restlessly entombed, Resurrection Cemetery along Archer Avenue in southwest suburban Justice, Illinois. No one seems to know her real name, or at least it has never been revealed. Cemetery records show that a Polish girl of about Mary's age and description is buried there.

The story told about her is that she was killed in an automobile accident in 1934 on her way home from a night of dancing at the old Oh Henry Park ballroom, a former outdoor dance pavilion built in the 1920s and named for the Chicago-produced candy bar. It was enlarged over the years and achieved national fame as one of the nation's premiere ballrooms, especially after it was renamed the Willowbrook in 1959.

Sadly, a multi-alarm fire destroyed the historic venue in October 2016.

Yet for ninety-plus years, Mary's appearances are legendary in that portion of Chicagoland. A song was written about her by singer/song-writer Ian Hunter, which includes this lyric:

> On a wild Chicago night, with a wind howling white
> I cheated time with Resurrection Mary
> And I felt tears form in my eyes for the first time, I felt something
> Deep inside and the first time I saw angels high in the air
> For the first time in my life, and I said, "Mary, go to the light
> It's gonna be alright.

It is generally agreed that Mary first made her presence known in about 1939 when motorists complained that a peculiar girl in a formal gown tried to get into their automobiles along Archer Avenue. In some cases she was able to hitch a ride to or from the ballroom. On those occasions no one suspected that Mary was anything but mortal. If she found a ride to the ball-room, she danced the evening away with the single men who frequented the nightspot. Folks noticed, however, that her answers were vague when anyone asked about her personal life. Her dance partners used the word "aloof" to describe her behavior. Her arm was icy cold when they touched it.

After the last dance, Mary shyly asked for a ride home and directed her impromptu chauffeur to head north on Archer. As they neared Resurrection Cemetery, she asked him to stop so that she could get out. Her home was nearby, she said. On at least one occasion, she kissed her escort good night.

A few claimed to see her vanish as she ran *through* the cemetery gates. That is when they knew they had given a lift to a ghost.

She was also seen on several occasions inside the cemetery. A man passing the graveyard late at night happened to glance toward the locked gates. Peering back at him was a young woman tightly gripping the wrought iron fence.

Mary seemed to be especially active after the cemetery's 1969 remodeling.

A taxi driver was cruising for a fare on a midwinter night when he caught sight of a coatless girl standing near the entrance to the Old Willow Shopping Mall. He thought the woman might have had car trouble, so he stopped. Into the front seat climbed a strikingly beautiful young woman dressed in white with black, patent leather dancing slippers fashioned with a thin strap over each delicate instep.

"The snow came early this year," she said, barely loud enough to be heard.

The taxi driver tried to get more information from her but with little success. She had to get home, she said, gesturing vaguely in a northerly direction. He thought she had imbibed a few too many drinks but took off anyway.

"Here!" she cried out after they had gone a few miles up Archer Avenue. The cabbie pulled to the curb and looked out his window toward a small, dilapidated shack set back from the road.

He turned to ask if this was indeed the right place, but the back seat was empty. The rear door had not opened. Across the street was a cemetery.

Devil Baby

Chicago

The three elderly Italian women chattered amiably as they scurried along the Chicago city sidewalk on an early spring morning. They kept close together, not daring to lose sight of one another, their pocketbooks clutched tightly against their ample bosoms. Should any one of the hundreds of strangers they passed have been asked to identify their mission, the answer might have been that the ladies were on their way to church, or the market, or perhaps to visit a favorite daughter-in-law. But that was as far from the truth as the women were from their native Sicily.

The trio turned a corner and paused. Their destination lay a few yards away. They looked at one another and nodded in quiet agreement. Yes, they would go forward. After all, it was not every day that they could see a living Devil Baby, the spawn of Satan himself complete with short horns, pointed ears, and cloven hooves.

A few more steps on this day in 1913 took them to Hull House, a city landmark since Jane Addams and Ellen Starr founded it as a settlement house for the city's large immigrant population in the late 1880s. Although Hull House moved to new quarters in the 1960s, the original building has been preserved as a memorial to Addams and Starr.

It is not clear what prompted the origin of the Devil Baby legend nearly a century ago, for that is what it was, a tale without substance, as that trio of elderly women soon sadly discovered.

The Hull House receptionist pleasantly greeted them, sat them down, and asked them their business. And then as gently as possible she told them that there was no Devil Baby. Never had been, not then and not in the quarter century the shelter had existed. The story was untrue. Gossip. Nothing more.

The women insisted they knew what they were talking about and spoke at length about the child and his incredible attributes, about how he looked and about how he could speak from the moment he was born. Why with his first breath he had cursed his father, grabbed a cigar right out of his mouth, and smoked it on the spot.

Fantastic as it sounds, Hull House was inundated with hundreds, perhaps thousands, of similar requests to see the Devil Baby over the course of the next several months.

Letters, telephone calls, and personal visits by the curious fully taxed the resources of Hull House and its staff. A large group of Milwaukeeans wrote asking that their "delegation" be allowed to visit so they might "assess" the child. They would pay whatever the cost.

Italian, Irish, and Jewish versions of the peculiar child have been documented, each with its own strong moral implications. The "lesson" seemed to be to not question the teachings of one's own religion or family, to not stray from the fold. To do so invited hideous retribution.

The Irish and Italian versions of the Devil Baby reflected the centrality of Catholic teaching. In one telling, an Irish girl failed to confess to a priest that she had an affair with a married man before wedding her husband. For that transgression the girl was forced to give birth to the devil's baby as punishment. Her husband took the infant to Hull House, where workers decided it should be baptized. They unwrapped the swaddling clothes only to find them empty. That is when a nasty laugh erupted from the rear of the church. It was the baby, dancing across the pews and out the door.

In another story, a young Italian girl committed the grievous sin of marrying an atheist, despite the protests of her family. A few months later, pregnant with their first child, the young bride hung a painting of the Virgin on the bedroom wall. When her husband returned home from work that night, he ripped down the picture and burned it. He shouted that he would rather have the devil himself in the house than a holy picture. And he did.

Orthodox Jewish belief was at the center of another version of the story. In the tradition of pidyon haben, parents must pay the rabbi a fee for their first-born son no later than one month after he is born. A young Chicago Jewish mother had been asked if her son was her first child. Yes, she lied. She had given birth to a baby boy out of wedlock some years earlier. For that sin, she paid dearly—her next child was Satan's progeny.

The immigrant women of early twentieth-century Chicago fervently believed the stories and passed them along. Surrounded as they were by a foreign culture, they clung tenaciously to the ways of the Old World. Miracles, curses, the supernatural—all were considered possible in the cultures they brought with them to America.

The existence of a Devil Baby seemed perfectly normal. If a woman questioned the teachings of her elders, or her church or synagogue, or in any way ignored the behavior expected of her, the reckoning could be swift, the punishment harsh.

Jane Addams herself understood what motivated these women.

"During the weeks of excitement," she wrote later of the incident, "it was the old women who really seemed to have come into their own, and perhaps the most significant result of the incident was the reaction of the story upon them. It stirred their minds and memory as with a magic touch, it loosened their tongues and revealed the inner life and thoughts of those who are so often inarticulate. They are accustomed to sit at home and to hear the younger members of the family speak of affairs quite outside their own experiences in a language they do not understand."

Who started the story of the Devil Baby?

No one knows.

Was there ever any basis in fact?

Perhaps a child had been born with a birth defect and was taken to Hull House for care. If so, there is no known record from that period to indicate the identity of the child or whatever became of him or her.

Despite this lack of evidence, for a month and a half in the spring of 1913, a living, fire-breathing Devil Baby *did* exist at Hull House—if only in the fertile imaginations of the old, the superstitious, or the lonely.

The Telltale Hand

Chicago

Firefighter Frank Leavy seemed melancholy and preoccupied as he raised the soapy rag to scrub the winter's grime from another window in the Chicago Firehouse at Thirteenth and Oakley. It was Good Friday, April 18, 1924, so his mood was understandable.

Leavy was scheduled to work that day and on Easter Sunday, according to the recently posted work schedule. He was a thirteen-year veteran of the force, dedicated to his profession, but bothered by being away from his family on those days. They understood of course, but that did not lessen his gloom as he struggled to concentrate on the mundane task of cleaning windows.

The cold, harsh winter had taken its toll on the men of Engine Company 107 and Truck Company 12. They were thankful that spring seemed within sight and left open the large, red barn doors of the firehouse during the much-needed housecleaning.

Yet Leavy's friend Edward McKevitt was worried about him. He walked over to where Leavy was cleaning windows, one soapy palm, fingers spread, resting against a pane of glass while he wiped at the adjacent window with a wet cloth.

"Is there a problem?" McKevitt asked.

Leavy's shoulders sagged. He looked at his friend square in the face.

"This is my last day at the department," Leavy said quietly.

McKevitt was taken aback. His friend had seemed happy and content, talking about his future plans. But now something had changed. Whether it was working two important religious holidays or the multi-alarm fire spreading at that moment through the sprawling Union Stockyards, McKevitt did not know.

For several hours the ticker-tape device in all the Chicago firehouses rattling out updates about the stockyard blaze indicated it was extremely serious, but Leavy's firehouse was far from the scene and not likely to be called in. The real fear was that if another fire erupted somewhere in the city and Leavy's company had to respond, there would not be sufficient equipment to handle the new blaze.

Suddenly the unthinkable happened: the machine rat-a-tat-tatted a message from alarm box 372 nearly two miles across the city. A fire had erupted at Curran Hall, an imposing four-story brick-and-stone edifice southwest of the Loop. Within minutes Leavy's engine and truck companies were ordered to respond.

Leavy and McKevitt clambered aboard the pumper and truck with their fellow firefighters for the harrowing ride through the streets. There were few traffic lights in 1924; intersections were impossibly congested. New electric streetcars, rattling horse-drawn wagons, automobiles, and pedestrians all jockeyed for right-of-way. The screaming fire engines left a trail of bewildered citizenry and frightened horses.

Each city in America has its tales of heroic firefighters, those selfless public servants whose lives are often sacrificed to protect the public they serve.

Chicago is no different.

The files of that city's fire department are filled with the names of those who have died in the line of duty, and of the fires that have claimed them.

Of course most Americans know the story of Chicago's Mrs. O'Leary and her errant, lantern-kicking cow whose actions are said to have triggered the conflagration that nearly destroyed the city. But one of the strangest cases in Chicago fire history does not concern a particularly spectacular or even long-remembered fire.

It is the story of the Curran Hall fire to which Leavy and his mates responded.

Curran Hall was engulfed in flames as the fire trucks arrived. The building housed a number of small storefront businesses and offices. The heaviest smoke seemed to billow from the upper floors.

Truck 12's crew was ordered onto the roof to cut a hole in it to ventilate the upper floors. They hoped to reach the center of the fire in that way.

Leavy was among the men from Engine 107 ordered to the second floor. On their hands and knees, the men groped their way up a stairwell through the black, choking smoke, coughing and vomiting all the way. There were no oxygen masks in those days. Once they reached the second floor, the men took turns going out onto the fire escape for fresh air.

The minutes ticked by. It seemed the firefighters were gaining the advantage when suddenly a voice screamed from below.

"Get out! Get out!"

A fire captain outside saw what the men inside could not—the exterior brick-and-stone wall was falling in, crumbling.

Leavy and the others scrambled to the fire escape and started down. But it was too late. The wall caved in with a sickening crunch, like a giant roll of thunder, one witness recalled. It took the fire escape with it.

Heavy canvas hoses split, sending streams of water exploding in all directions. Ladders snapped in two, like so many matchsticks. Firefighters and their equipment were buried under an avalanche of brick and mortar.

Frank Leavy never had a chance.

He was only partway down the fire escape when the wall collapsed on him. Hours later the battered and broken bodies of eight firefighters were found under the rubble. Leavy was one of them; his face was the only one recognizable.

The next day was Holy Saturday, of course. Edward McKevitt did his best to explain to his fellow firefighters at the station house what had happened the day before. It was not easy—eight of their buddies were dead; twenty others were injured, two critically.

And yet what McKevitt most troubling were Frank Leavy's words of the day before—"This is my last day at the department."

Was it a premonition of death?

As McKevitt glanced around at his colleagues, trying to understand the senseless events, his gaze rested on the window Leavy had been washing the day before. He walked over and looked more closely. There seemed to be the perfect outline of a man's hand on the glass. McKevitt remembered Leavy resting his hand at that same position the previous afternoon.

"My God! It's Frank's handprint," McKevitt muttered, almost to himself.

Some of the men heard him and looked for themselves. They all agreed: it was the outline of a man's left hand.

Edward McKevitt grabbed a sponge and tried without success to wipe it off. The harder he rubbed, the clearer it became. Other men tried using ammonia and other strong soaps. One firefighter tried to scrape it off with a straight razor. Others thought it might be on the outside of the window.

By early the following week, the story of the firehouse at Thirteenth and Oakley and its mysterious handprint had spread throughout the city, fueled by newspaper stories and neighborhood gossip. Curiosity seekers showed up by the hundreds to see for themselves.

Experts from the Pittsburgh Plate Glass Company, the manufacturer of the window, were called in to solve the mystery. They used a special, highly reliable chemical compound to clean the window yet the handprint remained.

The weeks and months passed. The window was cleaned and cleaned again but with no obvious effect on what was now generally agreed to be the last vestige of firefighter Frank Leavy. A few people suggested that the glass ought to be replaced, but that idea was quashed. No one wanted to tamper with the unknown. Some thought there was a supernatural element to its origin.

So Frank Leavy's handprint remained there over the years. The firehouse at Thirteenth and Oakley saw dozens of firefighters come and go.

Older firefighters customarily told new men the story of Frank Leavy and showed them the handprint. Newspaper reports, usually on an anniversary of the Curran Hall fire, brought visitors asking to see "the hand."

However, Frank Leavy's widow and his children never looked at the handprint as far as it is known. That is perhaps understandable. Frank Leavy Jr. followed in his dad's footsteps and became a member of the Chicago Fire Department.

The nature of the handprint has been debated over the years. No one has ever satisfactorily explained what caused this strange legacy of the firefighter who died in service to others.

What happened to the window with Frank Leavy's handprint?

That is perhaps the strangest of all.

On April 18, 1944, twenty years to the date after Frank Leavy died, a newspaper delivery boy threw a rolled-up paper toward the firehouse. But rather than landing harmlessly on the ground, it struck Frank Leavy's window, breaking it into hundreds of pieces.

Red Rose

Chicago

Newspaper reporters are usually not given to hyperbole or a belief in the supernatural. Objectivity is the cornerstone of their profession, a world of hard information supported by verifiable facts and physical evidence.

Ann Marsters was just that kind of reporter. She worked for the old *Chicago American*, one of William Randolph Hearst's newspapers. Before that, she was the first female sportswriter for Hearst's *Boston American*. She was not gullible. That is why she was assigned to write a series of articles on Lily Dale, the famed upstate New York home of the controversial but popular American Spiritualist movement.

The Spiritualists began back in the mid-nineteenth century when the Fox sisters—Margaretta, Catherine, and Katie—purported to be able to communicate with a spirit in their Hydesville, New York, home. They called him Mr. Splitfoot, a peddler who had been murdered and buried in their basement by a previous occupant of the house.

The girls claimed they could communicate with him through a series of rappings. Eleven-year-old Katie worked out a code for talking with her "friend" Splitfoot.

Over a period of time other manifestations occurred. Furniture moved unassisted across the floors, beds rocked, and doors slammed shut. In a grisly scenario, the sisters claimed the peddler's murder itself was sometimes reenacted, replete with screams, the thud of a falling body, and what sounded like something heavy being dragged down the basement steps.

The eldest sister, Catherine, decided to exploit the mysterious events and American Spiritualism was born.

The girls' followers were not shaken when it was revealed that many of the so-called rappings occurred when they cracked the joints in their big toes. The reenactment of the peddler's death, and some of the other events, was still unexplained, the Fox Sisters' defenders maintained.

Scientists debunked the Fox sisters' claims and, later, magicians said they could duplicate all the noises the girls claimed Mr. Splitfoot made.

In 1904, after the sisters had all passed away, the *Rochester Democrat and Chronicle* trumpeted in a front-page story that a partial skeleton had been found beneath the foundation of the sisters' home. It seems rain weakened a section of the basement's stone walls and sections of the granite had fallen away, revealing a false wall behind. A human skeleton was discovered in the space between the false wall and the original foundation. The murdered peddler? The skeleton's identity was never determined.

The sisters' home was moved to Lily Dale in 1915, a town situated in north-central Chautauqua County, near Lake Erie, that became the headquarters of the American Spiritualist movement. The Fox Sisters' popularity did not wane; during the winter, the village's population numbered fewer than three hundred, but as many as two thousand people crowded into town each summer to study spiritualism.

Today, the permanent population numbers about the same, but over twenty thousand descend on the hamlet during the warm months to study spiritualism, New Age philosophy, and the paranormal. Unfortunately, the Fox sisters' small house was destroyed by fire in 1955.

Ann Marsters was given the opportunity in 1942 to "investigate" Lily Dale, then at its pinnacle as a spiritualist center. Her assignment for the *Chicago American* was to interview Ralph Pressing, the editor of the spiritualist newspaper *The Psychic Observer*, and to observe séances. Her editors wanted her to find out if it was really possible to communicate with the dead. The world awaited her answers.

Marsters later recalled her stay in Lily Dale.

"I had an open mind, not to write an exposé but to give an honest account of what I saw and heard. And I took along a staff photographer to make a pictorial record of my experiences," she wrote.

What Marsters saw was a mixture of obvious sham and truly puzzling events. She visited various "spirit" sessions, all conducted as "experiments" in spirit communication she was told, and transacted in darkened rooms that made searches for hidden gadgetry extremely difficult. From table rappings to trumpets floating through the air emitting disembodied voices to "materializations" of ghosts, the reporter saw it all. She dismissed some of it outright as hoaxes, but others raised questions in her mind. Could any of it be genuine? In some of the sessions, Marsters was addressed by voices from various "deceased" loved ones. She doubted they came from the dead, and certainly not from her relatives.

But then one afternoon Marsters met Red Rose, a so-called Indian spirit.

The two became acquainted during a séance led by one Ann Taylor, among the better-known mediums of the day. Red Rose became Marsters's "spirit guide," a kind of "buddy from the beyond" assigned (by whom was not clear) to assist Ann Marsters in contacting other spirits so that they, too, might communicate with the living.

In a mixture of Pidgin English and contemporary slang, Red Rose talked to her audience and sometimes directly to Marsters.

"You put a safety pin in the lining of your coat. Lazy!" Red Rose said to Marsters at one particular session.

She was flabbergasted. She had found a tear in her coat before leaving her hotel room. She temporarily fixed it with a pin. No one had seen her repair the coat, nor had she told anyone about it.

Ann Marsters returned to Chicago after a few days in Lily Dale. She outlined for editors a series of seven articles that she would write about her experiences. She decided against including her own encounter with Red Rose, figuring her editors would delete it as "too unbelievable."

Marsters did her writing at home. She completed the first article on a Friday and a copy boy came to collect the original manuscript and a carbon copy.

"Be sure to deliver these to the Sunday editor in person," she ordered.

Her series was due to begin that coming Sunday, two days hence. A heavy advertising campaign was underway to promote her findings.

But on Saturday, the Sunday editor telephoned. Where was the copy for her first story?

She could not believe her ears. Surely he had received it from the copy boy on Friday. Marsters even identified him by name.

"No!" her editor boomed before slamming down the receiver.

He found the copy boy and interrogated him.

The boy claimed to clearly remember collecting the copy from the reporter but had absolutely no memory of what he had done with it. Nothing succeeded in jogging his memory.

The editor phoned Marsters. She would have to rewrite the story. She shot back that there was no way she could remember the story line-for-line and, besides, the deadline for Sunday's edition was only hours away.

Marsters decided to go to the newsroom herself in the belief she might be able to find the copy boy's missing pages.

She arrived in a state of panic and stood at the editor's desk. What to do? Then she remembered Red Rose. Surely if the little spirit had found a safety pin in her coat she might be able to find the missing manuscript.

Oh, please, Red Rose, help me out! she pleaded silently to herself.

And then without conscious thought or deliberation, Marsters walked across the busy city room to a table next to the pay phone on the wall. She opened one of the phone books on the table. Inside was the missing manuscript.

Ann Marsters could never explain the reason she decided to go to the city room, nor why she looked in that one particular phone book. Nor were they ever able to figure out why the copy boy put the pages in a phone book. It remained a mystery.

The Attic

Equality

David Rodgers was grateful to have escaped the imposing antebellum mansion known benignly as Hickory Hill, near Equality, that particular Halloween morning. It had been a long night for the man from Harrisburg, Illinois. He claimed to have successfully challenged the ghosts of African American slaves that purportedly haunted a dismal third-floor attic.

While it is officially known today as the Hickory Hill Historic Site, after its builder, John Crenshaw, a man with a heinous reputation as a kidnapper and slave trader in the years prior to the Civil War, the imposing mansion and its ghosts Rodgers said he faced there make it understandable why so many know it simply as "The Old Slave House."

Although he heard plenty of strange noises that night, Rodgers did not encounter any of the spectral forms that had beset previous ghost hunters who supposedly fled the alleged third floor and its "slave cells."

Rodgers had heard other stories as well: of secret tunnels and whipping posts, of rushing, vaporous forms and horrific screams that would drive him out the door. A couple of Marines couldn't make it through the night and the wife of a former owner said human shapes materialized on the staircase.

Rodgers was a reporter for a local television station and saw a good story. During an earlier program, he had challenged the house's owner at the time, George M. Sisk II, to let him spend the night in the attic. When he was told no one had ever spent an uninterrupted night in the same rooms where the enslaved men, women, and children had been held, Rodgers found it to be a dare he could not resist.

John Hart Crenshaw—the man who built Hickory Hill in the late 1830s—came from a long-established American family. His parents moved to Gallatin County, Illinois, after their home in New Madrid, Missouri, was destroyed in the 1811 earthquake.

The Crenshaws settled on Eagle Creek, near one of the many salt deposits prevalent in that region near the Saline River. John's father, William, died when the boy was a teenager, leaving him as sole support for his mother and six younger siblings.

John Crenshaw went to work in the salt refinery. It was hard, backbreaking work. He grew sullen and resentful. He had, however, no other options at the time.

Shortly after John Crenshaw married Sinia Taylor in 1817, his life and his fortunes began to change. Illinois was a free state that ostensibly prohibited slavery. But the owners of the salt mines found it increasingly difficult to hire laborers to work the mines. In its 1818 constitution, Illinois provided a narrow exemption against slavery so the owners and operators of the mines could use slaves until 1825. The federal government, recognizing the economic importance of the salt mined there, agreed to let employers "lease" slaves from owners in Southern states and take them into Illinois to work the mines.

Crenshaw saw an economic opportunity. He leased several salt springs from the government and received permission to transport in slaves from Kentucky and Tennessee.

By 1834, John Crenshaw had amassed a sizable fortune. He owned three furnaces that reduced salty water to crystals, a mill on the North Fork of the Saline River, and nearly thirty thousand acres of land. Now he could afford to give his wife the home of her dreams. Before the year was out, John and his brother Abraham began construction of Hickory Hill. As the house took shape on a wind-swept hill near Equality, John Crenshaw's quest for riches and power grew. As soon as the house was completed around 1840, he undertook an even more reprehensible plan that would bring in even more money—he kidnapped free African American men and women that he then forced to labor in the salt works or in his farm fields; sometimes he sold them back into slavery in Southern states. The National Park Service has designated Crenshaw House a historic waystation on the "Reverse Underground Railroad," which secretly moved the kidnapped individuals to Southern states.

Some believe the house was planned with this aim in mind. From the outside it is of Greek Revival design with upper and lower front verandas, supported by massive columns, extending the width of the house. Not readily identifiable was a peculiar innovation that, according to local lore, Crenshaw built into his home: a carriageway that actually extended into the house. The shackled slaves or slaves-to-be were said to have been brought into the house in carriages with covered windows and then hustled up a rear staircase, where they were imprisoned in one of the third-floor "cells" scarcely large enough to hold a cot. The arrangement precluded curious neighbors and guests from learning this evil side to Hickory Hill.

However, archaeological and architectural investigations in the 2010s found evidence that the carriageway merely went to a broad back porch where passengers were unloaded in plain sight. That discovery cast doubt on the existence of any backdoor entryway for carriages full of slaves being slipped into the house.

There is another legend that a secret passageway once connected the house to the nearby Saline River. Slaves were brought up the Ohio River by steamboat to the Saline then transferred to smaller craft and moved up the river by night to a point near Hickory Hill. It was there that they were unloaded and taken through the tunnel and into the house. Archaeologists and architectual historians have not confirmed whether a tunnel still exists.

Although much of what could termed the lore of Crenshaw House cannot be proven one way or another, there is little doubt, and much on the record, to conclude that Crenshaw was a malevolent slaveholder with little compassion for the men, women, and children he enslaved.

In point of fact, Crenshaw apparently could not amass slaves fast enough to labor in his salt works, farm fields, or sell downriver to Southern slaveholders. According to one story, he began breeding slaves because a pregnant woman, or one with a small child, brought several hundred dollars more on the slave market. In one case, a slave named "Uncle Bob" was suspected of fathering three hundred babies.

There is evidence as well that Crenshaw sold forged contracts that purported to show free blacks were indentured servants (indentured servitude was legal in Illinois at the time) and sold the contrats to Southern slave owners.

The most well-known legend of the Crenshaw House is that two rows of "cells" on the third floor opened onto a hallway twelve feet wide by fifty feet long. Each cell had a narrow doorway and a single barred window overlooking the hall. The only ventilation came through windows in the front and rear gables of the house.

But that story appears to have given way to modern architectural detective work as well. Pieces of iron rings, chains, shackles, and a "whipping post" found on the third floor were left over from slave times, past visitors were told. However, according to findings by academic experts, many of the pieces are not accurate to the period or are erroneously labeled—the so-called whipping post is really a tool for making wood shingles. Recent paint and wood analyses did indicate the room was built at the same time as the first two stories.

Further research determined that the rooms were not cells but more closely modeled after those on a steamship or riverboat. Crenshaw may have built them as lodging for travelers.

Crenshaw did not escape notice that many of his activities were illegal even in those years when slavery sometimes was condoned even in free states. He was charged with kidnapping four times but acquitted by juries each and every time. He came close to being held accountable only once. In 1842 he was accused of selling into slavery a free woman named Maria Adams and as many as eight of her children. A Gallatin County jury trial found him not guilty, possibly because of his financial and political importance. It is speculated that at one time one seventh of the State of Illinois's entire revenue came from the taxes Crenshaw paid. Abraham Lincoln was a state representative when he spent a night in a second-floor bedroom at Hickory Hill after attending political debates in Equality and Shawneetown.

Although the reason is not clear, in time, Crenshaw moved his family to Equality and leased out the farm to a German family. He sold Hickory Hill outright in 1864 and died seven years later. John and Francine Crenshaw are buried in Hickory Hill cemetery.

The Sisk family bought Hickory Hill in 1913 and began giving public tours. They may have been the first to call it the Old Slave House. In the mid-twentieth century, George Sisk II and his wife, Janice, operated the house as a museum and tourist attraction. It was also their home. They restored the exterior and used the first and second floors as their living quarters.

The Sisks left the third floor virtually untouched. The cells remained, as well as various "instruments of torture," and the scarred wood on the wood casings where doors once hung. One window remained intact . . . and barred.

Even if they do not believe in ghosts, most visitors are understandably uneasy after visiting the attic. Sisk himself did not believe in ghosts, but respected them, he said.

Over the years, many psychic investigators tried to establish the presence of supernatural elements there.

An exorcist by the name of Hickman Whittington went there to write a story about what he might find. There is a legend that Whittington was in splendid health when he climbed the stairs into the attic, yet he was dead a few hours later. Sisk believed that he was literally scared to death.

Perhaps it was the same thing that terrified two Marines decades later. In their report, the men said that close to one o'clock in the morning a kerosene lantern—their only source of light—began to flicker. A terrible moan shook the walls and then swirling masses of vaguely human forms enveloped the frightened men. A hideous moan seemed to come all at once from nowhere and yet everywhere. Suddenly the kerosene lamp sniffed out and a final, bloodcurdling scream sent the pair bounding down the stairs.

Janice Sisk, George's wife, understood their panic. She would not stay alone in the house. She was so frightened of the place in the early years of her marriage to George that she temporarily left him. She had to quit taking baths alone in the evening because she would hear a voice whispering her name. The rooms were always cold, even on the hottest, most humid day of summer.

And both she and her husband, George, always thought they were being watched.

The Sisks retired in the 1990s and closed the museum. The State of Illinois bought the house and ten adjacent acres for a half-million dollars in 2000 with the goal of restoring the house and grounds and opening the property as a museum. However, only minimal progress has been made toward that goal during the ensuing twenty years. The estimated $7 million-plus it would take has been the stumbling block in the cash-strapped state budget.

Working with temporary grants, however, archaeologists and historians from Southern Illinois University and elsewhere have worked to separate the factual record of Crenshaw House from the legends that grew up around it. They are looking for the future day when the property can be reopened to the public with a full and accurate account of its place in Illinois's pre–Civil War history.

Despite the dubious likelihood for many of the supernatural legends, there is little doubt that they will not go away anytime soon. And that is understandable. John Hart Crenshaw visited unimaginable evil upon hundreds, perhaps thousands of innocent human beings in his quest for wealth. If there is anyone deserving to be haunted for all eternity, it is this man.

The Hickory Hill Historic Site is closed to the public.

Cave Dwellers

Burton

About five and a half miles east of Quincy, Illinois, is the beautiful Burton Cave Nature Preserve, an eighty-five-acre tract of public land with the water-carved limestone cave as its centerpiece. Dedicated in 1987, the preserve, including the cave and its environs, has been a popular destination for picnickers and hikers alike for well over a century.

But what every visitor does not know is that the cave is the subject of a most curious ghost story.

Back many years ago on a late Sunday morning, a group of young people from Quincy, intent on a leisurely picnic and then an afternoon's exploration of Burton Cave, found themselves lounging in a shaded meadow not far from the cave entrance. A thunderstorm cut short their outdoor plans and their cave exploration began earlier than expected.

The suddenly blackened sky made the soggy trail toward the cave difficult. A few of the teenagers had candles cupped in their hands, using the light to avoid becoming entangled in the exposed tree roots.

As they neared the entrance, the group was startled to see a hooded, dark-robed figure spring from the cave and scurry away. The quick glimpse gave little clue as to the person's identity except that the robe had a hem that dragged along the ground.

Nevertheless, not to be thwarted in their adventure, the group made its way into the cave. None had ever been in Burton Cave. Oddly, there was a faint glow from a ledge several yards away. They walked toward it. The corpse of a woman garbed in white was laid out on the ledge as if prepared for a funeral. Candles burned near her head and slippered feet.

The suddenly silent band of picnickers quickly streamed out of the cave and ran for their horses and wagons.

Later the skeptical Adams County sheriff and several deputies, led by a couple of the braver picnickers, returned to the cave. There was no trace of the body. Indeed, it seemed as if no one, save the frightened young people, had been in Burton Cave for a very, very long time.

Today Burton Cave is still a popular warm-weather destination (it is closed during the winter months) for those interested in its 330 million-year-old Burlington limestone and the many fossils, fauna, and invertebrate animals found inside, including five species of bats, some endangered. Some of the invertebrates remain hidden away inside the cave all their lives, blind and colorless.

To Do Good

Kingston

Ezra and Betsey Hawkins drove their farm wagon filled with their meager possessions along a dusty trail in north-central Illinois. Betsey held their infant son, Samuel, on her lap. The family needed rest; their two mules needed water.

"We'll stay here for a time," Ezra said, nodding toward an abandoned cabin in the near distance. It looked sturdy enough to protect them from the elements. Betsey readily agreed. It had been a long trek so far.

"Maybe I can find some work at that farm back down the road," Ezra added.

He unhitched the team while his wife carried their sleeping infant inside. The place needed a thorough cleaning, a few broken windows boarded, and the door put back on its hinges, but at least there was a solid roof over their heads. After they unloaded what they would need overnight, Ezra took two pails and went in search of the freshwater spring they had passed earlier.

A few minutes later Ezra heard a scream come from the direction of the cabin. He dropped the buckets and ran back.

Betsey was in the yard, clutching little Samuel.

"This house is haunted!" she blurted out. "Soon as we got inside, a skinny old man with a cane was suddenly there. He walked around us then went out the front door."

"You just imagined it," Ezra sighed. He took her back inside.

"You see, nothing in here at all," Ezra said with a sweeping gesture.

With that he went on to the spring for water.

After lunch he told his wife he was going to the farm up the road to see about work.

"That's part of my property," the farmer who lived there told him. "If you need work and want to stay I'll let you. But let me warn you. No one stays there more than one night. You stay there tonight and come back in the morning if you still want work."

Ezra was puzzled but accepted the offer.

Meanwhile, the young man's wife had another visit from the old man. As before, he seemed to materialize out of nothing and walked around. Betsey and the baby started crying. That seemed to distress the ghost greatly.

He stopped his pacing.

"Don't be afraid, I'll not harm you," he whispered. With that he vanished.

Betsey insisted to her husband that they must leave.

"I'm scared, Ezra. I don't know why he's here or what he wants."

Her husband was resolute despite the farmer's words. He did not tell her of the farmer's odd warning.

"Let's stay the night at least and see what happens. I promise I'll stay awake to look after you and the boy."

Early the next morning after an uneventful night, Ezra left to work on the farm. Betsey was packing away dishes. The old ghost returned.

"I will not hurt you," he said, raising a hand in a calming motion. "I'm here for a reason."

Betsey shrank back, her child clutched to her breast.

"I have come to do you good. My wife and I were murdered here, murdered for our money. But him what killed us did not find it. I want you and your husband to do something for me. We are buried out yonder in a small cave. You will find us where the earth has been disturbed. I want you to find our bones then give us a proper burial in that graveyard up on the hill."

With those words he opened the cellar door and beckoned her to follow. Terrified yet curious, she picked up a lantern and followed him down the ladder.

In the dank cellar he hovered in a corner and scuffed a mark in the packed earth.

"Dig here and you will find some money."

He climbed back up the ladder and beckoned her to follow him outside.

At a corner of the house he pointed downward.

"And here below the surface you will find even more money and the deed to this property. It is yours if you do what I tell you. Now, do you see that cave over there?"

She followed his gaze to see a small opening in the hill behind the cabin.

"That is where we are." He pointed and vanished.

Betsey quickly found a shovel and took it back down into the cellar. She began to dig. Within a few minutes she hit something solid. She carefully unearthed an old pitcher stuffed with currency—more money than she had ever seen before. She set about to count it.

Late that afternoon when her husband returned from his farm work, she merrily danced out to greet him.

"I've made more money than you have today," she said gaily.

She told him the tale of her mysterious visitor. Ezra grabbed a shovel and dug where the ghost had pointed at the corner of the house. Buried a foot below the surface was a metal trunk filled with gold coins and the deed.

The next morning the couple made their way into the cave. It did not take long for them to find the buried bones.

Ezra built a plain coffin out of scrap wood. The couple bore the remains to the small graveyard, where they laid their nameless benefactor and his wife to rest, a simple wooden cross to mark their passing.

Ezra and Betsey were able to claim title to the house and lived there with their family. As for the ghost, he was never heard from again.

The Devil's Bake Oven

Grand Tower

A few miles north of Grand Tower on the Mississippi River, a rocky promontory has been used for centuries as a landmark for travelers. The oddly named Devil's Bake Oven is a rock outcropping marking the eastern terminus of a stone ledge, termed the Devil's Backbone, which runs beneath the Mississippi River. Before the river was dammed, boatmen on their way upstream had to leave their crafts and walk along the shore, pulling their vessels behind them with long towlines. Going downstream, they repeated the same procedure, only they had to hold their boats back lest they break loose and swamp.

Dangerous river pirates infested the region in the nineteenth century, launching surprise attacks on keelboats with camouflaged canoe-like craft called pirogues. They would take what merchandise could be sold and dumped the rest in the muddy waters. Passengers and crewmen were murdered or left stranded on the desolate shore.

In time civil authorities and increased population made the piratical attacks too perilous for the lawbreakers. An iron foundry was built on a hill at Devil's Bake Oven. Several large homes went up to house the foundry managers.

The superintendent's home was especially striking, towering above the tree line, and commanding wide vistas of the river. Traces of the house could be found well into the twentieth century on the eastern side of the stony hill near its summit.

But that house sheltered more than families. The ghost of a foundry superintendent's beautiful daughter haunted it.

The child is said to have been somewhere in her teens and protected by her doting parents from the roughness around her. Yet in time, she had many suitors longing for her hand in marriage, but her father turned away the rougher men who wanted to pay a call on her.

But as so often happens, the girl had her own mind and soon fell in love with a man her father strongly disapproved of—a dashing young fellow who was, unfortunately, quite a ne'er-do-well. He enjoyed gathering about him the finer things in life even if he might not always have the funds available to pay for them.

The girl's father strongly objected to the romance, yet she persisted in loving him. He forbade her from seeing the young man, even confined her to the house for long periods of time in the vain hope that absence would make her heart grow less fonder, at least toward this particular suitor.

Whether from grief over her lost love, or some other equally serious malady, according to the legend, the young lady fell ill and soon died.

It was not long before her ghost—a misty presence in the pale moonlight—was seen floating along the narrow trail that led up the mound. On storm-swept nights when black clouds swirled overhead and streaks of lightning split the sky, pitiful wails erupted into screams that shook even the bravest man's spirit. Long after the superintendent's house was razed and the timbers used to build a railway station, the girl's ghost continued her mournful ways.

There is little to remind the modern visitor of the tapestry of history that unfolded below the Oven's stony summit. A bridge carries natural gas lines across the river not far away while a bridge tower is near the Oven's south side. And there is certainly nothing to note the passing of a bereaved young maiden who returned in death to find her roguish beau.

Old Man Lakey

McLeansboro

Old Man Lakey was an early settler in McLeansboro. That is about all anyone knew about him, except that his name got attached to a small creek that meanders through the countryside near the city and that the old man's restless ghost haunted his former neighborhood for many years.

It all started one spring day when he decided to build a more permanent cabin for himself on the west side of the creek. The cabin may have been where a roadway now passes over the stream, though no one is quite sure. But there was no bridge at that time, only a muddy ford that animals, wagons, and people had to wade across.

After many weeks of labor, Lakey completed his new house save for the clapboard siding he was fashioning from an oak tree that he had taken down. On the evening before Lakey hoped to finish his work, he warmly greeted several travelers who had stopped to admire his handiwork. Tragically, his corpse was found early the next morning propped up against a tree stump; his roughly severed head lay on the ground a few feet away.

It looked as if Lakey's own broadax, now driven into a stump, was used as the murder weapon.

Who would want to kill old man Lakey? That was the question rippling through the community as soon as the crime was discovered. Those who had seen him the night before denied any knowledge of the murder and said Lakey seemed happy and excited about finishing his project.

As far as anyone could tell, he had no known enemies—his reputation was that of a kind, simple, if not reclusive, man not known for his extravagant ways. He possessed no hidden wealth that anyone knew of. Local authorities investigated but without apparent success.

The townspeople took up a collection to bury Lakey, for he had no kin, in a grave adjacent to his never-finished cabin.

He did not rest well.

On the night following the burial, two fishermen returning home on horseback near the Lakey cabin nearly fell out of their saddles when the horrible specter of a headless horseman joined them not far from Lakey's Creek crossing.

The men spurred their horses to a gallop, but the ghost easily kept abreast. As the anglers reached the stream, the phantom horseman disappeared into the mist downriver. The pair eventually made it safely home, but the men were reluctant to tell their story. A few nights later, however, two other horsemen returning from the east encountered the same ghost.

Word spread quickly that the ghost of old man Lakey would not stay in its grave, though without a head it is a wonder anyone knew who it was.

Witnesses claimed the thing appeared immediately after sundown and usually to eastbound riders crossing the stream. Mounted on a tall, black stallion, the ghost rode along the downstream side of the unlucky witnesses. The specter invariably vanished halfway across the creek. The ghost never communicated and, so far as is known, did no one any harm.

The stories of old Lakey and his ghost were told for decades, but they have faded away with time. A concrete bridge crosses Lakey's Creek at about where the old crossing used to be.

The Reincarnation of Mary Roff

Watseka

On the afternoon of July 5, 1865, eighteen-year-old Mary Roff from Watseka, Illinois, died in a Peoria insane asylum. She had been committed after she tried to slash her arms with a razor, the last tragic incident in the girl's long, harrowing descent into madness.

In the first stages of her illness, she heard voices or fell into a sort of hypnotic state during which she took on other identities. Later, she became obsessed with the need to rid her body of blood. She used leeches to suck blood from her veins, giving the creatures names much like family pets.

One day her parents found her on the floor with her arms slashed, the razor still in her hand. Days later they took her—still unconscious—to the Peoria asylum.

Unfortunately there was no real effective treatment or even much of an understanding of mental illness in the nineteenth century. Mary Roff was subjected to what passed as scientific "treatment": the so-called water cure, a practice originating in the Middle Ages that was still used in 1860s America. A naked patient was alternately—and repeatedly—immersed in a tub of icy water then dumped in scalding hot water.

A female patient like Mary Roff also received a cold-water douche administered with a hose. Although victims were nearly senseless from this "cure," the horror continued with water-soaked sheets tightly bound around the body as to literally squeeze shut blood vessels. Finally, if the patient had so far survived, her skin was vigorously rubbed to "improve" the circulation.

The treatments were repeated several times a week, despite their noticeable lack of success in bringing anyone back to a healthy mental state. It is little wonder that after Mary Roff died in the asylum, her father, Asa B. Roff, declared that his daughter was "in a condition terrible to behold, among maniacs, ruled and cared for by ignorant and bigoted strangers."

Lurancy Vennum was not yet fourteen months old when Mary Roff died mad and alone. But their lives became forever intertwined twelve years later in one of the strangest cases of possession ever recorded in the United States.

Lurancy was, from all accounts, a normal, healthy child raised in a loving and religious home. Born on April 16, 1864, she and her family moved to Watseka in 1871, when she was seven. Although Asa Roff, his wife, and several children also lived in Watseka at the time and still grieved for their dead daughter, the Vennums apparently did not know the Roff family beyond the casual acquaintanceship not atypical in small towns.

Yet on July 11, 1877, shortly after the twelfth anniversary of Mary Roff's death, a series of events began that would plunge Lurancy into the netherworld of the supernatural.

On that morning, when sewing with her mother, thirteen-year-old Lurancy complained of feeling ill. Before her mother could react, the child fell to the floor, unconscious. For the next five hours, Lurancy was caught in a deep, almost catatonic sleep, oblivious to her surroundings. She recovered later that day without any visible adverse effects.

The next day, however, Lurancy again fell into the same deep faint. This time, while apparently still unconscious, she began talking. She was in heaven, the child told her bewildered parents, and could see and speak with spirits, including her brother, who had died several years before.

After that, Lurancy's lapses into unconsciousness become more and more frequent. When she was lucid, her visions took on a nightmarish tinge. She would sometimes shout at her parents, calling her father "Old Black Dick" and her mother "Old Granny." After one particularly long siege, she told her mother that "persons are in my room calling 'Raney! Raney!' and I can feel their breath upon my face." Raney was her nickname.

Continuing attacks lasted for periods of up to eight hours and occurred three to twelve times per day. While Lurancy could speak, her words seemed to be directed by someone, or something, the Vennums could not understand. Once her spells had passed, Lurancy remembered nothing of her strange jabbering.

The story of Lurancy Vennum's peculiar visions spread quickly through Watseka. The local newspaper published articles about the child and her dialogue with the spirit world. Among the townsfolk who closely followed the case was Asa Roff, Mary Roff's father. His interest was more than casual. In the early stages of Mary's sickness, she too had said she could communicate with spirits. From what he read in the newspaper or heard from others, Lurancy's symptoms sounded disturbingly similar. Now her father was determined not to let another young girl die at the hands of "ignorant and bigoted strangers" whose ideas of medicine and mental health were more akin to medieval torture. He said nothing, however, until Lurancy's family had exhausted every known treatment for their daughter's illness without success; doctors and their minister were advising them to commit the girl to the Peoria state hospital.

That was too much for Roff. On January 31, 1878, he intervened, persuading the skeptical Vennum family to let him bring Dr. E. Winchester Stevens, a dedicated spiritualist like himself, into the case. Both men were convinced that Lurancy was not insane or catatonic, but rather the vessel through which the souls of the dead were communicating with the living.

Lurancy was sitting near a parlor stove when Asa Roff and Dr. Stevens first visited the Vennum home. Her unblinking gaze seemed riveted on the wall, her legs pulled up under her on the chair. She rested her elbows on her knees, her hands clasped under her chin. Roff said later she looked every inch a mean old woman not to be trifled with. Even her voice had the raspy sound of age.

Lurancy growled that she did not want to talk to anyone.

After a few minutes, however, her mood changed. She said that since Dr. Stevens was a spiritualist she would answer any question he might pose.

Dr. Stevens quizzed the strange girl: "What is your name?"

"Katrina Hogan."

"And how old are you?"

"Sixty-three years."

"Where are you from?"

"Germany."

"How long have you been here?"

"Three days."

"How did you come?"

"Through the air."

"How long can you stay?"

"Three weeks."

Lurancy's mood suddenly shifted.

She had been lying, she admitted. She was actually Willie Canning, a young man now in the spirit world but who had shown up "because I want to be here." He had led a wild life and implied that he may have committed suicide.

For over an hour, Lurancy spoke to Dr. Stevens in the guise of Willie. She then suddenly flung up her arms and fell backward onto the floor.

The doctor said she appeared to be rigid as a plank. He grasped her hands in his own, talking quietly but firmly in an attempt to "magnetize" her, as he later wrote but did not explain. Gradually, she regained the use of her body.

Now she had entered heaven, she said, with spirits of a far gentler persuasion than Katrina or Willie.

Would she not like to be controlled by a happier, more pleasant spirit than Willie? Dr. Stevens asked.

39

Lurancy agreed that would be nice. In fact there was a nice spirit nearby, Lurancy said. The spirit of a girl named Mary Roff.

Asa Roff had been silently taking in the proceedings but now sat bolt upright.

"That's my daughter! Mary Roff is my girl!" Asa Roff said. "She has been in heaven these twelve years. Yes, let her come. We'll be glad to have her here."

The trance continued into the next day, February 1. Lurancy Vennum had now taken on the persona of Mary Roff. All she wanted was to leave the Vennum house and go home with the Roffs.

When Mrs. Roff heard of the supposed reincarnation of her beloved child, she hurried to the Vennum home with her married daughter, Minerva Alter. As the two women turned up the walk, they saw Lurancy sitting by the window.

"Here comes Ma and Nervie," Lurancy/Mary cried out.

She rushed to the door and showered the startled women with embraces. No one had called Minerva "Nervie" since Mary died. That had been Mary's pet name for her.

Those watching the scene believed the spirit of Mary Roff had taken complete control of the mind and body of Lurancy Vennum.

She seemed to know everything about the Roff family, treating them as her own. To the Vennums, her real parents, she remained polite and courteous as a child might with adults present. Dr. Stevens later wrote: "From the wild, angry, ungovernable girl, to be kept only by lock and key, or the more distressing watch-care of almost frantic parents; or the rigid, corpse like cataleptic . . . the girl has now become mild . . . and timid . . . knowing none of the Vennum family, but constantly pleading to go 'home.'"

She went home with the Roffs ten days later.

Lurancy's family, with the happy acquiescence of the Roffs, agreed that it was best at least for the time being. They hoped that in time Lurancy would regain her true identity. Having lived through hell during the past seven months, they viewed this new persona only as another phase of the insanity, but they were willing to go along with almost anything to keep their lovely daughter from being locked up in an asylum.

For the Roffs, on the other hand, it seemed a miracle. Their Mary had returned from the grave, though she looked nothing like her old self but rather as a girl they barely knew.

An incident on the way home that day strengthened their belief in what they were choosing to call Mary's reincarnation.

In 1865, the year Mary died, the family had been living in a house near the center of Watseka. That was the home Mary knew. As Lurancy, with her new family, passed the old place, she asked why they did not turn into the drive. When Mr. Roff told her that their home was now elsewhere, Lurancy insisted that was not correct. Only after strong persuasion did the girl agree to accompany them further.

For a time, Lurancy Vennum was content living as Mary Roff. Although Mary's personality occasionally vanished for short periods, Lurancy seemed to have completely forgotten her pre–Mary Roff life. Yet she seemed to sense impermanence in the arrangement.

"How long can you stay with us?" Mrs. Roff asked.

"The angels will let me stay until sometime in May," Lurancy/Mary said.

As the days and weeks passed, Lurancy continued to display remarkable knowledge about Roff family matters. She recognized most of the family possessions that had been part of Mary's world; she welcomed "old friends" when they visited; on one occasion she recited the entire itinerary of a long trip the Roffs had made to Texas in 1857. Of course, the Roffs were ecstatic.

"Truly our daughter has been restored to us," Asa Roff said.

Likewise, Mary's sister, Minerva Alter, with whom Lurancy lived for several weeks during the spring of 1878, was convinced that Mary had indeed returned from the dead. She told interviewers that on at least two occasions, Lurancy had shocked her with specific remembrances. One time she pointed to a spot beneath a currant bush and accurately described how her little cousin Allie had "greased the chicken's eye." On another occasion, Lurancy/Mary correctly identified an area in her yard where they had buried a pet dog. Both incidents occurred several years before Lurancy was born.

Later, as an experiment, Asa Roff asked his wife to place a velvet bonnet Mary had often worn on a hat stand in the parlor. Lurancy ran to it, mentioned the store where it had been purchased, and reminisced about some of the things that had happened those times when she was wearing it. She wondered if the Roffs kept her box of letters from friends and relatives. They produced her old box of letters and some sewing materials.

"Oh, Ma!" she said, "and here is the collar I tatted! Why didn't you show me my letters and things before?"

Not everyone in Watseka believed that Mary Roff had taken possession of Lurancy Vennum.

Several of the doctors who had treated Lurancy before the arrival of Dr. Stevens ridiculed his diagnosis of "spirit possession."

One woman who knew the Vennum family well echoed the sentiment of many when she lashed out at the role spiritualism appeared to be playing in Lurancy's treatment.

"I would sooner follow a girl of mine to the grave than have her go to the Roffs and be made a spiritualist!" she said.

A local minister—who had unsuccessfully tried to persuade the Vennums to have Lurancy committed—told Mrs. Vennum, "I think you will see the time when you will wish you had sent her to the asylum."

Meanwhile, Lurancy Vennum's life as Mary Roff continued. Any new test designed by Dr. Stevens to gauge her ability to recall distant events in that other life purportedly met with complete success.

Still, the girl did know that she was not actually Mary Roff.

Dr. Stevens asked her if she remembered a cut she had received as a child.

"Yes, indeed, I can show you the scar."

She rolled up her sleeve, pointing to the place on her arm where the real Mary had scarred herself in a childhood accident.

"Oh, this isn't the mark. That arm is in the ground," she said matter-of-factly.

Lurancy-as-Mary also seemed to have had some power of clairvoyance.

Early one day, she told the Roffs that her "brother" Frank would become sick that night. He did.

The girl then instructed her parents to take Frank to Dr. Stevens's home. Mr. Roff protested that Dr. Stevens was out of the city and not expected home. An insistent Lurancy disagreed. They did, indeed, find Dr. Stevens at home and he treated the boy for "spasms and congestive chill" from which he soon recovered.

In early May, Lurancy took Asa Roff aside and said it was nearly time for her to go. She choked back sobs at the thought of forcing the Roffs again to say good-bye to their daughter. Over the next few days, Lurancy's true personality steadily returned, not understanding where she was or what had happened. Lurancy would hold sway one moment, Mary the next. On May 21, Lurancy announced it was now time to return to her real home. Then, Mary took control, addressing Asa Roff as "sir." She wept bitterly at the thought of leaving.

But leave she did. Once back with the Vennums, Lurancy displayed none of the alarming symptoms of the past year. Her parents were convinced that their daughter had been cured by the intervention of the spirit of Mary Roff.

Lurancy remained in touch with the Roffs.

As did the spirit of Mary Roff.

Lurancy sometimes allowed Mary to take control so the Roffs could communicate with their late daughter. Mary never wanted to stay long and allowed Lurancy to regain her identity whenever she wished.

Can this case of spirit possession be explained?

Perhaps Lurancy Vennum suffered from a genuine mental illness. Based on reports of that period, she appeared to have the memories, emotions, recognitions, physical nuances, and personality of a person dead twelve years. In most cases of multiple personality, however, the individual does not have this knowledge of the early life of another, sometimes fictitious, personality.

Or perhaps Lurancy was merely an actress putting on a very convincing performance. Shortly after the possession became common knowledge, rumors spread that she had a crush on one of the Roff sons and for that reason wanted to be close to the family. The allegation was never substantiated, and it seems unlikely that Lurancy had somehow acquired her knowledge of the Roff family and applied it so expertly.

Whatever the case, after she left the Roff house, Lurancy became a happy, healthy fourteen-year-old girl, having survived with few ill effects one of the most bizarre experiences anyone could ever imagine.

Eight years after the extraordinary chain of events, in 1896, Lurancy Vennum married a farmer and devout nonbeliever in anything to do with spiritualism or religion itself. She moved with him to Rollins County,

43

Kansas, where they lived out their lives. Lurancy died an old woman, never again to be possessed by the spirit of Mary Roff.

Lincoln and the Supernatural

Springfield

President Abraham Lincoln did not stray far from the telegraph key in the U.S. War Department offices in Washington, DC, on June 7, 1864. As the day wore on he awaited word from General Ulysses S. Grant, who was nearing Richmond. Oblivious to everything but the Civil War, he paid scant attention that day to the opening sessions of the Republican Party Convention in Baltimore. He left the office only to eat a hasty lunch in the White House.

It was not that the president did not care about his own renomination taking place forty miles away. No, he did not give it a thought, because he knew he would be nominated and elected to a second presidential term.

And he knew that he would not survive.

Shortly after his election in 1860, on a day when the news of his victory over Stephen A. Douglas was still being transmitted to his private offices in Springfield, Lincoln retreated to his quarters to rest. He caught nearly his full-length reflection in a mirror atop a chest of drawers.

Hardly odd, except for what Lincoln said he saw in his own reflection. He later confided to a friend:

> My face, I noticed, had two separate and distinct images, the tip of the nose of one being about three inches from the tip of the other. I was a little bothered, perhaps startled, and got up and looked in the glass. The vision vanished. On lying down again, I saw it a second time, plainer . . . than before; and then I noticed that one of the faces was a little paler . . . than the other. I got up and the thing melted away. [In] the excitement of

the hour I forgot all about it, nearly, but not quite, for the thing once in a while came up and gave me a little pang, as if something had happened. When I went home that night, I told my wife about it, and a few days afterward, I made the experiment again, when sure enough the thing came again.

Each time Lincoln tried to reproduce the image in his Springfield home he succeeded. His wife, Mary Todd Lincoln, never saw it but was deeply troubled by her husband's unhappiness after seeing the image. Claiming to have the gift of prophecy, she said the healthy, vigorous face was her husband's "real" face, and indicated that the president would serve out his first term. The paler, ghostlike image, however, was a sign that he would be renominated for a second term, but he would not live to see its conclusion.

Lincoln apparently dismissed it all as an optical illusion caused by an imperfection in the glass or his own nervousness about the election.

Even so, he seemed preoccupied on that day of the 1864 Republican Convention, oblivious to the political events swirling around him.

One of Lincoln's aides later wrote an account of the day. The president returned to the War Department after lunch in the White House. As he strode toward the telegraph offices, he was handed a telegram from Baltimore. It said that Andrew Johnson of Tennessee had been nominated as vice president. Johnson was Lincoln's military governor in occupied Tennessee.

Lincoln looked perplexed. "This is strange. I thought it was usual to nominate the candidate for president first."

"But Mr. President," his aide replied, "have you not heard of your own nomination? It was telegraphed to you at the White House two hours ago."

The president shook his head and said he had not paused in his private office to receive the information. Later he attached great meaning to that inattentiveness and recalled his strange encounter with the mirror four years earlier. Surely, he thought, a hand was guiding him toward a destiny over which he had no control.

Abraham Lincoln always had a melancholy nature. The loss of his mother as a child, the ceaseless hard physical labor he endured as a youth, and the struggle to acquire even a rudimentary education all combined to make him somber, even when cracking a joke.

The Civil War shadowed his countenance with constant sorrow. The heavy losses on both sides and the divided loyalties the war called up pained him deeply. His wife's brothers fought for the Confederacy; Lincoln's own family ancestry was Southern.

Lincoln paid fanatical attention to even the minutest details of the war. By the time of his reelection the physical strain was self-evident; deep lines etched his face and heavy black circles underscored his eyes. He slept little. During his five years in the White House, he took less than a month's vacation. His only escape was an occasional theater outing or a late-night buggy ride. Reading Shakespeare or the Bible gave him solace late into the night.

But there may have been more to his sadness than even he would admit. The disturbing mirror image in his Springfield home was but the first incident that seemed to foreshadow his tragic fate. Lincoln is widely reported to have dreamed of his own death.

One account comes from his close friend and self-appointed bodyguard Ward Hill Lamon. He said the president told him the following on an evening early in 1865:

> About ten days ago I retired very late. . . . I soon began to dream. There seemed to be a deathlike stillness about me. Then I heard subdued sobs, as if a number of people were weeping. I thought I left my bed and wandered downstairs.
>
> There, the silence was broken by the same pitiful sobbing, but the mourners were invisible. I went from room to room. No living person was in sight, but the same mournful sounds of distress met me as I passed alone. . . . I was puzzled and alarmed.
>
> Determined to find the cause of a state of things so mysterious and shocking, I kept on until I arrived at the East Room. Before me was a catafalque, on which rested a corpse wrapped in funeral vestments. Around it were stationed soldiers who were acting as guards; and there was a throng of people, some gazing mournfully upon the corpse, whose face was covered, others weeping pitifully.
>
> "Who is dead in the White House?" I demanded of one of the soldiers. "The President," was his answer. "He was killed by an assassin."

Abraham Lincoln became even more depressed as April 1865 approached. Although Northern forces now firmly controlled the war, Lincoln did not rejoice.

A few days after his horrifying dream, on Friday, April 14, 1865, President Lincoln called a meeting of his cabinet. Secretary of War Edwin M. Stanton arrived twenty minutes late with apologies. The meeting then proceeded as scheduled.

At the meeting's conclusion, Secretary Stanton and Attorney General James Speed left together. The secretary noted that they had completed a good deal of work.

"But you were not here at the beginnings," the attorney general said. "You do not know what passed. [We] found the President seated at the [head] of the table with his face buried between his hands. Presently he raised it and we saw that he looked grave and worn."

"Gentlemen," the president began, "before long you will have important news."

The cabinet members were anxious to hear what news Lincoln might have. They pressed him, but he demurred.

"I have heard nothing," he said. "I have had no news, but you will hear tomorrow."

He hesitated, Speed said, but then continued.

"I have had a dream; I have dreamed that dream three times before, once before the battle of Bull Run, once on another occasion, and again last night. I am in a boat, alone on a boundless ocean. I have no oars—no rudder—I am helpless. I drift!"

Shortly after ten o'clock that evening, while the president and Mrs. Lincoln enjoyed a rare night at the theater watching a performance of *Our American Cousin* at Ford's Theater, an unemployed actor and Southern sympathizer named John Wilkes Booth shot Lincoln in the back of the head. The president died the next morning, April 15, 1865. It was the anniversary of the Southern assault on Fort Sumter, the opening salvo of the Civil War.

The eerie incidents connected with Abraham Lincoln did not end with his death. Little Willie Lincoln, the president's favorite son, died while his father occupied the White House. Mary Todd Lincoln never again set foot in his bedroom. But others say they have seen the ghost of a little boy in there.

The life of Lincoln's oldest son, Robert Todd Lincoln, was also touched with a perplexing psychic cast. Robert Todd was at his father's bedside when he died of the bullet wound inflicted by Booth.

Sixteen years later, in 1881, James A. Garfield, less than four months after taking office as the twentieth president of the United States, strode through a railroad station in Washington, DC. Robert Lincoln, his secretary of war, was at his side when a crazed man named Charles Julius Guiteau leaped forward and killed the president.

In 1901 President William McKinley invited Robert Lincoln, by then the president of the Pullman Company, to tour the Pan-American Exposition in Buffalo, New York. There, the anarchist Leon F. Czolgosz fired a fatal bullet at President McKinley.

Robert Todd Lincoln had now personally witnessed three deaths of American presidents.

As a result, this son of a revered president, a prominent statesman and lawyer in his own right and a graduate of Harvard University, refused ever again to meet or associate with a U.S. president. Although he had many invitations, Robert Todd turned them all away. His presence was a curse, he insisted. He died in 1926.

In the years since then, several presidents and visiting dignitaries have encountered Lincoln's ghost in the White House.

During the thirteen years Franklin D. Roosevelt lived there, his wife, Eleanor, often sensed the presence of the Great Emancipator. She used his former bedroom as her study. She wrote that sometimes she felt someone watching her. Even when she turned to look and found no one else in the room, she believed it was Lincoln standing alongside her.

A young clerk who worked in the White House during Franklin Roosevelt's first term in office said she saw Lincoln's ghost sitting on his very own bed, pulling on his boots.

Queen Wilhelmina of the Netherlands spent a night in the White House during Roosevelt's presidency. She reported that a knock brought her out of bed to answer the door. The ghost of Lincoln stood staring at her from the hallway.

Lincoln seems to prefer knocking on doors. Presidents from Theodore Roosevelt to Herbert Hoover and Harry Truman all said they heard tap-tap-tapping, often at their bedroom doors in the middle of the night when no one was about in the family quarters.

Also, there is that certain window in the Oval Office. First Lady Grace Coolidge said she saw his ghost gazing through that portal on several occasions, his hands clasped tightly behind his back, his attention focused on the bloody Civil War battlefields that lay beyond the Potomac.

Indiana

Diana of the Dunes

Indiana Dunes State Park

The naked young woman walks nimbly across the Indiana sand dunes, sheltered by a grove of black oak trees that nearly shut out the sun. Emerging on the wide beach, she stops to watch the shore birds tottering along on spindly legs as they search for breakfast at water's edge. They pay little attention to this odd, two-legged creature.

The woman plunges into the frigid water. She swims gracefully, her strong, swift strokes carrying her body effortlessly along.

Back on shore, she races back and forth over the sand to dry off. She stops, arches her back, and raises her arms. She tilts her face skyward as if giving thanks for the glory of the day. With a determined stride, she vanishes across the dunes in the direction she had come.

Who is this mysterious young woman and why is her life at the heart of a century-old northern Indiana ghost story? Her reputed appearances—virtually none of them verified—have been told and retold as if they were hard fact.

The first part is easy enough to answer, though much of her life remains veiled in mystery and ambiguity.

Alice Mabel Gray was her given name, but she came to be known to the world as Diana of the Dunes. From 1915 until her untimely death on

February 9, 1925, this mysterious, free-spirited Chicago native, University of Chicago Phi Beta Kappa graduate, and early dunes conservationist chose to eschew civilization and live in primitive conditions in the wild and rugged Indiana dunes country along the southern Lake Michigan shoreline.

Alice/Diana might have lived and died in obscurity had not someone seen her frequent nude swims, which was in reality simply the way she bathed, often twice a day, as she had no running water or steady water supply. Most likely it was a fisherman casting a line who first caught sight of her, though it is the man's wife who probably spread the salacious rumor of her nudity in an era when women's bathing suits were heavy, baggy woolen affairs that covered the wearer from neck to midcalf. But however the news spread among the scattered dunes residents, by the summer of 1916 the life of this skinny-dipping "bronzed goddess" would be forever changed.

Alice was in her midthirties when local newspaper reporters heard the rumors and combed the dunes to find this woman "costumed as Eve," as the *New York Times* described her in its obituary years later, flouncing around the region. It was a story they could not ignore in an era when facts often did not get in the way of a juicy tale. And that it certainly was.

She was not hard to find.

Alice Mabel Gray/Diana of the Dunes (sometimes *nymph* of the dunes) was living alone in a sand-floored, abandoned fisherman's shack that was "ten-foot square and without windows," as she later wrote. She had named it "Driftwood." She had been there since October 31, 1915. Now, some nine months later, Diana tried to tell the peering reporters that all she wanted was her privacy, to be left alone. She had fled Chicago and the severe limitations placed on women for the solitude of a more natural life among the sand dunes and as an advocate for its preservation.

Sadly that was not to be.

A century later, her story has been printed and reprinted in hundreds of newspapers and magazines. It is among the best-known legends of northern Indiana. Even today, visitors to what is now Indiana Dunes State Park look for the ghost of the mysterious Diana hurrying over the sands at dawn, or her sobs coming from the location of the old fishing shack that was once her home. Her tears shed because her dying wishes were not carried out.

The legend has arisen partly as a ghost story because so few firm facts are known about Alice's Gray's life. She was wont to exaggerate, obfuscate, or downright lie about her own background and intentions when reporters were hounding her. A biography published in 2010 gathered what information was known and could be verified.

Diana of the Dunes was not the child of a prominent Chicago physician, as was thought at one time (and may have been promoted by Alice herself), but the daughter of a hardscrabble working-class family, one of six children of Ambrose and Sallie Gray, born on March 25, 1881, when the family was living on South Hermitage Avenue in the McKinley Park neighborhood of the city. Her father was listed in city directories variously as an ironworker, spectacles maker, and lamplighter. He spent a year recovering from a gas lamp fire that burned his arms. Ambrose died in 1898 at the age of fifty-seven. Four years later, in 1902, Sallie Gray died of pulmonary tuberculosis.

Alice graduated from South Division High School at age sixteen in 1897 and immediately enrolled at the University of Chicago, where she primarily pursued math studies but also took foreign languages, theology, and astronomy classes.

She spent six years there, earning Phi Beta Kappa distinction and graduating in 1903. She had moved out of her family home by then and seemed to be headed for graduate school in Europe when she instead took a civil service job at age twenty-two with the United States Naval Observatory (USNO) in Washington, DC. She left Chicago alone for the nation's capital. She had been hired as one of the USNO's earliest women "computers," employees working for hours at a time with columns of logarithmic equations. The women, Diana included, made $1,200 annually, an amount not changed since 1892.

The woman who became Diana of the Dunes seemed to begin the mysteries connected to her life while in college and the two years she spent at the USNO.

University of Chicago yearbooks contain virtually no information about her, no list of activities, no photographs.

The same holds true for the USNO. A biographer found in their archives nothing but the most perfunctory information about her two years there. She was one of the few with not a single photograph in the files. Her life in Washington is a blank canvas.

How did she pay for it all? Her parents certainly did not have the money to send her to the University of Chicago (their own home had been bought for them by a relative). Evidence suggests she may have earned some of her way through college working part time as a stenographer or editing journals; she may have had relatives who helped her out as well. One story—which was recounted in her *New York Times* obituary—is that a high school friend did not need her scholarship to the University of Chicago and so she gave it to Alice.

Alice was showing her independence at a time when women could not vote, were barred from all but the most menial workplace jobs, and were certainly not supposed to travel alone halfway across the country to take a job with the government. But the Civil Service System was one of the few that openly encouraged female applicants for many levels of employment.

After about two years, Alice left the USNO to study mathematics as a "guest listener" at the University of Göttingen in Germany. The question that lingers here is why would she leave a relatively well-paying job for the era—and certainly for women—to take up the life of a graduate student? One possibility was that her former professors, who knew that university, encouraged her. The university was also one of the few European ones at the time to accept female students on an equal footing with their male counterparts.

Perhaps the thought of spending time living in and traveling through Europe was another step on her path of adventurous independence. Hour upon hour of hand-calculating mathematical figures must have become excruciatingly dreary to an intelligent twentysomething woman who wanted to push against the boundaries of what society considered "acceptable" female behavior. She may have also discovered the glass ceiling was already in place at the turn of the twentieth century—even in the Civil Service—and she was not going to advance very far in either the public or private sector despite her brilliant academics.

Records of her time in Germany were sent home with her so the only real details known are that she returned to the United States in 1908 and enrolled in graduate school back at the University of Chicago.

For about the next four years she studied, among other subjects, advanced math, "physical culture," beginning Sanskrit, and elementary Italian. She also signed up for philosophy but seems to have dropped the course. It is speculated that she may have helped edit a book and a university academic journal to help ends meet.

She dropped out of grad school in 1913. No records exist of the next two years of her life . . . nothing until the few residents and, eventually, the press discover this single woman taking up residence in the harsh, inhospitable Indiana dunes country.

Why would an undoubtedly brilliant woman like Alice Mabel Gray again make such a radical departure from the life she was leading? One theory is that she got fed up with society and its treatment and limitations of women and wanted to adopt a simple, back to nature existence like the dunes offered.

"I was tired of working under the conditions and the lighting in offices, so I came out here," she told one interviewer. "Then I wished never to go back to Chicago—to the learned and the officious. Out in the dunes I wished to regain my poise once more and trust."

On another occasion, she said, "The life of a wage earner is slavery."

But in another interview, she told a reporter that she left Chicago because her eyesight had begun to fail and a physician gave her the wrong medicine, which made it impossible for her to continue the close work her magazine job required.

Perhaps it was something more personal. Several writers have suggested it was a broken love affair with someone named "L," whom she references in a few of her surviving diary excerpts. Others put forward that her inability to compete with men in access to the workplace or rise at all above menial (to her) labor had led her to contemplate suicide.

One clear reason for choosing the dunes as her unlikely front yard is that she had visited the region as a child because her older sister and family lived in Michigan City, Indiana.

She also claimed to have written a naturalist's dissertation about the dunes when she was at the University of Chicago.

Whatever the truth, she adapted to her new natural world with enthusiasm if not adequate knowledge of how to set up housekeeping in little more than an unheated hovel amid miles and miles of the "trackless wilderness" of towering sand dunes, dense woods, and only scattered settlements that was the region a century ago. It was commonly termed a "wasteland" by those not enamored of its wildness.

According to most accounts, Alice Mabel Gray arrived in the Indiana dunes country with few possessions on Halloween day, October 31, 1915. One version is that she had the clothes on her back, a glass, a knife, a spoon, a blanket, and two guns. After sleeping on the moist sand for some time, she found a deserted fisherman's shack built years before by one George Blagge, a Civil War veteran and well-known character of the region. Hermits, recluses, and even criminals on the lam had ended up living among the dunes over the years. They would simply move into one of the many abandoned cabins. But they had all been men, of course. And that was probably the first thing that set tongues wagging.

Fortunately no one objected to her occupancy. She called the shack "Driftwood" because that was what served as her rough furniture . . . and because she felt like a piece of driftwood herself washing up on various shores.

That is the factual beginning of Alice's ten years in the Lake Michigan dunes. There is still much that we do not know. The first public notice of her occurred in the popular press of the day in the summer of 1916, but much of what was written was simply made up by reporters in pursuit of a sensational story. Adding to the complications is that Alice herself exaggerated or lied to curiosity seekers and reporters about her own personal background and intentions, probably to keep them from pestering her. She often did not tell visitors her real name.

At first Alice lived on the fish she caught or netted by hand and the wild fruits that grew on berry bushes sprouting among the dunes. She had a gun with which she reportedly bagged the ducks that flew overhead and was proclaimed an excellent shot. (If she was such a good shot, that would seem to be at odds with the belief that her move away from Chicago came about because of failing eyesight.)

With her hair chopped short and uneven (she had no mirror), shod in stout boots or often barefoot, and wearing formless khaki clothing, she trudged miles to the nearest communities to buy essentials and, extremely important to her, check out library books. People who spoke with her said she was shy but always kind and courteous, an eloquent speaker with a masterful vocabulary. She could converse on a wide range of topics and advocated forcefully for preserving the dunes' wild habitat, a conservation effort gaining support at the time.

So a well-educated, independent woman had turned her back on civilization to lead a solitary, Thoreau-like existence in a sandy wilderness less than an hour away from downtown Chicago. That must have been an exciting subject of speculation to those who lived in the area and who first encountered her.

Here was a woman who defied all sorts of boundaries to live "off the grid" in search of personal fulfillment.

Rumors and stories about this strange woman and her unconventional lifestyle soon reached the ears of reporters in Gary, Michigan City, and other regional newspapers anxious to track her down, and that they did.

First those local newspapers sought her out, then the Chicago press sent reporters in search of her. Within a few weeks, newspapers from California to New York carried scores of stories about this unconventional "female hermit," as some called her: "Diana of the Dunes Loses Fear of Men," "Diana of the Dunes Dissects Soul in Diary," "Mystery Still Hangs about Hermit Woman," "Woman Hermit of Sand Dunes Tells Sad Tale." (Female, most certainly. Hermit, hardly.)

The stories exaggerated her looks (a "beautiful nymph," though pictures show her to be quite plain) and her lifestyle ("takes her plunge [into the lake] like a goddess of the wave," when that was how she bathed) and treated her as possibly deranged and sometimes "hostile" or "hysterical" (who wouldn't be toward strangers nosing around one's domicile?).

A Chicago newspaper was the first to label her "Diana of the Dunes," after the Roman goddess of hunting, in the summer of 1916. That's the name that stuck—it is even chiseled above her birth name on her Gary, Indiana, cemetery marker.

Newspapers ran outlandish stories of this female "discovered" like some runaway from a lost civilization. Much of what was said or implied was wrong. Some newspapers simply reprinted the news item, adding their own spin whether it was true or not.

At first she tried to ignore the pack of newspeople (mostly male; there was at least one female reporter on her story) looking for her but in time she relented, perhaps realizing they would never give up. While she tried to promote conserving the dunes, most of the reporters were after a sensational story about her unconventional lifestyle.

In the modern era of social media, we would say the story of Diana of the Dunes "went viral." It was everywhere. Tourists and curiosity seekers showed up to talk to her. Front page stories followed her every move.

The attention caused her to question her decision to settle there, but in time she seems to have become comfortable in using her fame to help protect the dunes from encroaching civilization. She was even a speaker at a large gathering on the subject at Fullerton Hall, the Art Institute of Chicago, in April 1917.

In 1918 Alice's life alone ended when a twenty-six-year-old drifter who called himself Paul Wilson came into her life. Although he claimed to be from Texas (he may have served in the army there), he was actually Paul George Eisenblatter, born and raised in Michigan City, a ne'er-do-well and minor criminal. But for reasons still hard to fathom, Alice fell in love with him.

He was a man with a hair trigger temper, constantly picking frights with neighbors and visitors to the dunes, and was continuously in trouble with law enforcement. Shortly after they met he began serving a six-month sentence for petty theft. They corresponded regularly during his incarceration.

Whatever his background, he was tall, strong, and resourceful. One newspaper called him her "caveman."

He improved Driftwood immeasurably, peddling the fish he caught, selling his handcrafted driftwood furniture, and even building small boats by hand. At some point they found new lodging in a larger cabin (Wren's Nest) at Ogden Dunes. By most surviving accounts Paul was devoted to her. He even told a reporter sometime later that they had gotten married, though they probably had a common-law marriage. Their finances improved, Alice was content. Perhaps she had at last found someone with whom she could share her distaste for societal norms and her desire for solitude and independence.

She could not know that violence would destroy this promising new life.

In June 1922 a dunes hiker found the grisly, charred remains of a man close to Waverly Beach. The coroner was unable to identify the victim. Although the remains were some distance from Paul and Alice's cabin, suspicion settled almost at once on Paul Wilson and by extension Alice. He was known for his hot temper, his great strength, and his strong dislike of strangers. Newspapers did term him her "caveman." She was still viewed with suspicion by many dune residents.

Newspapers jumped on the story, headlines screaming: "'Diana of Dunes' Being Sought in Slaying Mystery," "Husband of Diana Gives First Clue," "Original 'Diana of the Dunes' and Mate Flee as Civilization Intrudes," "Diana's Cottage Broken into by Curiosity Seekers."

The stories generally focused on Paul Wilson's "criminal" background and all but convicted him in print. They claimed both Paul and Diana were seen near the scene of the crime. There was no evidence of that.

Reporters, police, and curiosity seekers made life miserable for the couple.

Alice Gray was livid at the accusations.

When Eugene Frank, a deputy hired to guard dunes cottages and a purveyor of rumors about Paul Wilson's guilt, confronted an angry Alice and Paul, a fight broke out. Frank shot Paul in the foot and fractured Alice's skull with the butt of his pistol.

Police arrested both Paul Wilson and Deputy Eugene Frank. Alice was transported to Mercy Hospital in Gary, where she hovered near death.

Someone vandalized the shack while the couple was gone, taking many of Alice's books, diaries, and other writings.

Meanwhile, Wilson insisted that a stranger committed the murder. No one fitting Wilson's description was ever found. Perhaps he was the victim? If not, whose charred remains were these? And why was he slain?

The body was never identified, the case never solved, Paul Wilson never charged in the murder.

Alice was discharged from the hospital, but she never fully recovered her physical and emotional health. It had taken a toll that put her on a downward spiral.

To make matters worse, within a short time progress—in the form of automobiles and people—closed in on Alice Mabel Gray and Paul George Eisenblatter Wilson. The solitude and independence both cherished were growing more elusive.

With the completion of the Dunes Highway (U.S. Highway 12) through northern Indiana, parts of Lower Michigan and north through Illinois, city residents from Chicago and elsewhere were vacationing there or even putting up homes. The same man who owned the property with Wren's Nest on it was developing a new beachfront housing development at Ogden Dunes. His name was Samuel Reck. He told the couple they could stay in their cabin for the time being.

But it all seemed to be too much for them. Angry and upset with encroaching civilization, the accusations of murder against them, and the newspaper inaccuracies that continued to be published, they made plans to "escape" by taking an open boat Paul had rebuilt down the Mississippi River. Maybe he would hunt rattlesnakes in Texas. He had done that at one time, or so he said.

Yet within only a few months, their flight south ended and they were back at Wren's Nest . . . with Samuel Reck's *permission* this time.

Part of the reason for the return may have been connected to what they did next: they brought a libel lawsuit against several newspapers for the alleged falsehoods written about them. After eight years! Alice and Paul filed the federal lawsuit in the Hammond, Indiana, federal court in June 1924 asking for in excess of $100,000 in damages, a significant sum in those years.

Alice never got her day in court.

Alice Mable Gray Wilson became desperately ill in the shack they called Wren's Nest in early 1925. Despite Paul's frantic pleas, she did not seek treatment from a doctor or go to the hospital. After a week or more of a worsening condition, she fell into a coma on February 8. Paul found Samuel Rock and together they took Reck's car to fetch a doctor from Gary. He diagnosed uremic poisoning (kidney failure) and prescribed hot water bags and "stimulants." Neither that remedy nor the additional medicine worked. Alice died in the early morning hours of February 9, 1925.

Knowing she was dying, Alice asked to be cremated, her ashes scattered from Mount Tom, the tallest of the dunes. But cremation was a rare and expensive burial procedure then. Paul had no money to speak of and her own family would not allow it. Paul wanted to build a funeral pyre on the beach to perform the cremation himself, but the authorities refused.

Paul Wilson was nearly crazed at Alice's funeral because he would not be allowed to carry out those final wishes of hers. He packed a handgun at the funeral and threatened anyone who attempted to bury her. Authorities jailed him until the funeral was over

Alice's remains were interred in Gary's Oak Hill Cemetery. Her marker reads simply

Diana of the Dunes

Alice Gray Wilson

Nov. 25   Feb. 9

1881   1925

There is some irony that today, as with most mortuaries, Oak Hill offers the services of a crematory.

Within days, news of the death of Diana of the Dunes made the pages of newspapers from coast to coast. The *New York Times* devoted seven paragraphs to the story: "'Diana of the Dunes' Dies of Privations; Chicago Woman Who Took Up the Primitive Life in 1916 Refused Hospital Aid"; while the *Helena* (Montana) *Independent* took a more ethereal, albeit erroneous, approach that may have helped formulate the ghost story: "Diana of Dunes Is Dead, Dancing in Moonlight on Sands of Shore at End."

What of Paul Wilson? He married again—this time to a wealthy Wisconsin native who owned dunes property and with whom he had two children, got into frequent trouble with the law, and at some point ended up in California.

Alice and Paul seemed to have shared an unconventional life with each other. Her death nearly drove him mad. Newspapers for a while were curious about how Diana's "caveman" was going to cope without her. Not well, it seems. One story published two months after her death (in a Fresno, California, newspaper, of all places) described Paul as saying Diana's ghost haunted him because he was not able to carry out her final wishes . . . She came to him as he sat at Mount Tom and watched for her.

It was that tender image that helped spread the ghost stories of this beautiful Diana haunting for all time her beloved dunes.

The press eventually stopped writing about Paul until news of his death came in 1941 in Bakersfield, California.

There are dozens of variations told about all aspects of Alice Mabel Gray's colorful life, many of them propagated by Alice herself, her husband, her friends, people who had never met her, and, most frequently, the newspapers of the day. But in the end all that we do know is that Alice Gray was an independent woman perhaps decades ahead of her time in advocating for conservation of this natural treasure, brilliant and nonconforming, who only wanted to be left alone in peace during life and united with her beloved dunes in death. Sadly neither would come to pass.

Is it any wonder then that stories of her ghost are such a part of the dunes lore? And beyond. There is the Mabel Gray Restaurant in Hazel Park, Michigan, a suburb of Detroit, where "everything is handmade from scratch."

So it is not so hard to believe that by the light of a full moon, Diana of the Dunes stands silhouetted on the beach, perhaps near Mount Tom, giving thanks for the glory of the night and the peace and solitude it brings to her.

The Haunting of Hannah House

Indianapolis

Are ghosts naturally attracted to empty houses where they are less likely to be disturbed? Or do they occasionally prefer the livelier company of the living?

Stories of ghostly activity in the Hannah House, a stately, nineteenth-century, red-brick mansion in Indianapolis, began after it had sat empty for several years in the 1960s. Since then, eyewitnesses have described a mysterious man in a frock coat who wanders the hallways, sickening smells of decaying flesh wafting through the air, crashing unseen glassware, pictures falling off the walls for no apparent reason, and encounters with sudden, numbing cold spots.

The history of Hannah House certainly lends itself to colorful legends and absorbing stories. Built three years before the American Civil War, the twenty-four-room mansion is part of the legacy of Alexander M. Hannah, an Indiana state legislator, postmaster, sheriff, and clerk of the circuit court. When it was first built, it was supposedly used as a way station on the Underground Railroad. Hannah used the basement to hide the African Americans escaping slavery in the Southern states. One tale is that a lantern tipped over in the basement one night and the subsequent fire killed many of the slaves awaiting their journey north. They were buried in rude caskets in the basement.

From all outward signs, Alexander and his wife, Elizabeth Jackson Hannah, whom he married in 1872 when he was fifty-one years old, lived a peaceful life in the lovely Italianate-style home on Madison Avenue. The couple may have had a stillborn child, but they certainly did not lead the sort of tragic lives that often beget unhappy specters.

Alexander Hannah died in 1895 and four years later, Roman Oehler, a prosperous Indianapolis jeweler, bought the house. His daughter, Romena Oehler Elder, inherited the mansion upon her father's death. In 1962, with all the children gone, Romena moved out and left the care of the place to her youngest son, David. The house remained empty for six years.

David Elder was the first to suspect that the vacant Hannah House was "occupied" by otherworldly beings.

He was working alone there one bleak and rain-soaked day in the late 1960s when the distinctive crack of breaking glass came from somewhere in the basement.

Elder investigated the noise but found nothing disturbed. Interestingly, the jars Elder suspected had somehow fallen and broken were stored in the area where it is suspected the slaves had been buried more than a century before. So far as is known there was no attempt to unearth and rebury the remains.

From time to time, the odor of rotting flesh seemed to emanate from a second-floor bedroom, a smell so strong that it sent more than one visitor reeling out the front door. Attempts to eradicate it with cleaning solutions, bleach, perfume, and other potions failed. However, at other times a much more pleasant rose fragrance was produced. But there were no flowers kept in the room; normally it was locked up and used for storage.

In addition, the door that opened from the aromatic room into the hallway seemingly possessed a will of its own—it swung open even when the handle was securely locked. Once it opened, an increase in other unexplained activity in the house would occur, including strange noises, footsteps, cold drafts, and voices mumbling in shadowy passages.

Lynn Dohrenwend, an Indianapolis psychic, once insisted that she "saw" a pregnant woman in that room, a woman obviously in severe pain with abdominal cramps apparently caused by the child she was carrying. The child had later been stillborn, said the psychic.

There was no official record of any child having been born to the Hannahs. However, a later investigation at Crown Hill Cemetery, where the Hannahs were interred, revealed a third, smaller tombstone next to their own. No name was on it. Some speculate it was the grave of that still-born child.

Gladys O'Brien and her husband, John Francis O'Brien, operated an antique business in the house from 1968 and 1978 and lived there part of that time. During their stay, the couple said they were subjected to an array of strange incidents.

Early one evening, Gladys O'Brien caught a glimpse of a man in a black suit walking across the upstairs hallway. She thought a customer had somehow ventured onto the second floor, which had been closed to visitors. Yet by the time she reached the top of the stairs, the mysterious visitor was gone.

On another occasion, a painter sprucing up the interior claimed that he became the unwitting target of whatever it was that haunted the house. Doors would swing open as he walked by, and pictures slid from their moorings. In the most bizarre event, a spoon Gladys had placed on a tray flew across the room. The painter fled.

The O'Briens' son volunteered to finish the house-painting job. An uneasy feeling of being watched made him very uncomfortable that first night. So the next evening the young man's wife and two daughters accompanied him to the house. His younger daughter, Cheryl, played on the stairs while her father, mother, and sister worked in an adjoining room. Soon, he heard Cheryl talking to someone.

"Hi, Dad," the girl said. That was the affectionate name the children used not for their own father but for their grandfather, John O'Brien.

But the elder O'Brien was not in the house. Cheryl continued to talk to her "grandfather," while the rest of the family looked on. In a few minutes, Cheryl's father asked what "Dad" was doing now. She replied that he was climbing the stairs.

John O'Brien once encountered the Hannah House mystery man. The transparent specter was standing in an archway on the staircase, sporting mutton-chop whiskers and wearing a dark, old-fashioned suit of clothes.

Quite often, the rustling of clothing and the sound of footsteps of varying loudness were heard on the staircase; some steps were light, others heavier. Oddly, the stairway was carpeted at that time. When either one of the O'Briens checked on the source of the sounds, they ceased.

The door to a staircase leading to an attic from the second floor also had a mind of its own. John O'Brien heard something upstairs as he worked on the lower floor. He rushed up the staircase and down the hall-way, throwing open each closed door. His eagerness waned, however, once he reached the attic door and saw the handle itself turning slowly. The door swung open, emitting a cool draft from the unused loft. He did not go in.

The O'Briens often watched television in a room on the second floor. Once John heard what he identified as loud groaning. A few minutes later it began again. He yelled to the ghost to stop its "bellyaching" and leave them in peace. The groaning stopped for that night.

In the early 1980s, the house's ghostly reputation led the Indianapolis Jaycees to use Hannah House for their annual Halloween haunted house project. They sponsored tours of the old mansion for youngsters, replete with rigged, spooky effects—except that some of the effects were not planned.

Dick Raasch was once the Jaycees' coordinator for the project. One day he was relaxing with fellow workers in the old summer kitchen, a part of the original house. A scratching suddenly arose from inside the staircase wall, the rear staircase originally used by servants. David Elder, who was there assisting the Jaycees with their setup, dashed beneath the stairs looking for the sound but could not locate a source for it.

A local television station got in on the supernatural action when it visited Hannah House for a Halloween segment. One of the cameramen stood in the dining room doorway in order to take a shot across the room. An old chandelier hung from the ceiling.

"Wouldn't it be eerie if the chandelier moved?" he said, looking up. At that instant, the chandelier started to swing in about a half-foot arc.

On that very same day, the television crew brought a psychic to the house. She sensed cold spots. The crew then moved into a room where they were going to film some "exit" footage. The cameraman stood in one of two doorways to the room, and a reporter stood near an empty coffin that had been propped up against a wall. Suddenly, a picture above the coffin fell to the floor. The two-penny nail holding the picture had not moved. In fact, it was nailed into a stud at an upward angle. The wire on the old picture remained attached.

"There is no conceivable way the picture could have fallen of its own accord," Dick Raasch observed. "It lifted up and fell. It looked like somebody dropped it to the floor."

How to explain these incidents?

"I can't explain them," Raasch confided. "Something was in [the house] . . . I just don't know what it was."

The Vigil

Terre Haute

Deloris Hart opened her eyes and tried to focus on the unfamiliar surroundings. Where is this place? What am I doing here? So many questions for a young child.

The bed was much bigger than the one she had at home. The sheets were pulled taut, a light blanket drawn over the top, so tight in fact that they practically pinned her to the mattress. She could barely turn her body. Her legs and arms felt as if rocks held them down. Something white was wrapped around them. She could not move her head, which hurt terribly anyway.

The child's eyes shifted slowly about the room, noticing the window with the drawn curtain, and the shade pulled down that cast the room in a veil of darkness. A door in one of the walls went somewhere, she surmised, and two, simple, wooden chairs were positioned next to the bed.

This was not her home. Of that she was certain.

But where was she then?

The pleasant lady standing at the foot of her bed was definitely not her mother. Deloris tried to speak to her, but the woman pressed her right forefinger against her lips. There was something peculiar about her, the little girl thought. She looked a lot like a pretty lady from her fairy-tale books. A kind of haze shimmered around her. She had such a nice smile that Deloris was not a bit afraid—she felt very warm and comfortable in her presence.

Deloris drifted in and out of consciousness over the next several days. She could not remember exactly what had happened, only that she had been in the car with her grandpa and greatgrandpa when something bad happened; of that much she was certain. And then there was darkness.

Now she was someplace where men and women in white coats often came into the room. Oddly, Deloris thought, they never acknowledged the nice lady who never moved or spoke.

One man peered into Deloris's eyes and throat with a small light. She tried to ask him where her mama and papa were, but somehow she could not make the right sounds.

What Deloris Hart did not know was that her parents, Herbert and Rose Hart, in an earlier time of hospital care policies, were not allowed into their daughter's Terre Haute hospital room for the first few days after the accident. She was in critical condition and not expected to live.

On an earlier afternoon, an automobile had swerved across the center-line directly into the path of her grandfather's car, in which she was riding. Her great-grandfather had been killed instantly. Grandfather lingered close to death in another hospital room.

Deloris was terribly injured; flying glass had sliced off nearly half her scalp. Despite all this, Deloris Hart recovered. The doctors actually termed her recovery a miracle. Her parents were thankful; their prayers had been answered.

Although she remembered nothing of the accident and little of her days of recovery, she did know that the kind, smiling lady was always there in her room. The other people who silently entered her room ignored the woman. That was so silly, Deloris thought; why did they not say hello? Could they not see her? How rude.

The mystery woman had jet-black hair, deep-brown eyes, and a light complexion. She never touched Deloris or came any closer than the end of her bed. Once Deloris had sufficiently recovered, she was able to tell her parents about the nice lady. Hospital doctors and nurses insisted that no one of that description had been allowed into the girl's room.

Who then was the visitor who kept a vigil over Deloris?

Following Deloris's release from the hospital, her father became obsessed with discovering this mystery woman's identity. He firmly believed that someone only Deloris could see and interact with had been a constant, caring presence in the hospital room.

The answer came much later. As Herbert Hart was clearing out some boxes and trunks, he came upon a batch of old family photographs. Deloris's eyes shone when he happened to show the pictures to her.

That was the nice lady who was in my room, she told her dad, pointing to one of the photos.

Impossible, her father replied. It simply could not be.

Yes, the child insisted, that was the woman. "She made me want to live."

The photograph was of Herbert Hart's mother, Belle Hart.

She had been dead for twenty years.

One of the Family

Evansville

We only know him by his first name, Oscar. The kids in his Evansville neighborhood knew him as a friendly, outgoing nineteen-year-old who took delight in giving them rides in his car when automobiles were still a new and exciting way of getting around. They piled in, eager to meander the dusty roads around the city. Late in the evening Oscar brought them back to his house, and, calling good night, he watched as they scattered to their own homes.

The routine did not vary on that one evening in the early 1920s when everyone waved as Oscar went into his house. They never saw him again. His parents found him the next morning dead in bed of undetermined causes.

Yet Oscar's ghost apparently lingered for many years in Evansville, attached to a family that moved into Oscar's old home years after his death. Warren and Gladys Reynolds believed they were the targets of Oscar's friendly antics for over forty years, beginning when they moved into his home as a young married couple in 1942.

"At first I thought they were ordinary noises," soft-spoken Gladys Reynolds remembered. "But my husband thought from the beginning that something peculiar was going on. He always seemed to have the most experiences. I worked during the days, and he was on the night shift as a deputy sheriff. Oscar seemed to be around more during the day when my husband was at home."

The Reynoldses' first indication that Oscar was still in "his" house came during a thunderstorm. The family was in a downstairs room when footsteps suddenly pounded down an upstairs hallway. What followed sounded like windows being shut in the bedrooms. Sure enough, when the family went upstairs to close them, each window that had been open was now firmly closed against the developing storm.

On another day, the couple's twelve-year-old daughter was home alone finishing homework at the dining room table. Someone came pounding down the staircase. The child was so frightened she slid under the big round table and covered her eyes. The footsteps stopped abruptly. She carefully peered out from under the table but saw she was quite alone.

Oscar, it seems, was a very shy ghost.

On only two occasions did he allow himself to be seen. The witness in both cases was Warren Reynolds's mother. She lived with her son and his family for several years.

Grandmother Reynolds occupied the same bedroom in which Oscar was reputed to have died. The first time she saw Oscar was quite late at night, when a sharp noise forced her awake. There was Oscar standing with his back to her, bending over the fireplace grate. She pulled the blanket over her head and waited a few moments before peeking out again. The shadowy figure lingered for a few moments before melting into the darkness.

Oscar's second visit to his old bedroom was a bit shorter, and again at night. He was standing stock still with his back toward Grandmother Reynolds. And as before, after a few seconds, he seemed to dissolve into the darkness.

Oscar liked to prowl about the partially finished attic.

"My husband heard someone up there one afternoon," Gladys Reynolds said. "He thought some kids had broken in through a window."

Since Warren was a deputy sheriff, he took out his revolver and headed up the stairs. All the windows were locked and nothing had been disturbed. He was convinced someone had been walking around up there.

Another incident involved a friend of Gladys who came to visit for several days. Late the first evening, after her friend had gone to bed, from upstairs Gladys distinctly heard drawers opening and slamming shut, footfalls across the squeaky floorboards, and doors slamming. She thought perhaps her friend was walking about. At breakfast the next morning, however, the friend emphatically denied being the source of the nocturnal activity.

The Reynolds family eventually moved out of Oscar's house. It was taken down long ago.

Might he have moved with them into their next home? The family thought so.

Gladys Reynolds says there were two occasions when objects mysteriously disappeared, only to be found later in places the family had thoroughly searched.

"When I couldn't find my makeup compact in its usual drawer," she said, "I thought my granddaughter had taken it to play with. . . . I looked everywhere and after a few days I just gave up. My daughter and her family left and I still couldn't find the compact. Well I opened a cabinet and there it was right in front of my eyes. I had looked there and would certainly have seen it if it had been there earlier."

Gladys thinks these were Oscar's pranks. After forty years of living with him, the Reynoldses treated the ghost like one of the family. There was no fear of him and, indeed, the family responded to his infrequent visits with a matter-of-factness characteristic of people who have accepted what is sometimes so hard for others to believe.

"I never did believe in ghosts either," Gladys Reynolds laughed. "But I know what I heard, what my husband believes, and what my mother-in-law saw."

That was good enough for her. Oscar was "their" ghost. He was a member of the family for all time.

Tippecanoe and Tecumseh, Too

Warren County

William Henry Harrison, the ninth president of the United States, and the great Shawnee Tecumseh were of two different worlds, yet their lives were intertwined.

Each was a great leader of his people, each was a bitter enemy of the other, each would die an untimely death—and each has become the center of beguiling Indiana legends: that ghost soldiers from the army Harrison commanded in the Battle of Tippecanoe still march across the Indiana soil, and that the most devastating earthquake in American history occurred shortly after Tecumseh promised to "make the earth tremble" as retribution against his faltering Indian allies.

Although he was born in 1773 to wealthy parents near Richmond, Virginia, William Henry Harrison spurned the comfortable life of a gentleman for the privations of the military. After dropping out of medical school, Harrison joined the fledgling U.S. Army in 1791, where he served with merit in the early Indian wars in the wilderness that became Ohio and Indiana. He rose quickly to the rank of lieutenant.

President John Adams appointed him governor of the Indiana territory in 1800 when he was still commandant of Fort Washington, Ohio. In later years, Harrison served as congressman, U.S. senator, ambassador to Colombia, and, of course, for only thirty-one days, as the ninth American president. On the rain-chilled day of his inauguration, the old soldier contracted pneumonia and died a month later, on April 4, 1841. He became the first American president to die in office.

Harrison is also remembered for the famous political slogan of that 1840 presidential campaign, "Tippecanoe and Tyler, Too." John Tyler of Virginia was his running mate, and the man who became the tenth president of the United States when he finished Harrison's abbreviated term.

The Tippecanoe phrase came about from Harrison's victory over the Shawnee at the 1811 battle on the Tippecanoe River, a few miles northeast of present-day Lafayette, Indiana.

As governor of the Indiana Territory, Harrison banned the sale of liquor to the tribe and ordered that they be inoculated against smallpox.

But his largesse did not extend to treating them with respect or as equals. In 1809 he negotiated a treaty with Shawnee leaders whereby nearly three million acres of wilderness on the Wabash and White rivers were forfeited to white settlers.

Several Shawnee leaders, however, objected vehemently to the new treaty, including the celebrated Tecumseh, and his brother Tenskwatawa, the Prophet. Both declared their intentions to regain the land surrendered to the U.S. government . . . by any means necessary.

Early in 1811, Chief Tecumseh set out on a long, more or less campaign journey that took him to tribal villages throughout the West, Middle West, and South. From the Sioux and Apache in the West, to the Alabama people along the southern Mississippi River, Tecumseh boasted that he could deliver a war that would drive the white settlers back into the sea.

He met with only partial success. Although many young men joined with him, others doubted Tecumseh's promise of eventual victory over the whites.

One tribe of Alabama people that made its camp on the banks of the Mississippi was especially contemptuous of Tecumseh.

"Your promises are like the wind," their chief scoffed when Tecumseh finished his speech. "The wind is free. Talk is nothing."

As the snow of late winter swirled through the Alabama camp, Tecumseh made a promise to his hosts of what he would do when he returned to his own people near present-day Detroit: "I will stamp the ground, the earth will tremble and shake down all your wigwams. You will remember Tecumseh!"

71

The Alabama people laughed and shook their heads.

Yet did Tecumseh's "curse" come true only a few months later?

On December 16, 1811, the most violent earthquake in the history of the United States roared through the lower Middle West. The New Madrid Earthquake, so named because the epicenter was located near that small Missouri town, destroyed homes, wigwams, and much more, from Cincinnati to Kansas City. The Mississippi River itself actually cut new channels and even reversed its southerly flow for a time, throwing riverboats against the shore.

Forty thousand square miles of undulating earth swallowed farms and villages. The exact number of human casualties is unknown because the land was so sparsely settled, but estimates range from several hundred to many thousands.

The Alabama said it was Tecumseh's prophecy come true.

"He has stamped his feet at Detroit!"

A tragic and bizarre coincidence? Probably. But Tecumseh *did* say he would make the earth tremble.

The Indian nations that joined up with Tecumseh terrorized white settlers up and down the length of the Wabash River Valley in late 1811. Westward immigration had steadily increased the number of settlers in Indiana and eastern Illinois. The land was being stripped of the virgin wilderness by European settlers, replaced by farms and settlements. Tecumseh, his brother the Prophet, and their followers refused to accept the prospect of being driven from their homes to new land in the West.

Thus it was that the Indiana territorial governor General William Henry Harrison took control of the militia and marched northward from the capital of Vincennes to Terre Haute, where he built a fort to defend the Wabash Valley.

General Harrison left Terre Haute with his troops in the first week of November 1811 to forcibly remove the remaining native people from what he declared to be newly designated "federal" land.

As the general's well-armed force approached the mouth of the Tippecanoe River, near present-day Americus, Indiana, in Tippecanoe County, the soldiers were met by a delegation of Shawnee from the village of the

Prophet. They wanted to talk. Although he was suspicious, Harrison agreed to meet with them the next day, November 7, 1811.

In a freezing drizzle just before dawn, however, the Shawnee warriors swarmed upon Harrison's troops. Harrison had wisely ordered the militia to sleep in full battle attire, and thus they were able to keep the Prophet's men at bay until daylight, when the soldiers mounted a bloody counterattack.

In the hand-to-hand combat, sixty soldiers were killed and more than one hundred were wounded. Scores of Shawnee fighters were also killed and wounded. The Prophet's men fled but General Harrison was not content. He marched on the main Indian encampment and burned it to the ground. The Prophet and most of his followers escaped. Harrison returned to Vincennes a hero.

Meanwhile, Tecumseh was in southern Indiana when his brother attacked Harrison's soldiers. He had not approved of the foray, and in fact publicly criticized the Prophet for upsetting his careful plans to wrest control of the territory from the Americans.

In the end, Tecumseh and most of his followers fled to Canada, where they joined the British in their fight against the United States in the War of 1812. The Indian wars in the Middle West had ended for all practical purposes when Tecumseh was killed in the Battle of Thames, Ontario. The British had virtually abandoned their posts in the Middle West by 1813.

Are the wars really over for General Harrison's militia, or do their ghostly remains still march across western Indiana on their way to a phantom Battle of Tippecanoe?

For well over a century, a two-story, wood-frame house, about twelve miles north of Williamsport, in Warren County, has been noted in local legend as the scene of curious activities that some have linked to the paranormal. Indeed, the house was on the precise route that Harrison and his militiamen took on their way to the Tippecanoe engagement.

On certain nights in early November, the unmistakable cadence of hundreds of marching feet approaches from a southerly direction. With drums rolling and steps reverberating against the cold, fall air, the spectral sounds grow louder as they approach the house and then gradually recede as the procession passes to the northeast. There are never any apparitions, only the resonant echoes of a vanished army.

Moody's Light

Rensselaer

What is the peculiar shimmering orb that so many people claim to have seen between Francesville and Rensselaer in northwest Indiana? The glowing, evanescent light in an isolated wood mutates in color from red to white, chases cars and people, and, according to local folklore, is connected to several deaths.

The origins of Moody's Light, or the Francesville Light as it is sometimes known, reaches back over a century, although its specific source is unknown. There are some unsubstantiated claims that scientists have investigated it, but it is most widely known in the folklore of northern Indiana.

The light's geographic center is hard to pinpoint. It is not listed on county maps, of course, making it necessary to ask a local for directions. The core of its activity is often said to be along rural Meridian Road, about fifteen miles west of Francesville; it is most often reported across an open field in a dank woodlot. It flashes red to white and back again. Once, a young woman watching the light with some friends claimed it shot across the field with bullet-like speed. The light was so bright, the young woman said, that she and her friends had to shield their eyes. The edges of the sphere were clearly visible to them.

One man who claimed to have seen it offered that the light looks quite like an automobile's headlights, though he did not see how that was possible. "We've been out there when it will come right up to the car. It illuminates the whole area. It's scary. It sits way out in the woods and as it comes close it changes colors back and forth. It scares you to death when it comes up like that."

There are several legends connected to the origin of the Moody name.

The most commonly held belief is that it originated with a family by that name that lived in the neighborhood long ago. Late one night, the father returned home to find his family trapped inside their burning home. The light is said to be the father swinging his lantern, searching for his lost family. However, that would not explain why the light turns various colors.

Some investigators say rotting organic matter, light reflecting from a fog bank, or periodic emissions of natural gas deposits may be possible causes for the light.

The Indiana University Folklore Archives has collected several versions of the legend. More recently, Indiana-based ghost hunters have created YouTube videos purporting to show the light.

Whatever its origin, Moody's Light adds a touch of the unknown to the bucolic countryside of rural Indiana.

The Stump

Bloomington

The worn, narrow dirt trail to Stepp Cemetery begins at a curved rock wall near a state highway in a dense Indiana state forest not far from Bloomington. The path winds up a short hill, skirts a broad, brushy thicket, then finds its way through a stand of massive oak and poplar trees, emerging at the graveyard. A few dozen headstones are all that remain. Most of the markers date to the nineteenth and early twentieth centuries. Faded plastic flowers are strewn over some of the simple graves.

It is a peaceful atmosphere.

Along the south boundary there is a row of broken, lichen-covered tombstones, including one on which time and nature have expunged the deceased's name. The barely visible outline of sunken earth is less than three feet in length. A child's grave, it would seem. Nearby is a small stump in the shape of a chair.

It is here, on what some have termed a natural "throne," that the legend of Stepp Cemetery may have originated, for it is said the ghost of a nameless old woman sits there each night—watching . . . and waiting.

Or so the legend associated with this hallowed place would have you believe. It is one of the state's most enduring ghost tales.

Folklorists identify one popular version of the woman's presence this way:

> [Many] years ago, a woman gave birth to a child who was struck and killed by a car when just a toddler. She buried the child in Stepp Cemetery. The woman had a tree with twisted branches next to the grave cut down and the stump shaped into a chair. She desired to sit in it and protect her child from strangers. When she was not on her chair, she put a "curse" on it to protect the grave. If anyone sat there, or even touched it when she was not there, that person would die one year later—to the day.

Presumably, it is the woman's ghost that has taken over the chore of guarding the small grave.

Other "witnesses" to the ghostly guardian are more precise.

The child's mother had long, white hair, was quite old but not ugly, and always dressed in black. A strange triangular mark scarred her forehead. The woman rarely accosted visitors, preferring to sit on the stump swaying back and forth as if the child lay nestled in her arms.

Folklorists at the nearby Indiana University-Bloomington have collected some of the other popular origin stories for the ghost.

In one version, sometime during the 1950s a girl was killed and her body dumped in Stepp Cemetery. The girl's mother comes to the cemetery nightly in search of the killer. If he runs, he will die as the girl did—stabbed and beaten beyond recognition.

In another story, during a drive through the state forest, a girl told her boyfriend that she did not love him. He shoved her from the car and sped away. She was never seen again. Several days later, the girl's mother also vanished in that same area. When couples go into the forest in search of the girl's body, her mother's ghost secretly checks their car to see if her daughter might be hiding in it.

A final variation is disturbing albeit poignant for any mother. In it, a mysterious woman in black visits the grave of her small daughter every midnight. She disinters the girl's corpse and cuddles it through the night.

The tales of Stepp Cemetery have also taken on some of the characteristics of modern horror folklore.

In every state, for instance, tales are told of a character called "The Hook," a nefarious being who skulks about lovers' lanes waiting to pounce on unsuspecting couples. He is generally described as an escaped convict who can be easily identified: he has a steel hook where a hand ought to be. The lovers generally learn of the man's escape over the car radio and become so afraid they decide to leave their isolated location. At home, they find a steel claw—or a deep scratch from one—embedded in their car door.

The Hook of Stepp Cemetery, however, is female and she is not an escaped convict.

A local version of the tale explains that a woman and her small son were involved in a horrible automobile accident. She was seriously injured and her son killed. He was buried in Stepp Cemetery. His mother's hand was smashed in the accident and replaced with a steel claw. The boy had always been afraid of the dark. His mother decided to use the tree stump as her perch to watch over the grave each day after nightfall. She continued to do so until her own death; her ghost now sits on that stump. But she is so shy she flees when a car approaches yet manages to shake her hook-hand at the intruders. Her only companion is a ghostly white dog.

Detailed written encounters with the ghost of Stepp Cemetery are scarce, as one might suspect. The legends rarely include actual physical encounters with the ghost. However, several late-night visitors claim to have been frightened by something. A teen girl remembered the following harrowing experience:

> Connie and Jeanne and I went out to Stepp Cemetery. They had told me stories, but I had never been there. I really didn't want to go, but they talked me into it. I really didn't believe the stories.
>
> I wouldn't get out of the car, but Jeanne finally got out and said we should just walk around. After awhile, we got back in the car and started

to drive out. Right where the road curves and goes back to the highway, we suddenly heard the wind, like things rushing through the trees. It was really dark, too. I was driving, and then, right in the middle of the road, there was this image, rippling right in front of the car. The car lights went off. The motor died, too.

We all screamed, and I closed my eyes. Connie started to cry. We locked the doors and rolled up the windows. We tried turning the key, but the car just wouldn't start. We could hear that wind on both sides of the road. That image drifted on across the road. Then all by itself, the car started. No one touched the ignition. Connie wanted to get out and look at the battery and engine, but I wasn't going to let anybody out of the car. We took off!

The three girls never again ventured into Stepp Cemetery.

Perhaps the oddest legend associated with this old cemetery has nothing to do with women in black.

State forest rangers will tell visitors the cemetery was begun by area families in the early 1800s. (The earliest identifiable graves are from the Civil War era.) However, some believe in the legend of the Crabbites, an alleged nineteenth-century religious sect that is supposed to have used it for their bizarre church services, which included speaking in tongues, handling live snakes, and sexual promiscuity.

A longtime resident of Monroe County told an earlier researcher that her father had been called to the cemetery late one evening to help quell a particularly frenetic Crabbite sexual rite. He snapped a bullwhip above their heads to break up the orgy.

Despite the scant evidence to support orgies among the tombstones or phantom women in black mourning a deceased child, Stepp Cemetery continues to draw visitors fascinated by legends that will not go away. These visitors want to discover for themselves if it is perhaps only the occasional teenager who finds a "twisted tree stump" to sit on and say boo, or if there might not be another thing that perches there in the darkness. Waiting.

Iowa

Gone Too Soon

Southeast Iowa

Travelers through southeastern Iowa can find a quintessentially rural American landscape with serene country roads stretching straight on until the asphalt highway disappears beyond the horizon.

Interspersed throughout the twenty-two counties, drowsy country villages and small cities struggle to retain their dignity and basic essential services in the face of twenty-first-century challenges; yet most of the concerns they face are of human origin.

Experiences from outside the expected routine of daily life—especially incidents that might be labeled supernatural in origin—can disturb this outward calm.

Take what happened to the Sterling family on their 350-acre farmstead in that part of Iowa. Thirteen children had been born to Blanche and Clarence Sterling. Three of the children died young. Clarence himself died in the late 1990s.

It is their daughter Linda Sterling who talks about her brushes with the "other side." Despite the passage of some years, neither Linda nor her family quite understands *what* was happening and perhaps more importantly *why* it all took place. Although her experiences may seem of minor consequence to those expecting visits from the netherworld to be accompanied by howling winds and yowling wraiths, Linda's episodes fit into that category. They were defining moments in her life.

It was all a very frustrating experience for her. Nearly everyone she told the stories to thought they could not possibly be true. To not be believed may have been the hardest part of it all. Yet she calmly accepts that assessment from others: "I'd probably say the same thing if it had happened to someone else."

Linda's experiences with the supernatural seem connected to the tragic death of her older brother by nine years, Brad Sterling, when he was only fourteen and Linda five. The circumstances are so ordinary as to make his passing even the more agonizing. He was doing what typical Iowa farm kids have done for generations—riding a small motorcycle around the family farmstead. He especially enjoyed zooming to the end of their long driveway, in and out of the ditches along the county road, and then turning around to peal back up the Sterling driveway.

"It had been very dry and dusty" that day, Linda says. At the end of one swing down the long drive, Brad rode his cycle onto the gravel country road—directly into the path of an oncoming car that had been enveloped in a cloud of dust caused by a car in front of it. A neighbor was driving the car that struck him. Brad was killed instantly.

As one would expect, the boy's death had a tragic and lasting effect on his family. He was his father's favorite, for one thing. Everyone knew that. Linda said her father, Clarence, never fully got over the cruel way fate had snatched his boy away from him.

Linda said the family never spoke of the accident: "It was just like Brad had never existed because none of us could say anything. Dad was just a basket case. He never did recover."

"Dad told my brother Mark that he'd have to take Brad's place. That bothered Mark so much. He realized later that dad was [really] saying he'd never be as good as Brad, that he'd have to become *more* like him. Mark is a doctor now, a very smart man, but he just never got over that."

Nearly twenty years passed after the boy's death and Linda Sterling was still living at home when she encountered some things that made her wonder if Brad had never truly left the family. She remembers that the first incident was in the middle of the night. She woke up with a sudden chill, like being aware that someone else was in the room with her—someone she could not see.

"I wasn't truly scared, so I just lay in bed. Then my mom came in and asked me if I was okay." Linda realized that she must have called out or made some noise that brought her mother to her room.

Not wanting to upset her mother, Linda assured her that she was having a bad dream and all was okay.

Linda's mother, Blanche Sterling, actually had awakened earlier because she had one of those sixth-sense episodes moms sometimes have that one of her children was in distress. Blanche wanted to check on her own brood still living at home. She had started with Linda, who was in her early twenties at the time.

As Blanche turned to leave, mother and daughter were stopped cold when they heard "Mom!" cried out from a corner of the bedroom. It was a clear, distinct male voice.

The women stared at one another. Each had heard the same thing. Later, Blanche confided to Linda that she heard it repeated a few hours later but in a different part of the house.

But at that moment, Blanche quickly left the bedroom to check on her son Jeff. Perhaps he was playing some sort of mean-spirited prank. Blanche found him asleep, as she did another son.

A religious woman, Blanche went to the living room and prayed. Linda fell back to sleep. Neither one heard the voice ever again.

Later Linda realized something else: her bedroom had been Brad Sterling's old room.

"My mother doesn't believe in ghosts," Linda said of that night. In fact, Blanche did not think Brad was the source of the disembodied voice at all but rather thought it was the product of "demonic activity."

Linda disagreed but kept her opinion to herself.

"Who else could it have been?" Linda asks, if not her long-dead brother.

The aftermath of young Brad's death also touched her brother Mark in another way. He sometimes experienced a distinctive, albeit disturbing and terrifying, pull toward the location on that gravel road where Brad had been killed.

Is it possible that the spirit of a boy who died too young could have returned with an attitude and behavior uncharacteristic of him during his few brief years on earth? Although he could be "ornery" or mischievous, Linda said, he was at heart a "good boy."

That may well be a central question because Linda Sterling herself faced far more than an utterance by something unseen in an early morning hour.

For a period of several weeks, Linda was terrified by what she termed a "perception of evil" so keen that she was barely able to stay in the house.

It all began on an evening near dusk on a routine drive home with her sister. That harmless trip was punctuated by a most disturbing conclusion.

As they neared the family farm's driveway, Linda saw what looked like a man staggering toward them. She quickly turned to ask her sister if she saw the man, but when Linda looked back he had disappeared. "I looked along the ditch to see if maybe he had fallen. But there was absolutely nobody there."

The man she saw on the road was in dusky light, so she could not distinguish his age or what he might have been wearing, but she could tell he was tall and lanky. Linda thought it might be her younger brother Jeff who fit that description. Maybe he had wrecked his four-wheeler and was trying to get back to the house.

Then another thought occurred to her. Brad had the same build at fourteen as Jeff did.

"I suppose it could have been Brad I saw," she speculated.

Sometime later she found out a neighboring farmer had been killed near that spot many years earlier when his tractor accidentally turned over on him. Perhaps it was his ghost she had seen.

Once Linda and her sister got home, there was another mystery waiting, that "evil presence," she called it, so distinctive that for her it permeated the house and its surroundings.

She was sure somebody was in the house with her, somebody who meant to do her harm.

"I had to get out. It was frightening to feel that way in my own house. I still try not to think about it too much."

She compares the sensation to what she felt on the night she heard that voice cry out "Mom!" That someone was around you could not see, someone in the shadowy corners of a familiar room.

Although the dreadful feelings passed in time, Linda still harbors some reluctance to return to her family's farm.

"I do go back occasionally, but not often, though. I don't really like going there. You'd think I would since that's where I grew up."

Linda Sterling does not directly connect the vanishing man on the road to the malevolent atmosphere in the house, and she certainly cannot understand why a brother who has been dead for three decades would return to call out in the nighttime, thereby frightening his mother and sister. In the end, however, she does not like to dwell on these disquieting incidents from her past, nor does she think about them very much.

She knows some mysteries will remain unsolved.

The Guttenberg Poltergeist

Guttenberg

Some fifty years ago the Meyer house near Guttenberg, Iowa, was the most exciting place in Clayton County. In fact, it was so thrilling that on a cold December night, the family fled their home—they claimed a poltergeist had taken over the premises. The events leading up to their flight are truly amazing.

It all began late one evening as Bill and Annie Meyer were sitting in their living room. A booming crash from the kitchen shook the house right down to its foundation. The couple hurried into the kitchen to find their refrigerator tipped over. In the next instant, a flower stand flew across the kitchen and slammed against the stove, splintering into dozens of pieces. Then an egg rose from a basket on the windowsill, soared through the air, and bounced off a door.

Annie Meyer was speechless; her husband was bewildered. How could these things be happening? Yet that was only the beginning.

Too upset to prepare dinner that night, Annie insisted that the couple eat out. She felt more relaxed away from home and out among people. In fact, while she was gone she almost forgot about the destruction in her home.

At home later that night she decided to read herself to sleep. She placed a glass of water on the nightstand and climbed into bed with her book. That glass rose from the table, hung in midair, and exploded over her head, showering her with water and shards of glass.

Her husband, who had witnessed the incident, was as frightened as his wife. He suggested that they move into one of the other bedrooms, which they did. But no sooner were the Meyers settled in bed than soot began falling on them from the ceiling.

In the morning, Bill called the sheriff, who tramped through the house, looking unsuccessfully over, under, and inside their possessions.

The sheriff was called home suddenly but promised to check back later. When he returned to the Meyer place later in the afternoon, he found the couple huddled in their front yard. They claimed that several chairs had scooted across the floor and that every window in the house had cracked. The sheriff examined the windows and shook his head. He confessed that he could not help them. This particular problem was beyond the long arm of the law.

Word soon spread of the strange goings-on at Bill Meyer's house, and visitors from Guttenberg and neighboring communities besieged the family with tour requests. A towboat captain on the Mississippi River a few miles away arrived one night with some friends.

"I was just wondering, ma'am," he began, "if I could spend the night. You see, I don't believe in ghosts."

Annie courteously offered the captain a bedroom. Shortly after he had gone to bed, his friends and the Meyers were drinking coffee at the kitchen table. Then they heard a loud commotion in the bedroom. They rushed into the room. There the river pilot lay on the mattress, which was now on the floor eight feet away from the bed frame. The perplexed captain claimed he had no idea how he and the mattress had gotten there.

Sometime later, an expert on parapsychology reportedly came to study the unexplained phenomena. He said that the activity was a result of "some intelligent motivation." He explained that a young person who, unconsciously, transfers his suppressed rage and energy force to inanimate objects usually sets a poltergeist in motion.

By that time, however, the Meyers did not care much for theories. Weary of visitors, of assaults by unseen tormentors, and of too many sleepless nights, they moved out. The house, however, had become so notorious that curiosity seekers could not stay away; they arrived regularly, uninvited, tramping through the place and spreading stories about the antics of the "ghost."

Eventually the Meyers sold the house to their former neighbors, the Wallace Finnegans. Vandals then began vandalizing it, smashing windows and breaking down locked doors. Young people came from near and far to hold all-night beer parties in the place. Mr. Finnegan, in desperation, filled the house with hay and turned it into a barn.

The Guttenberg poltergeist at last was laid to rest.

Mildred Hedges

Indianola

It was a Monday morning, May 6, 1935. A new week had begun at picturesque Simpson College, Indianola, and classes were changing. Students rushed along the sidewalks on the tranquil campus and in and out of the charming brick campus buildings.

In Old Chapel, the college's oldest building, a vivacious young home economics major named Mildred Hedges balanced a handful of books in her arms as she started to make her way down the steep, open staircase from the top floor. No one knows precisely how it happened but one of her high heels caught on a top step. She lost her balance and tumbled over the handrail, plummeting thirty-five feet to her death below. Mildred was gone at the age of twenty-two. But she has not been forgotten.

Old Chapel became College Hall after it was remodeled in the 1980s. It is an imposing, three-story, brick building with white trim and a grand bell tower; it is a campus centerpiece.

Today College Hall is home to administrative offices and meeting rooms. The admissions office is on the first floor. Yet up on its third floor is a reminder of Mildred Hedges's tragic death. The Red and Gold Room is a re-creation of a college student's room in the 1930s. In fact it may have been where Mildred lived during her brief life there. One former student described it as a perfect little bedroom: "There should be a little old lady living in there."

The idea of *someone* living there may be close to the mark. And it is definitely not an old lady.

The haunting of what is now College Hall by the ghost of Mildred Hedges is an enduring legend on the Simpson College campus.

College Hall was built in 1870. For years students, faculty, alumni, and employees have both cherished and feared the building that once held the library and conservatory. The first religious chapel was there. However by 1980 it was condemned because of crumbling ceilings and unsafe staircases, prompting its remodeling.

Since Mildred Hedges's death over eighty years ago, some have reported strange things inside College Hall: floating lights nod and dip, something invisible but weighty seems to climb the creaking stairs; shadowy forms pace the halls or peer out of third-floor windows.

Some of the College Hall ghost legends are quite vague, while others are based on historical events, like those associated with young Mildred.

One story holds that in the late nineteenth century a young man distraught over a failed romance hanged himself in that early chapel's belfry. After his death, friends believed he was the one they saw wandering the gloomy halls or gazing out a window. Skeptics, however, say the suicide tale was a myth handed down after a professor was hanged in effigy in the tower.

Two female students purportedly committed suicide by hanging. The words "In Memoriam" follow one student's name in a 1924 yearbook. Alumni who were there in the 1920s recalled only that "something happened" and not specifically a death by hanging. Another woman is alleged to have hanged herself from a massive chandelier that was visible through the Palladian window on the second floor.

Dark deeds have been unjustifiably attributed to the building. In at least one instance from the 1880s, a young student who fell to his death in another campus building was reported to have died in College Hall.

Past students tell of meeting the apparition of a young woman on a College Hall staircase. One insisted the ghost talked to him. It said in no uncertain terms that she wanted to be left alone.

A security guard was badly frightened one night after stumbling upon a translucent figure in the corridor. And a cleaning lady once told a news reporter that she knew mysterious things went on "all the time." She claimed that she and her coworkers witnessed what they could not explain — basement lights turning on when no one was in the building, lights on the third floor blinking on and off. Electricians were not able to find any reason for the erratic behaviors in the otherwise empty building.

Through the years these legends have intertwined, been told and retold, until fact and fiction are inseparable.

Famed Connecticut ghost hunters Ed and Lorraine Warren looked into the ghost legends of College Hall during a visit to campus.

Accompanied by a crowd of students, photographers, and press reporters, the Warrens worked their way up the old, three-story staircase, throughout the drafty corridors, and all the way to the third floor, gathering their own psychic vibrations and impressions.

The couple reported the building was occupied by something not of flesh and blood.

The old hall had "an earthbound spirit," they concluded.

"She died here, but she's convinced herself that she didn't. She might have been contemplating suicide. But she didn't want to die at the end."

That did not seem to jibe with Mildred Hedge's untimely death. But another conclusion by the ghost hunters did seem to make sense.

In a trance, Lorraine Warren said the ghost was that of a dark-haired woman in her twenties wearing a skirt with a calf-length hem.

That description was close to the one obtained by Twyla Dillard in her research on the ghosts of Simpson College that included information about Mildred Hedges's 1935 death. Period photographs of her matched the Warrens' description.

A few nights after the Warrens' visit, a hypnotist and psychic led another group of students through the hall. He suspected that as many as five students had died there over the years. Although the man knew nothing of College Hall's history, he said that there were no ghosts left there.

But, he added, "I believe they were here."

Whether the ghost of Mildred Hedges remains or not, her story will not fade away anytime soon. The college has produced a video about her and posted it on YouTube for the world to view.

Its title?

"Mildred: The Spirit of College Hall."

The Man in the Doorway

Oskaloosa

In 1949 Hal and Elaine Worrel lived in a century-old house in Oskaloosa that a short time before had been remodeled into apartments. The Worrels lived at one end of the top floor. At the opposite end lived Patricia Burns, a young widow. The landlady told the Worrels that Patricia had recently lost her husband, Raymond Burns, in an industrial accident. She moved to Oskaloosa to try to rebuild her life.

Patricia was an accomplished pianist. Elaine often heard music coming from the woman's small apartment. When they passed one another in the hall going to or coming from the shared bathroom, Elaine exchanged smiles with her, perhaps a quick hello, but not much conversation. Elaine respected her neighbor's privacy as she grieved over Raymond's death.

Elaine felt uneasy one Saturday while Hal was away at work, though she did not know why. Perhaps a warm bath would relax her. Slipping into a robe and slippers, she headed toward the bathroom. As she opened the door and groped for the dangling ceiling-light cord, the pungent aroma of pipe smoke suddenly filled the air.

Elaine spun around. A young man lingered in the doorway, his head of black, curly hair spilling down over his collar, a faint horseshoe-shaped scar outlining his left cheekbone. Cupped in his hand was a briar pipe. He was not looking at her and he did not speak; he seemed to be intently staring off into the distance.

Elaine's scream caught in her throat as she shrank back in surprise, for the stranger most definitely did not belong in this house.

The young man turned and moved toward Patricia Burns's apartment. Elaine was swept by an unaccountable compulsion to follow him, which she did, from a distance. At the door of Patricia's apartment, the man disappeared.

Concerned about her neighbor, Elaine knocked on the door several times but there was no answer. She tried the doorknob. It turned in her hand and she pushed open the door. Just visible through a doorway was Patricia lying across the bed, her arms red with blood. She had slit her wrists and was barely conscious.

Elaine quickly put tourniquets above the gashes and then phoned her husband at work. He arrived a few minutes later with a doctor in tow.

The next day Patricia thanked the couple for saving her life. She told Elaine that she had been overcome with despair after a night out drinking and decided to join her husband in death.

Elaine said nothing of her own mysterious encounter outside her apartment. It was clear to her that Patricia had slashed her wrists at about the same time she had seen the ghost.

Later that evening, Elaine again checked on her young friend. Patricia sat on the sofa clutching a photograph. She showed it to Elaine. "His name was Ray," she said.

There was the black, curly hair, the scar on his left cheek, even a briar pipe.

Raymond Burns was the man in the doorway.

Ham House

Dubuque

Dubuque pioneer Mathias Ham built his home to last. The twenty-three-room Victorian gothic mansion straddles a wind-wracked bluff on the city's north end, its massive native limestone walls as sound today as the day they were completed. This antebellum house has long been the pride of Dubuque, a symbol of wealth and a statement of the owner's faith in the future of his Mississippi River hometown. The house is on the National Register of Historic Places.

As with many old mansions, it seems natural that the Ham House has been the subject of ghost stories over the decades, eerie incidents in which it is claimed that strange lights move through the vast, dark corridors and cold, sudden breezes seem to have no natural origin. And then there's the story of an old river pilot whose ghost seeks revenge on the woman who killed him with a fatal shotgun blast to the abdomen.

The history of the house would certainly support more than a few remarkable tales.

The energetic Mathias Ham prospered in lead mining, lumbering, and agriculture and operated a fleet of vessels to ship his products up and down the river. He married Zerelda Marklin, his childhood sweetheart, in 1837. Three years later, he built a five-room, two-story, stone-block house. It was considered lavish for the time, as most of the surrounding homes were log cabins. In 1856 Zerelda died, leaving Ham with five young children to raise. He was devastated by his wife's death and by a number of business setbacks that followed, but nevertheless made plans to vastly enlarge his original house.

In 1857, while the Dubuque Federal Customs House was under construction, several loads of stones shipped from southern Illinois were rejected because of inferior quality. Mathias Ham bought the shipment and started on a twenty-three-room, three-story addition made of limestone to his Lincoln Avenue home for himself and his family. Then in 1860 he married Margaret McLean, who bore him two more children. As Ham was recouping his losses, he completed his Dubuque mansion, furnishing it with taste and elegance.

Soon the Hams, Mathias and Margaret, opened their luxurious home to entertain the socially prominent in the city.

Their parties became well known and guests felt honored to be invited. Many partygoers remarked that Matthias Ham had thought of everything, noting the exquisite plaster rosettes and moldings of the fourteen-foot ceilings, the beautifully decorated window casings, and the burnished walnut staircases.

But there were things about the Ham house that fawning guests would probably never see: for instance, those twentyfive steps that led from the third floor up into a tall cupola that, like a giant crown, topped the building and afforded a splendid view of the river. Ham built it to observe the movement of his riverboats, an important part of guarding his steamboat fleet.

Pirates still roamed the Mississippi River in that era, plundering steamboats carrying lumber, foodstuffs, and various supplies. The story is that Ham's spying out of the cupola eventually led to the capture of a band of pirates. When the pirates vowed vengeance, the Ham children seemed more excited than frightened. Nothing came of the threat. Then.

Margaret Ham died in the house in 1874, and in 1889, just short of his eighty-fourth birthday, Mathias himself passed away. Of the children, all but May and Sarah had already moved away. After May's death in the 1890s, Sarah was left alone in the old mansion.

One late night as Sarah was reading in her third-floor bedroom, she thought she heard a prowler. The pirates' threat of years ago crossed her mind, but she was too afraid to get up to investigate. In the morning, Sarah told a neighbor that if she heard the prowler again she would put a light in the window as a call for help.

Several nights later Sarah was again reading in her room. A distinct but distant clatter came from somewhere deep within the house, probably the first floor. She put aside her book and called out, "Who's there?" There was no answer.

This time Sarah locked her door, lit the lamp, and put it in the window, hoping her neighbor would see it. Then, taking up a gun she kept always at her bedside, she waited. All was quiet for several minutes until she heard a set of heavy footsteps in the hallway outside the bedroom. Sarah Ham fired two shots through the door and heard a cry.

Later, neighbors found a trail of blood leading from the hallway, through the house, and out into the night. They found the body of a river pirate at the water's edge, dead from Sarah's gunshots. Some say that the mysterious light now seen moving through the Ham mansion at night is the lamp carried by the murdered brigand searching for his assailant.

The Dubuque County Historical Society operates the Mathias Ham House as a historic home and museum. Society employees and volunteers have reported a number of peculiar incidents over the years.

For example, a window in an upper hall may be found open from time to time though it was securely locked the night before—a strong spring holds the lock in place and workers believe the window could not open accidentally, even if buffeted by gusts of wind. In that same upper hallway a light worked only part of the time.

Lights in the front rooms of the Ham House once could only be turned on and off by screwing and unscrewing a fuse. One summer night an assistant curator who was closing the museum for the night heard music coming from a pump organ when she unscrewed the fuse. When she screwed the fuse tightly back in place, the music ceased.

There is a pump organ in the house, but it is closed and never played.

On still another occasion, Dubuque police officers, conducting a routine check of the premises, noticed a light burning in the hallway of the house's original section. They called an employee, who later told a news reporter that it was a frightening experience. After he turned off the burglar alarm, he turned on the lights. It was the first time he had been in the house alone at night. He said he felt a "presence."

On another night, a tour guide also thought that someone or something was in the house. He spent the night there, hoping to catch a prowler. Sometime after three o'clock in the morning, he heard women's voices in the yard outside. He looked out the windows but saw no one. Returning to the house, he heard someone walking overhead on the second floor of the original section of the house. He investigated but again found nothing.

Sometimes workers and visitors feel ill at ease especially in the older sections of the mansion. On the third floor one can feel icy breezes and strange chills as well as hear, quite clearly, noises from other parts of the house. The stairway to the cupola seems to act as an echo chamber for sounds below. The legend of a man hanging himself in that tower has never been established.

Naughty George

Des Moines

Jim and Sue Anderson lived in a rambling clapboard house in Des Moines
in the 1960s. It had an upstairs sleeping porch, narrow double-hung windows, and gingerbread trim. Jim's grandparents once owned the house;
the young couple felt fortunate to be raising their family in such a spacious,
comfortable residence.

But one night shortly after they moved in, their delight turned to
dismay.

Jim was out late visiting a buddy. At about ten o'clock he phoned his
wife to tell her he would be staying a while longer. Sue was tired and, although she usually waited up for him, she went on to bed. The children
were already asleep. Sue was drifting off herself when the back door opened
and her husband walked into the kitchen.

At least that is what she thought was happening.

The bedside phone rang.

Sue lifted the receiver. "Hi, honey," her husband said. "I'm just leaving
for home."

"Wise guy," Sue chuckled. "I just heard you come in."

"But honey, I'm not in the house. I'll be right there."

Not in the house?

She eased the receiver back into its cradle, went to the bedroom door,
and cracked it open. Footsteps squeaked on the freshly waxed kitchen
floor. Sue tiptoed across the upstairs hallway to the children's room, gathered up her young son and daughter in her arms, and returned to the master bedroom. She locked the door and tucked the children into bed with
her.

A few minutes later, footsteps clattered up the staircase. She watched as
the doorknob turned.

"Sue, open up! It's me!"

She flung open the door and collapsed in her husband's arms.

When the front doorbell rang, Jim ran downstairs to open the door, calling over his shoulder that he had telephoned the police before leaving his friend's house.

Sue wrapped herself in a bathrobe and followed her husband downstairs. The officers listened to her account of the intruder then fanned out through the house. They searched from basement to attic, shifting furniture, trunks, and boxes, poking into dark corners with their flashlights. They found nothing. There was no indication the doors or windows had been tampered with.

After the officers left, Sue felt foolish; yet she knew that she had not imagined the incident. Someone had come in the back door and walked through the house.

The Andersons had nearly forgotten the incident when, a few months later, Sue was ironing in an upstairs room late one evening when something knocked at a window. She put down the iron and listened. It came again, knuckle-sharp rat-a-tat-tats on the outside of one of the windows.

Sue snapped off the light, walked to the wall of windows, and peered out, wondering all the time how taps like that could be possible on the second floor of the house.

Moonlight washed the high limbs of an old cottonwood near the window and the grove of walnut trees at the far property line. Otherwise all seemed quiet, nothing to account for what Sue heard.

She did not sleep well that night.

On another evening after dark, Sue finished washing the dinner dishes and set bags of garbage in an adjacent mudroom to be taken out the next day.

The bags were gone the next morning. The couple searched inside and out but never found their garbage.

Several times during that year the couple would come downstairs early in the morning to find lights blazing in the hallway and den, the front and back doors standing wide open. That truly frightened the couple as there was no sign of forced entry. The children were not sleepwalkers; the Andersons, not wishing to alarm them, said nothing to them about it.

Then came that day when she had to admit there was another possibility.

"It's silly, I know," she said. "Who'd believe stuff like that?"

The "stuff like that" was the presence of a haunting in their house, the idea that a ghost was causing all the mischief.

Her husband scoffed. He figured there was a logical explanation for everything, though he was at a loss for words in this instance.

The weeks rolled by, and the Andersons celebrated their second year in their house. One morning their small daughter announced that a man had been in her room during the night. He was standing next to her bed, smiling down at her.

She did not seem upset, so Sue explained to her that it must have been her daddy coming in to check on her.

"Oh no, it wasn't," insisted the child.

Although both parents were greatly distressed, they said it must have been a dream and dropped the subject.

A few weeks later, Sue invited a friend, Kathy, to spend the evening. During the course of their visit, Sue mentioned the odd events of the past year.

Kathy, who was interested in the occult and had some self-professed psychic abilities, interrupted. "There's a spirit standing in the corner of the living room."

Sue was taken aback. She could see nothing except a small cabinet.

Kathy said the ghost had a gentle smile and would not harm the family. Sue glanced nervously at her watch. It was ten o'clock. After Kathy left an hour or two later, Sue carried the coffee cups back to the kitchen. She returned to the living room to turn off the lights. She glanced at the wall clock. It had stopped at ten.

The same clock stopped at the same hour three nights in a row; then it quit running altogether.

For nearly a year, and to Sue's great relief, nothing more out of the ordinary took place. Perhaps it was all over.

That was not to be. The ghost paid a return visit.

It was the following fall. The Andersons were entertaining dinner guests Linda and Alan Peters. Linda and Sue lingered over coffee at the dining room table. Suddenly Linda gave a start and pointed into the adjoining living room. She said, "Look! There's someone in white pacing back and forth."

Again, Sue saw nothing. But then Linda leaned back in her chair and laughed.

"Of course, it's one of the guys clowning around."

Sue did not laugh. She knew Jim and Al were in the kitchen. Her fears returned.

Three nights later, Sue, Linda, Kathy, and another young woman had gathered at the Anderson house to work on a craft project for an upcoming charity bazaar. Midway through the evening's work, Sue served coffee and cookies, the foursome buzzing with friendly small talk.

Linda mentioned that her white cat had run off and had been missing now for four months. The animal never strayed from home before this, so Linda and her husband could not understand its sudden disappearance. They had searched and run advertisements in the newspaper, all without success. The cat had vanished.

When the women finished their evening's work and prepared to leave, Sue turned on the porch light. A white cat was curled up on the steps. Linda was astonished—it was her cat.

The Andersons were as mystified as Linda. However, they sensed that their mischievous ghost was somehow involved.

By now, Sue was desperate for answers. She suggested getting a Ouija Board. Her husband agreed. Perhaps they could learn the identity of their visitor and find out what he (or she) wanted.

The couple sat face to face in their living room, the board across their knees. When Sue asked about the ghost, the planchette spun around on the board, spelling out G-E-O-R-G-E. In questioning that followed, they found out that George had lived on this land in the early 1800s, that he did not want to be here, but that he would not harm them.

Sue checked property records at the Polk County Court House but deed transfers prior to 1866 were not available. She ultimately failed to verify the Ouija Board's message.

The Andersons said the ghost continued to be periodically active. Jim often awakened in the middle of the night to see a man he now knew to be George, the ghost, standing beside the bed, staring down at him. One night, Jim got up to use the bathroom. As he returned to the bedroom, George stood with his back against the hallway wall a few feet away, staring at him. Jim took a deep breath, carefully edged past the figure, and climbed back in bed.

Desperado

Winterset

Each year on the second weekend of October, the town of Winterset, forty-five minutes southeast of Des Moines, attracts thousands of visitors to the Madison County Covered Bridge Festival. Guests have come from every state and many foreign countries, drawn there to photograph or paint the half-dozen century-old covered bridges in the county, wander among scores of crafts booths, listen to country music, and watch or participate in a Civil War battle reenactment.

For several decades the romantic novel *The Bridges of Madison County* by the late Robert James Waller and later the popular Clint Eastwood and Meryl Streep film based on the book have made this idyllic patch of Iowa ground a national gathering place for people who want to savor the sights and sounds of what they believe to be a vanishing American landscape. Now, a highly successful Broadway musical keeps alive the bittersweet love story of globe-trotting photographer Robert Kincaid and the lonely farm wife Francesca Johnson. Cast members from the musical have performed at the Winterset celebration.

Winterset is also the birthplace of movie star John Wayne. The small, frame home in which he was born in 1907 is open year-round and is the only museum in the world to feature memorabilia from the actor's childhood and movie days.

But before there were literary characters there was *the bridge*, the Roseman Covered Bridge, the very special one that Robert Kincaid was seeking to photograph when he asked Francesca Johnson for directions, and the one on which she pinned a note asking him to dinner.

Five miles southwest of Pammel State Park, the Roseman Bridge's fame long predates Waller's use of it as the centerpiece in his best-selling novel. It is famous for an entirely different reason.

For well over a century the Roseman has been known as Iowa's most famous *haunted* bridge.

The story begins on a moonless night before the turn of the last century when the alarm spread through Winterset that a convict had escaped from the county jail there.

Even before sunrise, two posses formed, the better to spread out for a search. They strapped pistols to their waists, grabbed their rifles, and mounted up. The leaders of each band had mapped out their own routes and agreed to rendezvous at the Roseman Bridge.

They were off to give chase. Hours later, shortly before daybreak, as the posses approached the bridge from opposite directions, a cry went up from some of the men that they had seen someone crawl along the Middle River embankment before running onto the covered bridge.

The posse members took cover and prepared to go in after their quarry. The desperado heard shouts for him to surrender. He knew he was trapped.

Or was he?

In a frantic attempt to escape, he climbed the heavy oak support timbers and broke through a weathered section of the roof. The last anyone saw of him was of his legs disappearing through the hole.

What happened next is not known for certain, but deputies believe the man they were pursuing eluded capture by somehow making his way across the roof and then down into the swirling currents of the Middle River. He may have been swept away in the swift water or hidden somewhere in the wooded countryside until the posses dispersed.

Whatever took place, neither the suspect nor his remains were ever found.

Yet something of his presence seems to remain.

Fishermen report hearing jolly laughter from up along the bridge's roofline and footfalls across the roof on misty summer evenings. Although the "escape hole" was sealed up long ago, visitors still notice the repaired section through which the outlaw slipped.

Another more gruesome legend connected to the Roseman Bridge is equally difficult to verify, but that does not seem to lessen its popularity.

Desperado

The story is told that a young man in the region made the mistake of falling in love with the daughter of a mean and dangerous man. The old man did not want the boy anywhere near his sweet, young daughter, and so he planted evidence in the boy's possessions that would make it look like he had stolen from the man. He had not, of course, but that did not stop a mob from forming, which then dragged the unfortunate suitor to Roseman Bridge. He was hanged from a truss in the middle of the bridge and his body left there overnight. It mysteriously disappeared early the next day.

Some visitors notice a distinct cold spot in the center of the bridge about where the man was allegedly hanged. Dogs with their hackles raised sometimes howl and refuse to go all the way across.

During those Covered Bridge Festival weekends each October, experienced guides take visitors on a narrated tour of all the Madison County bridges. There is always a stop at the Roseman Bridge. Encounters with the ghosts of dead bandits, thwarted suitors, or fictional lovers are not on the advertised itinerary.

Kansas

Old Deg

Emporia

S. C. Dixon should have known something was not quite right when he went to work in the old street-level photography studio at one end of Emporia's Fox Granada Theatre building in 1974. Dixon had hired on with Udene Burnell, an elderly woman who had bought the business from its founder years before, in 1931. She was now getting ready to sell it herself. Dixon was an eager young man who found the selling price a real bargain for a college student like himself eager to start out in his own business. Udene Burnell stayed on for several months after he bought the studio to train him in photography and business practices. She put all that business acumen into the deal for no extra charge.

All in all it was a very good deal indeed: shop, inventory, customers, and business consulting. But maybe it was such a good buy because of something more, something Dixon could never have imagined. S. C. Dixon discovered the premises came with the ghost of its first owner, D. D. "Old Deg" Degler. He was part of the package.

To say that Degler might have been a sort of supernatural piece of the inventory is understandable. Photographing the people and places of Emporia and eastern Kansas had been his life beginning back in the 1920s. He also was apparently something of an eccentric, Dixon said, a showman of sorts. At one time he owned seven photography studios around Kansas. As an itinerant, traveling photographer, Degler had to hustle up business on his own—from weddings to school graduations, family reunions to business meetings. Many "shoots" were scheduled at one of his photo studios. The man hustled.

S. C. Dixon suspected that there was something Udene Burnell had not told him about the business. For instance, if she and Dixon were in the downstairs darkroom processing film and heard noises coming from upstairs or smelled pipe tobacco smoke, she would speculate that it was Deg checking them out.

Sudden noises.

Tobacco smoke.

A long-dead business owner curious about the new man in *his* shop?

All that and more became part of a peculiar fifteen years for S. C. Dixon, a time spent, he believes, fending off an aggresive spirit that never quite accepted the studio's third and, as it turned out, final proprietor.

Built in 1929 during the golden age of movie palaces and recently remodeled to near original, pristine condition, the Fox Granada Theater is resplendent in the plush, Spanish Renaissance design so popular in 1920s movie theaters. During the heyday of its operation, silent, then talking, motion pictures and sometimes live vaudeville entertainment featured stage and screen stars in what was called the finest theater "this side of Kansas City." Movie actress Ginger Rogers once danced across the stage.

D. D. Degler opened his Granada Photo Studio in the north wing of the Fox Granada Theater building a full year before the movie palace showed its first film in 1929. Degler's studio and the movie palace thrived until the 1960s, when film-going patterns changed, and a series of different building owners neglected the structure.

By the time Dixon bought the business in 1975, the fortunes of the old-fashioned portrait photographers had begun to wane. The bulky view cameras were virtual dinosaurs. Smaller, faster formats like 35mm had made location shooting more desirable by both photographers and customers. Wedding portraits were being made in churches, rarely in the studio, and much of the heavy old equipment had been relegated to the status of quaint artifacts of a bygone era. In many cases, individuals and families opted to take their own photographs with readily available and sophisticated consumer cameras.

"The most recent technology Mrs. Burnell had was a five by seven plate camera," Dixon recalls. "It even had the hood the photographer put over his head. The image was on a glass negative that you saw upside down and backward. She was still making a living, but she made a lot of her income from copying and restoration work."

Dixon managed to keep the photo studio open until 1989, even after the theater shut its doors. His was the sole business left in the original structure, which had suffered greatly from the owners' neglect.

The theater was placed on the National Register of Historic Places in 1986, but it was not until 1994 that a citizens group formed and rallied to restore and reopen the Granada, shortly before it was scheduled for demolition. The theater now features a wide variety of programming events year-round in a setting that makes full use of its original splendor.

When Dixon starts talking about the haunting of his photo studio, he emphasizes that he does not "see dead people." That simple declaration underscores his unnerving experiences in the fifteen years he ran Old Deg's photo studio.

For the most part, Dixon was a typical small-business owner. He worked at all hours of the day and night photographing clients, manning the upstairs shop full of photography-related equipment and supplies, and processing film in the basement-level photo lab/darkroom. But over the years, he grew weary—and wary—of the almost palpable sense of dread he felt in the shop that did not diminish with familiarity.

"Whatever this was, it was resentful [of me]. That was my overwhelming sensation. I noticed so many things long before I ever mentioned the [haunting] to anyone."

When he did start discussing his beliefs with friends or employees who helped out, nearly every one of them noticed two recurring sensations: a fragrant pipe tobacco and the overwhelming sense that someone was watching what they did, especially in the gloomy darkroom in the basement. Dixon said that any skeptic who worked with him for a time did not stay that way very long.

He admits that spending hours on end with no bright light in a film-processing lab can be disconcerting to some people. The only illumination usually comes from red safelights used by film photographers so as not to spoil images on white-light-sensitive photo paper. But what he felt in his own darkroom went beyond the normal discomfort in that setting.

He explained, "I thought there was something odd [in the darkroom], something vaguely out of sync. Blood didn't drip from the ceiling, nor did I have ectoplasm heads floating in midair, but there was still that oddness."

Dixon knew that his fears seemed illogical even though the darkroom itself—with twelve-foot-high ceilings—was eerie enough. Steep concrete steps led from the street-level studio down to the basement corridor that ended at what Dixon described as a kind of "dungeon" reborn with moist walls, a chemical-stained floor, and ancient corroded electrical outlets. In this setting, the high-tech photo enlargers seemed almost out of place. The whole setup was illuminated by the soft red glow from a safelight.

The ceiling of the darkroom was the floor of the gallery part of the photo studio. The floors overhead were poured concrete and steel a foot thick in places. Yet the room acted almost as an echo chamber for any sounds coming from the gallery. The softest of footsteps from above could be heard clearly.

The most disconcerting aspect of working alone in the darkroom was that disturbing feeling of being watched. Dixon called it a *presence* of some *one* or some *thing* there in the dark with him while he worked.

Oddly this presence exhibited a certain "tide" about itself, a kind of "ebb and flow," beginning as very pronounced during the morning hours and increasing steadily during the day, reaching a pinnacle as night descended.

Rarely did Dixon work in the darkroom later than early afternoon. Evenings were strictly off limits. "I noticed that the later the hour, the greater the sensation of uneasiness I would have," he said. He remembered Udene Burnell telling him that during the studio's boom years, the evening and night hours had been prime time for Degler and his staff to play catch-up on the day's accumulation of work.

At first, Dixon did not think whatever kept him company down there was necessarily out to "get him." He speculated, "Perhaps it was oblivious to my even being there, or maybe Old Deg was still there doing in death what the flesh and blood had enjoyed in life."

The malicious feelings grew as Dixon made changes and improvements in the business. Dixon thinks Old Deg began to consider him an interloper and wanted to squeeze out the new man in town. He said, "I got to the point near the end that hardly anything could convince me to go into that darkroom after two or three in the afternoon. It was just so incredibly uncomfortable, extremely oppressive."

All of this affected his ability to conduct his business. It was very difficult to focus on quality print processing, for instance, which was critical to establishing a solid reputation for a struggling small photo business. "I had this feeling that his was a malevolent force that just did not want me there. Period." He found even going to work difficult and that photography—which he had found so enjoyable—was now "nearly intolerable" to pursue.

Early on in the business, Dixon met another young photographer who shared his passion for photography. His name was Charles Evans and he eventually became Dixon's business partner.

"Charles was full of energy and ideas. What he lacked in acumen he more than made up for with enthusiasm," said Dixon. Plus they enjoyed working in the darkroom where both believed much of the "magic" of film-based photography took place.

Evans was quick to catch on that Dixon had a dislike to working in the darkroom after midafternoon. Dixon said, "He asked me why my aversion, why would I sacrifice the quiet early morning hours before opening to finish things up rather than during the evening and nighttime hours, as was his habit."

"I told him that I experienced several previous encounters with a certain foreboding, a presence that I had taken to calling Deg," Dixon explained.

In addition to the presence he felt, there was that smell of pipe tobacco even though neither man smoked a pipe.

And the cold—the steady, ever-present coolness that suddenly morphed into a narrow column of frigid air would abruptly encircle him.

"Then that sudden cold moved from one side of the room to the other," said Dixon, as if its source shifted position.

Although the presence seemed to manifest itself most frequently whenever Dixon was working alone, both Dixon and Evans noticed that a "deep chill" almost always greeted them as they made their way down the staircase, much more pronounced than one would expect in an old basement. Dixon felt it was as if someone was waiting there.

Evans, however, still did not understand Dixon's reluctance to work late hours in the darkroom. He was not being bothered in any significant way. Thus far.

Charles Evans's doubts were shattered in a disturbing episode one October afternoon.

Evans and his teenage daughter Mary Ann, who was working for him in the shop, decided to go in on a weekend and get a head start on the upcoming week's work by processing a roll of film, washing and drying it, then proofing each negative.

Since Mary Ann loved to help during the actual printing process, Charles decided that this would be a good time to send her to a store up the street to get some snacks. By the time she got back, the film would be dry enough to start making enlargements.

For the drying process, he had turned on the darkroom's only incandescent bulb. But now he switched that off and turned on both red and green safelights to acclimate himself to the darkness necessary to process prints. He was using a hair dryer to speed along the negatives' drying.

He gave Mary Ann the studio key and told her to take her time but to be sure to lock the door behind her.

Dixon said, "He told me he remembered quite distinctly the sound of her footsteps going up the staircase and across the old floor. It was that echo chamber effect."

Evans turned on the water to the print-washing drum and began cutting the dry negatives into work strips of six. It was then he caught the faint aroma of pipe tobacco, at the same time he noticed a stiff current of cool air blow through the room.

He ignored both and exposed the first sheet of photo paper; he was slipping it into the developer tray when he heard someone walk across the floor above him. He thought it was odd as he had not heard the outside door open and slam shut, which was usually the case. He had been concentrating on the print and did not know if his daughter had been particularly fast in running the errand or had forgotten to take enough money.

The footfalls seemed to pause. Evans moved toward the door and called out in a loud voice, "Come on down, it's all right. The safelights are on."

There was no answer.

Yet seconds later he heard her slowly coming down the steps. He had never known Mary Ann to take any staircase slower than two steps at a time. She rounded the corner and down the narrow hallway to the door going into the darkroom. There she stopped.

"Forget something?" Evans called out again.

Silence.

At that point Evans felt the hair on the back of his neck rise. He turned around and looked out the door. No one was there. Shadows and darkness, but no Mary Ann.

He stood stock still for seconds, perhaps a minute or more, his concept of time having escaped him. He did not feel the impact of what was happening until, still staring at the empty doorway, he heard the outside street door above him open and close once again, followed by footsteps across the bare floor and then someone pounding down the steps . . . two at a time.

"Daddy, it's me!"

When Mary Ann walked into the room, she saw her father standing stock still holding a pair of tongs dripping photo chemicals.

The image he had been working on had "come up" on the photo paper but had overdeveloped, leaving only a totally black image with a crisp white edge.

Evans felt an extraordinary mixture of panic and fatigue. He turned off the darkroom water, grabbed his daughter by the shoulders, and rushed her up the staircase to the brightness of the studio. He did not tell her what had happened. He turned off the lights and left with his daughter, locking the door behind him.

It was more than two weeks before Evans told Dixon about the episode. And that only came after Dixon pointed out to him that he was falling behind in his darkroom work.

"I never knew of a single occasion when he entered the old basement again after twelve noon. The joking stopped. He never mentioned that day to me again," said Dixon.

S. C. Dixon remained open in the old Granada photo studios until 1989 when the theater building closed. He was happy to be able to move his business to a new studio several blocks away, especially after one final episode that cemented his decision to relocate.

Dixon had installed a makeshift electric buzzer on the front door that emitted a loud buzz whenever someone walked in, loud enough for Dixon to hear if he was working downstairs—in the morning, of course. The problem is that it rarely, if ever, worked.

"I had tinkered with it time and again trying to make it work. I never had any luck. So I put a sign on the counter saying I was in the darkroom and I'd be right up," said Dixon, adding that he relied on hearing someone call out or their footsteps.

Dixon discovered on a late winter afternoon that something else could trip it, but exactly who or what it was he did not know.

On that afternoon Dixon securely bolted the door and left for the darkroom below.

"I absolutely had some project I had to get done, so I went down there and tried to immerse myself in work. But I was bothered to a dramatic degree that it was so late in the day. I wanted to get out of there. Finally I finished my work, and I'm going up those long, steep concrete stairs and I remembered I'd forgotten something down there that I needed. I went back down and that buzzer went off. I will not deny that I screamed like a little girl and jumped about four feet in the air."

Dixon had never, ever heard the buzzer except for an occasional short burst when he was tinkering with it. This time, he said, it was "ringing like a fire bell."

He scrambled back up the stairs and into the empty shop within seconds. The door was tightly secured.

Although he consulted with electricians, he failed to find an adequate explanation.

"That was actually one of the last times I went down there."

Even after Dixon opened his new photography studio, stories about his "haunted studio" continued to circulate.

Shortly after restoration work on the Fox Granada got underway in the 1990s, the local newspaper sent a reporter and photographer to meet Dixon at his old studio. The newspaper was publishing a story about the ghost of Old Deg and wanted to talk with Dixon in what remained of the darkroom. Perhaps against his better judgment, Dixon agreed. He had not been in the space for several years. It brought back all the old memories.

"I kind of knew the (newspaper) photographer. He was a young guy, very skeptical, and thought the whole thing was silly."

The newspaper men came loaded down with several floodlights, but since the electricity had been shut off in the basement, a long extension cord had to be run from the main floor down the staircase. The photographer unpacked his gear and had everything set up for the interview and photos.

He had been joking that he hoped something "scary" would happen that he could take pictures of, Dixon recalled. It did.

At the precise moment the interview got underway, the two big floodlights exploded, first one and then the other.

The three men were left standing in total darkness.

Dixon said, "Good job, pal! Now you're going to have to deal with the poltergeist in the dark."

Beverly Beers co-owns and manages the Granada Coffee Company in the north wing of the Granada complex, the same space once taken up by S. C. Dixon's photography studio.

She firmly believes that Old Deg is still around and that he is a kind of "guiding spirit" for her and the business she operates.

"The only thing I can figure out is that maybe Deg saw S. C. as a kind of competition, but we're not. We've had a friendly and warm embrace from him."

She does not advertise the presence of a poltergeist in her coffee shop.

"I don't talk about it much. People look at me a little funny if I do. But whether you believe in these things or not, once it happens to you there is no longer any doubt in your mind."

Since the coffee shop opened in 2002, Beers and her business partner, Rocky Slaymaker, had a sense that something unseen was hanging around the shop and that it liked playing the trickster.

For instance, Beers and Slaymaker were the only employees during the shop's first few months in business. To minimize their workload and maximize their small space, they were intent on making sure there was a specific place for every utensil they used. Once they were done with the implement, they put it back in its proper space. But even with that zealous commitment to organization, they would find that items had moved to some new location or even vanished.

"We had a stool that we used to clean the espresso machine. One day it just disappeared. We couldn't find it anywhere in the shop. The next day it was right back where it belonged," Beers said.

Beers thinks Deg has embraced the coffee shop owners because of their interest in conserving the building. She believes he has shown directly on several occasions just how much he cares.

At the end of long days—especially in the early months—she would count out the day's cash receipts. When she got tired or confused, perhaps losing track of the totals or becoming frustrated in some other way, she would often find a sense of calm suddenly settle over her. The answers she was struggling for, or some sort of clear solution, would soon be there.

"That happened on almost a daily basis. There's really no way to describe it," she said. "I think we were pure of heart in starting this business. We really had no clue about what we were doing. I taught school for sixteen years and my partner worked as an assistant to film set decorators. Perhaps because of that we were being embraced by Deg."

One winter afternoon shortly before Christmas and not long after the shop opened, Beers physically felt that embrace. She found herself alone in the shop. No one was about on the cold, snow-swept streets. She gave in to the quiet winter scene outside and dropped into one of the two big, comfy armchairs to relax and watch the snowfall through the front window.

She had grown used to dramatic temperature plunges in the shop—that was just part of having Deg around—but the temperature would always go right back up.

Deg was passing by, she figured.

But this time when she sat down in the chair, the air turned much, much colder. And it stayed that way.

She knew Deg was there in the other chair.

Ghost of the Purple Masque

Manhattan

Drama professor Carl Hinrichs was working alone late one night in the scene shops at the Purple Masque Theatre in its former location in Kansas State University's East Stadium.

The Lerner and Loewe musical *My Fair Lady* was well into rehearsal and Hinrichs, the scene designer, still had a great deal of work to do.

A few hours after midnight, Hinrichs poured paint from a five-gallon container into a smaller bucket that he carried back to the stage area.

Then he heard a tremendous crash.

"Who's there?"

With no answer, he went back into the scene shop to find the bucket of paint turned upside down in the middle of the floor. It was sitting at least ten feet from where he had left it.

The good professor may have had his first encounter with Nick, the mischievous ghost of the old Purple Masque Theatre.

Nick's origins date to the 1950s when the old East Stadium space was a cafeteria and a residence hall for athletes. The story goes that a football player named Nick was injured in a game, carried into the cafeteria, and placed on a table, where he died.

Nick, it seems, never left the building. He clomped through hallways and up and down stairs, and he talked on tape recorders. He also famously played tricks to get attention. He became one of the crowd, as it were, and generally was quite happy to share the small stage there with students and faculty.

Nick sometimes ran the show *his* way, however, frustrating the casts and crews.

In one case, rehearsals for the play *American Yard* were underway. After a rehearsal one evening, the theater doors and the building itself were locked. In the morning, a stagehand found all the chairs from the set piled in the hallway. The doors were still locked. The worker put the chairs back on stage. That night at rehearsal, after the houselights dimmed, the actors found their entrance blocked by the same chairs.

Later, when the stage manager ordered the stage lights to be brought up, the student running the light board was bewildered by what happened.

"I can't," he called out. "I gave them power. I can hear them, but they're not coming up."

A few moments later, the lights complied and came up slowly. The student was amazed. He said he had nothing to do with it. It was just Nick, others said, up to more pranks.

Sometimes Nick's pranks with chairs could be helpful. A theater major recalled that a stage crew once unloaded chairs in the Purple Masque to be set up later, then went outside. Less than five minutes later they heard a commotion from the theater. Once they got back in they found all the audience chairs set up and playbill programs neatly placed on the seats.

"There was nobody around," the student said. "It happened in five minutes, and it usually takes at least half an hour to do that job."

Nick's pranks were often purely playful. Two students setting up sound for an upcoming production ran into a puzzling scenario when, after finishing up for the night, they locked the doors and started out only to hear the show's music coming from inside the theater. They unlocked the door and found the tape running. Again they locked up and again the tape started up once they were out.

"It came on four more times," one of them said at the time. "We looked for someone playing a joke but there wasn't a soul around."

David Laughland was taping sound cues late one night. When he listened to what he had recorded, he heard a voice call out on the tape, "Hi Dave!"

Laughland rewound the tape and played it again.

There was no voice on the tape.

Nick's pranks usually startled, and sometimes even frightened, novice actors or backstage crew.

One night an actress was alone in a dressing room waiting for her cue. The room held a desk and several old wooden cubes. She made a quick costume change and sat down on the desk to rest.

One of the cubes in the room raised up in the air, turned over, and set itself gently down on the floor in front of the student, as if someone had invited her to put her feet up.

"Not nice, Nick," the actress said, quickly standing up, definitely not amused.

She edged toward the doorway and took a quick look back over her shoulder. The cube had moved back to its original position atop another one.

When Nick was not taking a hand in productions, he was often clomping through the theater.

Once, a former president of the K-State Players heard footsteps in the hallway even though he was alone in the theater. Another time, he and a friend stood at opposite ends of the hall and heard footsteps tread the entire length of the corridor between them. The pressure of invisible feet caused a number of the floorboards to creak.

One fall evening three students were working at the theater. During a break they all heard what sounded "like a two-hundred-pound person walking." The doors to the second floor remained locked. Although the students had keys, no one dared to go up and check.

It is not only students, however, who have experienced an unseen presence lurking in and around the theater. A visitor, touring the campus, told her guide that she felt a presence in the Purple Masque though she knew nothing of the supernatural history of the place. Her guide simply smiled and nodded.

When they entered the room where platforms were stored, the visitor stopped dead in her tracks, then fled, screaming. After she calmed down she said there was a dangerous element in that room; no one should ever enter it alone.

But one student who did said she always felt presences around her that made her uneasy. Others felt icy hands on their shoulders in that same storeroom. What was the "dangerous element" in that place? No one knew, but few believed it to be Nick. Mischievous, but friendly, he was never known to have knowingly harmed anyone.

Nick was such a familiar and beloved fixture that when plans were made to relocate the Purple Masque Theatre to West Stadium in 2014, students, faculty, and staff were hopeful Nick would move with them. A séance was planned to tell him about the move and invite him along.

"It just wouldn't be the same without him," one faculty member said.

A medium once claimed to have made contact with Nick's spirit. She asked him what they should do to put his soul at rest and relieve him of his need to haunt.

"Run a dalmatian through the theater at midnight," his spirit supposedly replied.

Some thought that sounded precisely like something Nick would say.

Ménage à Trois

Wichita

Billy Plummer was restless. He was tossing and turning in bed on that frigid night in December 1939 when suddenly he felt his wife, Gert, tickling his feet.

"No, Gert, no! Quit that!" he shrieked, jerking his knees up to his chin.

But when Billy glanced across the bed, he saw his wife sound asleep. In the next instant, she jumped.

"Billy, cut it out!"

"What d'ya mean, cut it out?"

Gert propped herself up on an elbow.

"You've got a sick sense of humor, Billy. You know I hate being tickled."

"But I never touched you!"

"You didn't?" Gert sat bolt upright.

Billy threw off the covers and snapped on the light.

"Look, if you weren't tickling me and I wasn't tickling you, then we've got bedbugs," he grumbled. Gert was horrified.

They jumped out of bed and together stripped it of sheets, blankets, even the mattress pad. They shook it all out yet found nothing.

At about four o'clock in the morning, taps and thumps from the bed frame awakened them. Billy reached over and turned on the light. The thumping continued. It seemed to emanate from the headboard, the side rails, the springs—indeed, from all around them. The couple lay rigid, bedclothes pulled up under their chins.

Night after night the Plummers' sleep was interrupted by the strange sounds. One night in February, their misery was taken to a new level when a deep, male voice called from beneath the bed, "Is the baby asleep?"

Gert Plummer, wild with fright, dashed into their toddler's bedroom. Their son was sleeping soundly.

Billy Plummer finally decided to take the bed apart. He found nothing unusual and put it back together again.

By mid-March the couple was getting desperate.

Billy tried setting a snare for whatever it was that was in the bedroom. He strung a copper wire from the bedspring to a gas pipe in the kitchen. Not a tap, a thump, or a tickle disturbed the couple all night. Gert rose happy and refreshed. Her joy was short-lived. The next night "the thing" was back in the bedroom tapping, thumping, and tickling.

Amateur ghost hunters from Wichita and the surrounding area decided it must be a ghost of some sort. The police were consulted. They all found the ghost accommodating as well as agile in producing noises anywhere on the bed, yet they were unable to learn its identity or to discover what it might have wanted.

At the end of March, Dr. William H. Mikesell, a psychologist and author, was brought in to the Plummers' Wichita home. Another seven witnesses, including a detective, were gathered when the professor arrived. His first command was to ask the ghost to thump the bed; it obeyed. Dr. Mikesell then ordered it to rap on one side of the bed and it likewise obliged. He asked it to rap a certain number of times in another place on the bed and it promptly obeyed.

"I could feel several raps near my hand on the bed," Dr. Mikesell told a news reporter. But when he asked the ghost to tap on the cedar chest in the room, it refused. It would touch no other piece of furniture than the bed.

Dr. Mikesell's rendezvous with the entity lasted several hours. By then the professor was tired and ill at ease because of the large number of spectators. He promised to return at some other time when fewer persons were present.

But the professor never had a chance.

On the first warm day of spring, the Plummers hauled the bed to the Wichita dump. Where it stayed.

Legend of White Woman Creek

Greeley County

Today, the streambed is dry and pocked with gravel. But once—many years ago—clear water flowed through the sweeping prairie of Greeley,

Wichita, and Scott counties in western Kansas. The meager stream would doubtlessly receive only a passing glance today, if that, yet the origin of its most peculiar name is one of the most enduring of Kansas legends. It is said that the ghost of a young woman captured by the Cheyenne people over a century ago haunts this creek.

The Cheyenne once roamed the vast grasslands of Kansas, hunting bison and antelope. Their quarry was numerous, their lives relatively untouched by the encroachment of white soldiers and settlers.

Cheyenne Chief Tee-Wah-Nee led a small party of hunters during one foray for game. They camped near the bank of a stream they called "River-That-Runs-Between-the-Hills-That-Are-Always-Covered-With-Smoke." The bison had been plentiful, and the men spent many days in this camp curing the meat and preparing the hide for clothing and blankets.

One night, a band of white men raided the camp. They stole the meat and hides and many horses. Chief Tee-Wah-Nee and his brother, Tan-Ka-Wah, were wounded; many of their brothers were killed.

At dawn, the Cheyenne rode after the enemy and seized ten men and two women from a white settlement to which the raiders had retreated and also recovered the meat and hides.

The prisoners were forced to return to the Cheyenne camp with the horses they had stolen. The women, two sisters named Anna and May, were given the job of nursing the injured Cheyenne men back to health.

The months passed, summer faded into autumn. Chief Tee-Wah-Nee and his brother were fully recovered . . . and deeply in love with the sisters. Both women returned their affection.

On the day set for the party's return to their village, Tee-Wah-Nee convened a council and proclaimed himself the husband of Anna. Tan-Ka-Wah stood next to him and repeated the phrase, asking May to be his wife.

Anna then sought permission to address the group, although women rarely spoke before councils. The men listened intently as she spoke in their own language:

> My heart is swollen with love for you, my people. To Tee-Wah-Nee I
> promise my love until the rain no longer falls from the sky.
> At first we were afraid. But no longer do we fear. The names by which

you call my sister and me, Anna-Wee and May-O-Wee, are signs of our acceptance.

I have only one request. We are now going home—to a home I have never seen. When five suns have gone, release the white men who are still with us. In return, they must promise never to steal the Cheyenne's horses or take my sister and me away from our husbands. Our only brother is among those you hold and we are thinking of him and his future happiness.

The council granted Anna's request. Then Anna-Wee's own brother, Daniel, rose to speak. None of the prisoners wanted to return, he said. None had families in the settlement, nor could they promise that other white men would honor a promise not to attack the Cheyenne. He asked that he and the other white men be accepted as brothers. The Cheyenne, who had long since stopped guarding the men as prisoners, granted their request.

Camp was struck and the party set out for the Cheyenne village. Scouts rode ahead to announce the arrival of Chief Tee-Wah-Nee, his brother, and their wives. A ceremonial feast of thanksgiving was prepared.

In time, Anna-Wee bore a son. The happiest lodge in the whole village was that of Tee-Wah-Nee and AnnaWee. The child was just learning to crawl when word came that Henrich, one of the adopted white men, had left the village. He had stolen one of Tee-Wah-Nee's finest ponies, but no attempt was made to stop him.

Henrich eventually reached Fort Wallace. He lied to the army commander that the white men and women held by Tee-Wah-Nee were still prisoners.

Tee-Wah-Nee heard of Henrich's tale. Before he could send a delegation to correct the story, cavalry troops lay siege to the Cheyenne village.

Henrich rode at the front of the first charge. The troops fell back many times after being repulsed by the well-fortified Cheyenne. Eventually, Henrich and Tee-Wah-Nee found one another at nightfall, realizing full well that one of them must die. Henrich fell upon Tee-Wah-Nee with his bayonet; the Cheyenne chief lay mortally wounded.

Henrich ran to the lodge of Anna-Wee. He killed her infant son, grabbed up the terrified woman into his arms, mounted his horse, and sped away with her down the streambed.

A short distance from the smoldering village, Anna-Wee spotted the body of Tee-Wah-Nee. She feigned illness, sat on the ground, and asked Henrich to allow her to take some beads and bracelets from her husband's body. Henrich sneered his assent. Anna-Wee knelt close, gathered Tee-Wah-Nee's bow and quiver of arrows, and hid them in the folds of her skirt. As Henrich turned to watch the fighting, she picked up the bow, slid in an arrow against the curved wood, and shot him in the back.

"You are a traitor to both your own people and to my adopted people," she cried as Henrich fell to the ground.

Anna-Wee took his rifle and ammunition, along with the bow and arrow, and returned to the battleground. At dusk, the body of Tee-Wah-Nee was carried to the ruins of his lodge. Anna-Wee kept vigil beside the remains of her husband and son, singing the Cheyenne death song and imploring Manitou, the Great Spirit, to take their souls. Cavalry attacked the Cheyenne village again the next day. Anna-Wee was killed as she bravely fought the troops.

On fall evenings, in those brief minutes of dusk, a mist rises from the sandy banks of White Woman Creek. Out of that mist, it is said, comes the ghost of Anna-Wee, singing her song for Tee-Wah-Nee and her son. Her soft voice drifts and rises across the tall grasses like a single white cloud in the endlessly blue Kansas sky.

Phantom Riders of the Pony Express

Hanover

Near the town of Hanover, in northern Kansas, stands the weather-beaten wood-frame Hollenberg Pony Express Station, the largest relief stop on that famed trail that stretched from Missouri to California. Hollenberg is today the only unaltered station in its original location.

It has another distinction too. Some claim it holds the specters of the Pony Express riders who pounded across the prairie, carrying the mail over a century and a half ago.

In 1860 the railroad and the telegraph ended at St. Joseph, Missouri. From there the mail was carried by stagecoach to California, a trip that took three weeks or longer. Nearly half a million Americans were then living west of the Rocky Mountains. Many had gone to prospect for gold or to take up lands, and all hungered for news from family and friends in the East. It was frustrating to wait for the slow and sometimes unpredictable stagecoaches to arrive, if they did at all. Besides, the rapid expansion of the young country required a faster means of communication between the federal government in Washington and the settlements on the Pacific Ocean. To fill this need, the Pony Express was born.

The hope was that horsemen, riding fast ponies in relays, could carry the mail across two thousand miles of prairie and mountain in half the time it took the stagecoach. It was a grand and daring scheme fraught with every imaginable danger. Even the Pony Express Company itself recognized the risks. Its advertisement of March 1860 read: "WANTED—Young, skinny, wiry fellows not over eighteen. Must be expert riders, willing to risk death daily. Orphans preferred."

Orphans or not, 100 to 120 riders were quickly hired, and at least 80 were in the saddle at any one time. One at a time, several hours apart, 40 riders headed westward from St. Joseph and 40 others started eastward from Sacramento, California.

The route followed the Oregon-California trail across northern Kansas then snaked along the Platte River in Nebraska, and on west by way of Fort Kearney, Scotts Bluff, Fort Laramie, South Pass, Fort Bridger, and Salt Lake City. The trail crossed Nevada and the Sierra Nevada mountains and ended at Sacramento. River steamers on the Sacramento River then carried the mail westward on to San Francisco.

At relay stations, set up about every ten to fifteen miles apart along the route, the rider cried "WHOOP!" as he galloped in on clouds of dust and switched to a waiting fresh pony. At every third station a new rider took over. The men rode day and night, through searing heat and deepest snow, for the mail had to go through.

The Pony Express lasted only eighteen months, but in that short time it changed boys into men and created instant heroes.

William F. Cody, Buffalo Bill, was only fifteen years old when he signed on as a rider. Galloping into his home station once at the end of his ride, he learned there was no one to take his place. Without a second thought, young Cody rode on, finishing the 322-mile trip alone. His sister Julia later wrote, "They sayed [*sic*] he was . . . the lightest and swiftest rider, and he seemed to understand the Country."

Another of Cody's rides is notable for a different reason. He was entrusted with a large sum of money destined for California. Cash was rarely transported, but in this case it was unavoidable. At any rate, rumors flew that bandits knew there would be cash for the taking and planned to ambush the rider. Cody, realizing he would be helpless in the face of a gang of armed men, devised a simple plan. He placed the money under the saddle, hidden in the blanket that lay between the leather and the horse's skin. The saddlebag, which he stuffed with blank paper, was in plain sight.

In changing mounts at relay stations, Cody carefully placed the blanketful of money under the new saddle. On the last lap of his trip the bandits waylaid him. Cody handed over the saddlebag and galloped off, the blanketful of money arriving sometime later in Sacramento safely intact.

The weather was another potential danger riders faced. Twenty-year-old Thomas Owen King lost his way in blinding snow. Coaxing his pony through drifts as high as his stirrups, he eventually found the trail and reached his next station.

Nick Wilson, at eighteen, was caught in early May 1860 in a conflict that blazed across Utah Territory between the Paiutes and the white settlers they were determined to drive out. Wilson was nearly killed when a barbed arrow pierced his skull above his left eye. Although he survived, Wilson carried the ugly scar for the rest of his life and usually wore a hat to hide it.

One of the youngest riders may have been the bravest. Billy Tate was an orphan and only fourteen years old when the Paiute war broke out. A dozen warriors charged after him on one of his Pony Express rides, driving him behind a rock. Friends found the youngster's body pierced by a number of arrows. Seven of his attackers lay dead before him.

While these daring riders faced the dangers of the long trail westward, the telegraph and the railroad were pushing back the frontier. By October 1861, the thin wires of the telegraph began flashing messages to the West Coast, and the need for the horsemen on their spirited ponies was gone.

With the demise of the Pony Express, many of the old stations fell to ruin. But the Hollenberg Station, also known as the Cottonwood Pony

Express Station, survived the caprices of weather and time. Located 123 miles west of St. Joseph, it occupied part of a ranch owned by Gerat Henry Hollenberg. He had built the station in 1858 originally to serve travelers on the Oregon and California Trails. The building housed a store, tavern, post office, and living quarters for the station keeper and his family on the ground floor. Overland stagecoach drivers and later Pony Express horsemen stayed in a second-floor sleeping loft. Fresh mounts for the riders were kept in a stable that could house a hundred head of horse or oxen. Countless wagon trains stopped at the Hollenberg Station for food and clothing, feed for the animals, and various supplies for the long westward journey. The station also serviced the Butterfield Overland Mail route.

In 1869 Hollenberg founded the nearby town of Hanover and later won election to the Kansas legislature. Residents of Hanover had a leading role in preserving the Hollenberg Station. In 1941 the Kansas legislature appropriated funds for the purchase of the structure and seven acres of land. The building, now a state historical park, has been restored and operates as a museum. It has never been moved and retains its original dimensions.

Some visitors to Hollenberg Station swear they hear whispered conversations and experience a sudden, cold breeze inside the building every time the door swings open.

Other visitors claim that the Pony Express riders and their mounts still travel the worn, familiar trails. Near quiet stretches of highway late at night, people tell of hearing pounding hooves and a faint *Hallooo!* as something passes them like the wind. Could it be an orphaned teenage Pony Express rider spurring his phantom horse on to the next station?

A Dog's Tale

Dodge City

The late Franc Shor was an associate editor of *National Geographic Magazine*. As such, he specialized in reporting from and photographing some of the most isolated places on earth. When Shor died at the age of sixty in 1974,

Supreme Court Justice William O. Douglas called him "the most traveled man I have ever met."

Shor's was a world of people, places, and confirmed information. He had very little if any interest in the ambiguous world of psychic phenomena. But a compelling incident one summer left him with questions he never thought he would be asking.

Shor's mother and other relatives lived in Dodge City, Kansas, while he himself was raised by his grandmother in Cimarron, Kansas.

His grandmother was an antique buff especially fond of Meissen porcelains that she had collected over the years. The delicate figurines fascinated little Frankie, his family nickname. His favorite was of a small child dressed in a smock, patting a dog that stood on its hind legs. Whenever his Aunt Ethel came from Dodge City to visit, she would tease her nephew by insisting that the figure in the smock was a girl. "There's little Frankie wearing a dress," she would say; Shor vigorously protested.

When Shor's grandmother died many years later, she left the porcelain collection to Franc's Aunt Ethel. Sometime later, Ethel died and willed the porcelains to her nephew, who was by now living and working in Washington, DC. After attending Ethel's funeral, he went back to her house. Ethel's husband had set out the china, and Shor readied it for shipment home.

While inventorying the pieces, Shor discovered his favorite one missing, the girl in the smock petting the dog. He searched the house and on a shelf in a corner of the basement found this figurine. Unfortunately, the tail had been broken off. He could not find it anywhere in the house. Sentimentally attached to the little statue, he decided to keep it anyway and took it for storage to his mother's home. Later he would arrange to have a ceramist craft a new tail.

Back in Washington, Shor became immersed in his work and forgot all about the broken porcelain figure until his mother died in June 1964. At her Dodge City funeral he remembered the figurine. It was still at her house. This time he took it home with him, sans tail.

A week after his return, he awoke suddenly late one night. In the center of his bedroom stood his Aunt Ethel, warm and lifelike in a loose-fitting, silk dress that he had often seen her wearing. Shor was wide awake, certain that he was not dreaming.

Aunt Ethel looked directly at him and smiled.

She said, "Why don't you look under the piano?"

Puzzled by the remark, Shor asked his aunt to repeat what she had said. She did and then added, "Frankie's little statue."

"I decided that I needed some strong coffee. In fact, I consumed two potfuls before dressing and going to the office that morning."

All day long Shor pondered the episode. Why had Aunt Ethel not retrieved the dog's tail herself at some point when she was still alive if she knew where it was? Had she died before she could reveal the location to anyone and now, after death, wanted to get that information to her nephew? Preposterous, Shor thought. He had no answers, but he had a plan.

That night Shor telephoned his sister, Camilla Haviland, a probate judge in Dodge City, and asked her if there was a piano in his Aunt Ethel's old house.

Haviland said there happened to be an old player piano in the basement. After Shor related the night's incident, his sister offered to take a look.

Two weeks later Haviland telephoned her brother. A housekeeper had found the dog's tail intact under the piano, just where Shor's Aunt Ethel had told him it would be.

The Cursed Knife

Topeka

Jane Armbruster was uneasy. Even though her husband, Peter, locked the antique bowie knife they had just bought in a strongbox in the bedroom closet and hid the key in the false bottom of a bureau drawer, that still did not seem sufficient protection. The knife was a rare find, but what really worried Jane was the disturbing encounter they had as they left the auction.

The auction took place not far from their Topeka home. The bidding had been intense. Many people admired the long, silver blade and the exquisitely carved handle inlaid with semiprecious stones. The knife gleamed in the afternoon sun, an almost electrical glow glancing off the blade. It looked as if it had never been used, but with a bowie knife nearly one hundred years old that seemed impossible.

The Armbrusters' bid was highest of the six people seeking the knife. As they left with their treasure, a swarthy young man with ebony hair and dark, penetrating eyes came up to Peter.

"Mister," he began, "I'd like to buy that knife from you. I'll offer you a fair price."

Peter shook his head.

"If you really wanted the knife, you should have kept bidding."

"I'm short of money just now," the stranger insisted as he walked along beside the couple.

"If you give me the knife today, I promise I'll pay you double what you just paid. That seems fair to me."

Peter had never seen him before. The couple knew most of the regular auction attendees around Topeka, and this nervous young man was not among them.

"But if I give you the knife," Peter countered, "how do I know I'll ever see you again?"

"I'll give you what money I have." He dug into his pocket and pulled out a fifty-dollar bill. "I'll get the rest of it from, er, my parents."

He sounded desperate and continued his pleading.

"Mister, that knife is special to my family!"

And then the young man added the words Jane Armbruster would never forget: "That knife can bring riches and pleasure . . . or misery and death."

Peter laughed. "So that's it! A bowie knife with an authentic curse! I suppose you'll tell me next that you're its immortal guardian. No sir! You can't buy it at any price!"

Peter took Jane by the arm and stayed close to her until they reached their car.

"You'll regret this day!" the young man shouted after them, waving his fist. "I'll get that knife one way or another! It will bring you only death!"

Jane Armbruster shrank against the car seat as those last words pounded through the window. Peter did not appear overly upset at the stranger's threats of harm, but he did worry that the man might follow them and try to steal the knife.

Armbruster locked it in a strongbox that night along with several other valuable possessions. There it remained for nearly two years.

On occasion Peter would remind his wife that nothing terrible had happened to them in all that time.

"That nonsense about a curse was just that creep's way of trying to get the knife at half what I paid," Peter chided her.

Jane almost believed him.

She had nearly forgotten the knife and the curse until she awoke early one morning to her husband gasping and shaking beside her. She reached out to him. There was a quick intake of air and he fell silent. Peter was dead of a heart attack.

About a month later, Jane was at a scheduled appointment with her own doctor. They ended up discussing Peter's sudden death. He thought a moment, and then said that Peter's death was so sudden it was as if someone had plunged a knife into his heart.

Jane shuddered at the words. A knife—the bowie knife and its curse.

She felt sick. She rushed home, anxious and agitated, remembering the words of that angry young man: *"I'll get that knife one way or another! It will bring you only death!"*

Jane had not been near the strongbox since her husband's death. She found the key in its hiding place and opened the box. Peter's old silver money clip was inside along with a few old coins and other small objects. But that was it. The cursed bowie knife had vanished.

Elizabeth Polly

Fort Hays

A merciless sun flattened the land from horizon to horizon as Ephraim Polly pushed his team westward. His hard, brown hands held the reins loosely, and half moons of sweat darkened the armpits of his shirt.

Beside him on the wagon seat sat his wife, Elizabeth, her back as straight as a newly driven fence post. Her wide, blue bonnet scarcely shielded her face from the sun and the hot wind that pushed dust up under the wagon wheels.

But Elizabeth never complained. She loved Ephraim deeply. She also understood him. He was a thoughtful man, but not shrewd. He wanted to give his wife the better things in life but did not know how to seize an opportunity. In her heart, Elizabeth knew she would always be the wife of a "drummer" peddling wagonloads of candies, tobacco, sewing kits, and other necessities to soldiers in lonely outposts along the Smoky Hill River trail and bringing news of the wider world along with the wares.

For Elizabeth Polly, that was enough.

At sunset, on this scorching day in 1867, the Pollys reached Fort Hays, in western Kansas. Elizabeth did not know that her travels with Ephraim were over. She would never leave the fort.

While the couple was at Fort Hays, a deadly cholera epidemic struck. Neither history nor legend recounts what happened to Ephraim Polly, but it is documented that Elizabeth volunteered to help the one doctor at the fort. She was not a trained nurse, but she was kind and brought hope to the sick and comfort to the dying.

Through the long, hot days she worked in the sick ward doing what she could to ease the suffering around her. She packed flannel cloths and hot bottles around the sick to help them retain body heat; she provided sips of barley water and beef tea to those able to drink. And she held the hand of more than one frightened child in the last hours of their lives.

Sometimes for an hour or two in the early evening, Elizabeth left the wardroom and walked to a hilltop a couple of miles southwest of the fort. There, alone under the vast sky, she welcomed the wind combing her hair and billowing her long skirts as she listened to the meadowlarks singing in the bluestem grasses far below. These peaceful moments renewed her strength. Then, in the fading light, she returned to the stench of sickness and the certainty of approaching death.

Elizabeth Polly ministered to the sick for many weeks. No one ever knew much about her; she was a quiet woman who did not even say where she was from. To the soldiers of Fort Hays, she was an angel of mercy.

Tragically the woman who spent so much time comforting others contracted the dreaded disease. As she herself lay dying, she asked if she could please be buried atop her beloved hill. She was assured that her wish would be granted.

Elizabeth Polly was given a full-dress military funeral in the fall of 1867, her body taken to the hilltop by a horse-drawn ambulance. Major Gibbs, the fort commandant, assisted in the burial service.

For years after Elizabeth Polly's death, local residents referred to her burial spot as the "Lonely Grave." Nearly inaccessible except on foot or by horse, the grave was rarely visited. From time to time a wooden cross appeared at the site, put up by a Boy Scout troop from Hays City. Then, in the 1960s, a group of citizens erected an obelisk on Elizabeth's hill. It was a fitting memorial to this selfless pioneer woman who rested there.

Or does she?

Fifty years after Elizabeth Polly's death, a sequence of peculiar events seemed to indicate that she may leave her lonely grave to walk the hill that she so loved.

Dawn was just breaking over the prairie on an April day in 1917 when John Schmidt, a western Kansas farmer, rode out to his pasture. It was his custom to go each morning to drive the cows the few hundred yards from the pasture back to his barn for milking. His dog trotted along at his side. Schmidt had ridden about halfway across the pasture when he noticed a woman afoot some distance away.

He saw first her light-colored, old-fashioned bonnet in the predawn light, and then, as the sky brightened, her ankle-length, blue gingham dress. She was quite tall, Schmidt figured, but he could not see her face very well, hidden as it was by her bonnet. She had the steady stride of a purposeful woman.

Schmidt had never seen her before; of that he was certain. To be out here, she would have to be one of the women from the Fort Hays Normal School perhaps, or from town, but her route perplexed him. She had come from the direction of old Fort Hays and was headed southwest. In that direction lay nothing but an abandoned one-room shack and about a quarter of a mile from that, the grave of Elizabeth Polly.

Schmidt cupped his hand to his mouth and called to her. She neither turned her head nor broke her stride.

Suddenly his dog yelped and took off for home, tail between its legs. Schmidt yelled after it but at that moment his horse reared.

The dog kept running, but Schmidt was able to drive the pony close enough to the lady in blue to have touched her with the tip of his horsewhip.

But she seemed oblivious to him. Irked by her indifference, Schmidt circled widely around and went on after the cows.

His whole family was waiting when Schmidt got back to the house. Because he was only a short distance across the field, they had seen the woman and all that had happened. They had not taken their eyes off the strange woman. His wife said she had gone into the old shack near the top of Lonely Grave Hill.

Schmidt asked his family to keep watch on the shack if they could, even though they would be busy doing morning milking and chores. They promised to take turns.

Schmidt hitched his team to the wagon and headed down to the Smoky Hill River bottoms where each day he dug and hauled sand for construction projects in the area. The job supplemented his inadequate farm income.

His brother-in-law, Anton Rupp, was working with him. Rupp saw that Schmidt was upset about something. He finally told Rupp about the morning's incident and asked if he would come with him after work to investigate the shack. Rupp agreed.

At supper, Schmidt's wife said she and the children had taken turns watching the shack and they had not see anyone go in or come out.

Their meal finished, the two men rode up to the old cabin, now cast in the shadows of a full moon. They called out. They banged on the weathered door. They called again. Schmidt said he was going in.

The old latch was rusted in place, so Schmidt gave the door a violent kick and it snapped inward. He stepped cautiously inside.

Cobwebs embroidered the corners and dust lay thick everywhere. Obviously the place had not been occupied for some time. There was no sign of a lady in blue.

Much later, in the 1940s, John Schmidt told a young friend, Robert Maxwell, the story that had perplexed the Schmidt family for nearly thirty years.

It was several days after hearing the tale before Maxwell got up the courage to ask the question that plagued him. "John, do you reckon that gal could have been Elizabeth Polly? Or her ghost?"

Schmidt took a long time answering.

"Bobby," he said softly, "I just don't know."

But he told Maxwell that after he saw the woman that day, he went to see George Brown, a night watchman at the coliseum on the Fort Hays state college campus.

Brown was a youngster when the original fort still stood. He herded cattle for the officers. Perhaps he would remember something of Elizabeth Polly.

Brown was eager to talk about those long-ago days, and he told Schmidt that indeed he had known Elizabeth Polly and remembered her husband as well. He described her funeral and recalled that she was buried in a wide-brim bonnet and a long, flowing blue gown, the same outfit the Schmidt family had seen the ghost wearing that morning in 1917, fifty years after her death.

On the hundredth anniversary of Elizabeth Polly's death in 1967, Hays City celebrated its own centennial. Men and women, dressed in nineteenth-century attire, gathered downtown for the festivities and a street dance.

Some say that at the edge of the crowd, amid the many bonnets and ankle-length gingham gowns worn that day, there was one particular lady, dressed in blue, who watched the bustling activities with a wistful smile on her face. At the coming of the night, the lady set off alone, back across the prairie to her lonely grave.

Michigan

The Soul of Stephen Strand

Battle Creek

Near Battle Creek, a decade before the American Civil War, a story unfolded so strange, so unbelievable, it reads like fiction. Even though the event originally appeared in an 1851 issue of the sensational *New York Mercury*, it was later cited by psychical research publications for its extraordinary circumstances. Did the events roll out as suggested, or was it a piece of fiction wrapped in the garb of authenticity? We may never know for certain, but what is alleged to have taken place was nothing less than an instance of long-term possession, the "transference" of a soul from someone dead to someone who lived on for many years.

In other words, a wandering spirit drove away the soul of a living person.

As incredible and unbelievable as it sounds, that is what is alleged to have happened.

Harper Allyn, a bachelor, worked as a wool carder at the mills of one Captain William Wallace in the years 1850 and 1851. He was a quiet man, given to long evenings alone by the fire, or to pursuing solitary sport such as hunting and fishing the shores of Goguac Lake, at that time a few miles outside Battle Creek. Little is known of him. His age was never reported, nor his personal history. The only characteristic of note is the crux of this story, Allyn's curiosity about a solitary "hermit" who lived on an island in Goguac Lake.

It was on a hunting trip that Allyn first noticed the tidy small cabin nestled among the pine trees. The man who lived there was Stephen Strand, a private character who shunned human interaction and lived alone except for an old dog and a black cat. As far as anyone knew, he never ventured into town and appeared to provide for himself through trapping, hunting, and fishing for bass, bluegill, and walleye in the abundant waters of the lake.

Allyn, the quiet bachelor, and Strand, the mysterious hermit, were thrown together in a most unusual way when a rattlesnake trapped Strand's black cat against a rock ledge. Allyn, who was hunting nearby at the time, happened along and killed the serpent. Strand showered Allyn with gratitude.

After that, the men frequently hunted and fished together. And although they spoke of many things, Allyn learned little about Strand's life and even less about the circumstances that brought him to such an isolated existence.

Their friendship might have continued uneventfully had it not been for a thunderstorm. Allyn and Strand had been fishing on the lake and had just made it back to Strand's cabin as the first wave of lightning-belching dark clouds erupted. Allyn could not make it back to the mainland and was forced to spend the night in Strand's cabin.

He had always sensed that something lay hidden within Strand, a dark secret that would provide the key to understanding the man.

On this wild night Allyn finally heard the astonishing tale. It all began with the first clap of thunder.

Never had Harper Allyn seen a grown man react with such abject terror to a thunderstorm. While it raged, Strand paced the cabin. From time to time he nervously glanced out the shuttered windows, as if waiting for someone. He noticed Allyn's curiosity but said nothing. At last the storm abated. Strand visibly relaxed and beckoned Allyn to join him nearer the fire.

"I apologize for what must seem to you peculiar behavior on my part," Strand began. "But you see, I have good reason to fear the storm. I, that is the person you hear speaking, am Stephen Strand. But the body you see is that of another."

Harper Allyn rose and made for the door. He was not going to spend the night with a madman.

"Please!" Strand reached out to grasp Allyn's arm. "Please, I am not mad, despite that rather odd statement. If you will allow me, I shall explain. But I warn you, it is a story you will find difficult to believe."

Allyn hesitated. Was he close to finding that hidden secret he knew was there? Or were Strand's words the ravings of a lunatic?

"Very well," Allyn said at last, resuming his seat and leaning forward. "Continue. Tell me how it is possible that you speak as one man and be another."

Strand took a deep breath and began his tale.

"That, sir, is why I fear the storm. I shall start at the beginning. I was born nearly six decades ago in the village of Becket Corner, Massachusetts. As Stephen Strand. At the age of sixteen years, I signed on with a whaler out of New Bedford. I rose steadily in rank until, at the age of twenty, I felt assured enough in my status to return home and marry."

His eyes clouded. He gazed into the deep, red embers of the blazing fire.

"Her name was Molly . . . Molly Lawton. We had known each other since childhood. After we married, I worked ashore for five years, first as a storekeeper and then at a livery. We had a good life together . . . but for me that wasn't enough. I knew I belonged at sea. Molly accepted that as a good wife does."

He shipped out on a merchantman bound for France. The trip was uneventful. He stayed with the ship, even though it was to be delayed several months before its return to America.

"At last we left France, bound for Ireland, where we were to take on cargo. Late one night, as we neared Cornwall, a violent storm descended upon us. We couldn't hold the course in the channel and smashed against the English cliffs.

"I was below decks when we hit. I was thrown across the sleeping compartment and must have struck my head for I remember nothing until . . . until I . . . woke up . . ."

He was struggling with the recollection. Allyn sensed it was the first time in a long while that he had talked about himself.

"Go on," Allyn gently urged. "You struck your head, but obviously you lived."

"Ah, but that's just it," Strand continued. "I did not live! I awoke, yes, but as I did I had the sensation of floating above the cabin deck, looking down upon the scene. I could not find my body. My soul or spirit, for that is what I presume I had become, had traveled some distance. I was in a different part of the ship."

Strand paused a moment, struggling to go on.

"I did not want to stay in that . . . limbo! I wanted to see my family again, to rejoin the world of the living. All around me, my shipmates lay dead. Suddenly, I noticed that one of the Frenchmen who had joined us as passengers was stirring.

"It was then I realized that perhaps his body could become mine! I tried to enter him, but his own soul prevented me. We fought. I remember little, except that after what seemed like hours I succeeded. His soul fled. But not far. It still . . . lingers. Close by. Always has."

Strand was breathing heavily, the sweat visible on his forehead, as if reliving the nauseous fear that must have gripped him on the English coast so many years ago.

"Whenever there is a storm, as tonight, the soul of that man tries to repossess what once was his—the body you see before you. I am the soul and mind of Stephen Strand, but this body, this *casing* belongs to the Frenchman I conquered that night so very long ago."

Allyn leaned back in his chair, not quite knowing what to say, or even whether to believe such a preposterous story.

"Did that Frenchman, er, did *you* find any possessions on that body you took?" Allyn asked at last.

"A few," Strand replied. "Some letters that I destroyed and a knife and a small bag I lost years ago." He reached into his pocket. "But this match safe I have kept since that night. You may have it. For saving my cat. Take it. Please. And for it, perhaps you would be kind enough to give me that daguerreotype of yourself you told me about. A fair trade? I want to remember you . . . and your many kindnesses."

Allyn took the exquisitely designed gold box. The workmanship was of the finest quality. Engraved upon the outside was the name Jacques Beaumont.

"I shall certainly give you that picture. I fear this is far more valuable, however. But are you . . . is that which I see the body of Beaumont?" Allyn asked.

"Yes," Strand said quietly, "although I know little of him. He is a vessel within which lives the soul of Stephen Strand. To me it is a stranger's name."

Even more questions crowded Allyn's mind.

"What then? How did you reach this country? And end up out here far from your, er, Stephen Strand's home?"

"I . . . or Beaumont rather was the only survivor. The ship broke apart, but I was able to ride a large piece of wood like a raft to shore. I made my way to Liverpool and thence to Boston. I must say, it was a peculiar experience. This body . . . I was not used to it! Silly things happened." Strand laughed. Allyn had never seen him laugh before.

"I began to crave French cooking! Of course I was in England so out of luck on that score."

Again he grew serious.

"It was as if I had suddenly been transported as a blind man into a new house, one in which I was expected to live and work, and yet I knew nothing of its rooms or furnishings. Each time I glanced into a looking glass, I expected to see Stephen Strand. Instead, this stranger stared back at me. I can tell you I was frightened more than once by the ordeal. And yet . . . I was alive!

"Well, once in Boston, I prepared to reacquaint myself with my wife. I made my way to Becket Center and . . ."

Strand covered his eyes and began to weep.

"Go on," Allyn urged.

"I'm . . . I'm sorry," Strand stammered between sobs. "It's so very painful for me. You see I hadn't reckoned with the shock my new . . . self . . . would have on those whom I loved. I poured out my story to Molly, my wife. She shrank from me. She said her husband had been drowned off the English coast. I tried to convince her it was I, her Stephen, but it was of no use. She took me for a madman. My friends shunned me. I was forced to flee for my life. I was afraid they would lock me up. I wandered for several years and finally settled here on this island where you found me."

His peculiar narrative at an end, Strand stared intently at his friend.

Allyn met his gaze but said nothing. The first light of dawn was knifing through the cabin, casting the cozy room's furnishings in an eerie, amber-colored glow.

Allyn replied at last. "I have to think about what you have told me. It is so . . . so unbelievable. But it has the texture of truth about it. I don't fully understand why . . . but I think I believe you."

Allyn saw little of Stephen Strand over the next few months, occasionally stopping by the cabin to check on his welfare, but never staying for more than a few minutes at a time. He tried to find proof to support Strand's assertions. He wrote a letter to the editor of a newspaper near Becket Corner, asking for information regarding Stephen Strand. Was there ever such a man in Becket Corner? Did he go off to sea? Marry? And, most importantly, was he still living?

In reply, the editor said that a man named Stephen Strand had lived in that village. But Strand had been lost at sea. However, many years ago a stranger had arrived in the village claiming to be Strand, but nobody believed him. The impersonator was driven from town.

Molly Strand and her children had left Becket Corner long ago to live with her wealthy brother in the West and had not been heard from since, the editor finished.

The letter did seem to confirm many of the details of Strand's baffling story.

About a year later, Harper Allyn found that Stephen Strand had vanished. A severe thunderstorm struck the Goguac Lake area, and when Allyn visited the cabin a few days later, the only living being was Strand's starving dog cowering in a corner. The black cat was also missing.

Had Jacques Beaumont's soul finally regained possession of its body? Allyn found the normally tidy cabin in great disarray—smashed crockery and chairs, an overturned table, windows smashed—as if there had been a tremendous struggle there. Allyn reported the missing Strand to the authorities and a search was made, even the lake was dragged, but nothing was ever found of the mortal remains of Stephen Strand, born Jacques Beaumont.

Harper Allyn did not stay in Battle Creek. He inherited some money, enough to allow him to spend his remaining life traveling and living in modest luxury.

A childhood friend of Allyn's, Charley Bushnell, had taken up residence in France, studying at an art school in Paris. Allyn decided to visit him. The saga of Stephen Strand had remained with him, and the thought of visiting Jacques Beaumont's native country intrigued him.

Bushnell was intimate with Parisian society and soon had Allyn attending numerous social functions. At one such gathering of artists and literary figures, Allyn was introduced to a particularly attractive woman. When she saw him and heard his name, she nearly collapsed. Allyn was at her side when she regained her composure.

"I am so sorry," she said. "It's just that your face and name are familiar to me."

Allyn was dumbfounded.

"How can that possibly be?" he said. "I have only recently arrived in Paris, and, to the best of my knowledge, I have never seen you before."

"But I have seen you. In a picture only last week," she replied.

"Please explain all this to me," Allyn requested. "I am quite confused."

"My name is Lily Beaumont," the woman said. Allyn paled. Beaumont. That name again. Could it be . . . ?

"Ah, my name means something to you?" she said. "Last week a very old man came to my mother in the village where she has lived since my father died. He was a sailor, lost at sea near the English coast. Anyway, this man, whoever he was, claimed to be my father. My mother didn't recognize him, nor did I. How could we? It's been over forty years. He told this preposterous story about being possessed by another man and said he was only recently able to regain his own identity. The prefect of police came and took him away. To an asylum. I . . . we . . . thought he was quite insane. But now I see that the picture he had in his pocket was a picture of you! And your name was written on the back."

"My God!" Allyn said. His voice was hoarse.

He quickly told Lily Beaumont the story of Stephen Strand and Jacques Beaumont and of Goguac Lake. She was speechless and nearly despondent.

Allyn left immediately for the asylum she had mentioned.

He found Jacques Beaumont in a tiny cell. He was very old, quite thin and sickly, but yes this was the same man he knew as Stephen Strand.

Strand/Beaumont did not recognize him, nor did he seem to understand English. Since he was in such ill health, Allyn stayed only a short time. Later, he showed Madame Beaumont, Lily's mother, the match safe Strand had given him. She collapsed at the sight of it. It was the same one she had given her husband before he vanished at sea.

The incredible story quickly circulated through the small village. Was the old man indeed the long-lost Jacques Beaumont? Some people claimed he looked like the man they had known decades earlier. Others were convinced he was an imposter preying upon the kindness of a respected family. Meanwhile, the old man had grown sicker and was taken to the hospital. Doctors could do little for him except to make his final hours as comfortable as possible.

Harper Allyn was notified, as was a Catholic priest who administered the last rites of the church.

Allyn sat at the old man's bedside. He knew not what to say or even where to begin. But he had to know. He asked the priest to translate his words.

"Will you now tell the truth? Are you Stephen Strand or Jacques Beaumont?" Allyn asked the dying man.

The priest translated: "In the presence of the Almighty and by the sign of the Cross, I swear . . ." but that was all. Strand/Beaumont sank back against his pillows and was dead.

The tale that Harper Allyn heard on that island in Goguac Lake remained forever in dispute.

Was this man Harper Allyn knew on Goguac Lake simply an imposter, claiming one of the most fanciful cases of possession in history? Or had he, for most of his life, lived as two men, inhabiting the body of one, the soul and mind of another?

If there was an answer, it went with him to the grave.

The Schooner *Erie Board of Trade*

Saginaw

It should not be surprising that the legends and lore surrounding lost ships and shipwrecks of the Great Lakes are legion. There is something about a modern lake freighter or nineteenth-century cargo schooner simply disappearing beneath the waves with all hands on board that excites and terrifies us at the same time. The first ship lost on the Great Lakes is an example. The French explorer Robert de la La Salle's barque, the *Griffon*, disappeared (in a storm, Father Hennepin wrote) during its return to Fort Niagara on Lake Huron after leaving Washington Island, off Wisconsin's Door Peninsula, on September 18, 1679. The rough-hewn ship was loaded with six hundred tons of furs. La Salle himself watched the ship leave port after deciding to set out with some of his men to explore lands to the south. There is no conclusive evidence that the ship's wreckage has been found.

Often the stories go beyond the ordinary and claims are made that particular ships, like the lost *Griffon* or the yawl *Western Reserve* in the story "Man on the Beach," have become *ghost* ships.

There is even a Lake Michigan Triangle (Ludington Michigan to Benton Harbor, then across the Lake to Manitowoc, Wisconsin, and back to Ludington) in which ships and planes are alleged to have vanished without a trace, much like its namesake in Bermuda, even though there is scant evidence to support the claims.

But sometimes the stories are not about an entire ship and crew condemned to sail as a Flying Dutchman for all eternity but rather a supernatural event on board that gives it notoriety.

Such is the case with a nineteenth-century three-masted barque that's named *The Erie Board of Trade*, though study has cast doubt that a ship with that specific name ever sailed the Great Lakes.

The ghost story connected to the *Board of Trade* has murky origins at best. A lengthy account was published in the August 20, 1883, edition of the *New York Sun* and then reprinted in newspapers all around the Great Lakes in the months that followed.

Whatever the case, the story is reputed to have been first told on a moonlit night in Saginaw, Michigan, in much the same way as it was later reported first in the *New York Sun* and then in the Saginaw *Courier*, from which this version is derived.

What makes it intriguing—irrespective of how much of it is true or not—is that the storyteller clearly had sailed on Great Lake schooners and knew what he was talking about. Perhaps he changed the name of the ship in the telling, but it is not hard to imagine that he went through exactly what he says he did.

A crew of Great Lakes sailors was sitting around a ship chandler's shop along the lower part of Saginaw's South Street, not far from the Saginaw

River. They had been exchanging ghost stories all evening and one man had just finished telling his own.

"Hah," snorted the chandler whose nautical supply shop it was.

"You're a sorry dog. You were drunk, and the spirits you'd taken made you see other spirits!"

Everyone laughed except for one man, the oldest sailor in the bunch. He had been listening in silence. Presently he tamped out his pipe and threw one leg over the anchor stock he was sitting on.

"Well, I saw a ghost once," he began, refilling his pipe bowl. "I saw it as plain as ever. The captain of the schooner I was on and the man in the waist both saw it too. And there wasn't a drop of liquor on board."

His audience quieted; they knew this old man always spoke the truth.

"It was a little over ten years ago. I was before the mast then. It was the opening of the season, and I was in Chicago. I heard at the boardinghouse that some men were wanted on a three-masted schooner called the *Erie Board of Trade*. The boys gave her a pretty hard name, but they said the grub was good and that the old man paid top wages every time, so I went down and asked him if he'd got all the hands aboard. He looked at me a minute, and asked me where my dunnage was. When I told him, he said I should get it on board right away.

"The *Board of Trade* was as handsome a craft as ever floated on the lakes. As I came down the dock with my bag under my arm, I had to stop and have a look at her. The old captain saw me. He was proud of her, and I thought afterward that he rather took a fancy to me because I couldn't help showing I liked her looks.

"I was in her two round trips. The last trip up was the last on the lakes. Not but what times were pretty good up there. We were getting two fifty a day for the first trip out and another two bucks the last. We messed with the old man, and, with fresh meat and vegetables and coffee and milk, it was first-cabin passage all around. But the old man made it hot for most of us. There wasn't any watch below in the day and we were kept painting her on the down trip and scrubbing the paint off again on the passage up.

"The first trip around to Chicago, every man but me got his dunnage onto the dock as soon as he was paid off. When I got my money I asked the old man if he'd want anyone to help with the lines when the schooner was towed from the coal yard to the elevator. He said he reckoned he could keep me if I wanted to stay, so I signed articles for the next trip there.

"When we were getting the wheat into her at the elevator, we got the crew aboard. One of them was a red-haired Scotsman. The captain took a dislike to him from the first. I don't know why. It was a tough time for Scotty all the way down. We were in Buffalo just twelve hours, and then we cleared for Cleveland to take on soft coal for Milwaukee. The tug gave us a short pull outside the breakwater, and we had no more than got the canvas up before the wind died out completely. We dropped anchor for the current, settling to the Niagara River, was carrying us down to Black Rock at three knots.

"When we'd got things shipshape about docks, the old man called Scotty and two others aft and told them to scrape down the topmasts. Then he handed the bosun's chair to them. Scotty gave the chair a look and then turned around, and touching his forehead respectfully, said, 'If you please, sir, the rope's been chafed off, and I'll bend on a bit of ratlin' stuff.' The captain was mighty touchy because the jug had left him so, and he just jumped up and down and swore. He told Scotty that, by God, he'd better get up there damn fast or he'd see to it that he never worked on the lakes again.

"Scotty climbed the main rigging pretty quick. He got the halyards bent on the chair and sung out to hoist away. I and a youngster, the captain's nephew, were standing by. We handled that rope carefully, for I'd seen how tender the chair was. When we'd got him up, the young fellow took a turn around the pin, and I looked aloft to see what Scotty was doing. As I did so he reached for his knife with one hand and put out the other for the backstay.

"Just then the chair gave way. He fell all bunched up till he struck the crosstrees, and then he spread out and fell flat on the deck, just forward of the cabin, on the starboard side. I was kneeling beside him in a minute, and so was the old man.

"I was feeling pretty well choked up to see a shipmate killed for he wasn't breathin'. I said to the captain this is pretty bad business, sir; this man's been murdered. Just then, why, Scotty opened his eyes and looked at us. In a whisper, he cursed the captain and his wife and children, and the ship and her owners. While he was still talking, the blood bubbled over his lips, and his head lurched over to one side. He was dead then a' course."

The old sailor brushed at his eyes.

"It was three days before the schooner got to Cleveland. Some of the boys were for leaving her there, but most of us stayed because wages were down again. Going through the rivers, there were four other schooners in the tow. We were next to the tug. Just at the big end below Port Huron a squall struck us. It was too much for the tug, and some lubber cast off the towline without singing out first.

"We dropped our bower as quick as we could, but it was not before we drifted astern, carrying away the headgear of the schooner next to us and smashing our own dinghy. We were a shaky lot going up Lake Huron and no lifeboat under the stern.

"There was a fair easterly wind on the lake, and as we got out of the river in the morning we were standing across Saginaw Bay during the first watch that night. I had the second trick at the wheel. The stars were shining bright and clear and not a cloud was in sight. Ever' stitch of canvas was set and drawing, though the booms sagged and creaked as the vessel rolled lazily in the varying breeze.

"I had just sung out to the mate to strike eight bells when the captain climbed up the companionway and out on deck. He stepped over to the starboard rail and had a look around, then the lookout began striking the bell. The last stroke of the bell seemed to die away with a swish.

"A bit of spray or something struck me in the face. I wiped it away, and then I saw something rise up slowly across the mainsail from the starboard side of the deck forward of the cabin. It was white and all bunched up.

"I glanced at the captain and saw he was staring at it too.

"It hovered straight up and then struck the crosstrees. There it spread out and rolled over toward us.

"It was Scotty, nah, his *ghost* that is.

"His lips were working just as they were when he cursed the captain. As he straightened out, he seemed to stretch himself until he grasped the maintop mast with one hand and the mizzen with the other. Both were carried away like pipe stems.

"The next I knew the square sail yard was hanging in two pieces, the top hamper was swinging, and the booms were jibing over.

"The old man fell in a dead faint on the quarterdeck, and the man in the waist dived down from the forecastle so fast that he knocked over the last man of the other watch. If it had not been for the watch coming on deck just then, she'd have rolled altogether. They got the head sails over and I put the wheel up without knowing what I was doing. In a minute it seemed we were laying our course again."

The old sailor stopped, took a deep breath, and looked around.

"Well, I see some of you don't believe me. Can't say I blame you but you can verify it all for yourself. On the next voyage the schooner was sunk. The insurance companies didn't want to pay on the ground the captain scuttled her. During the trial the whole story was told under oath . . . Scotty's deaths, the loss of her top masts under a clear sky . . . all of it."

And with that the old man relit his pipe.

Although this story or a close variant is sometimes included whenever Great Lakes ghost stories are discussed, the fundamental question remains: Is it true?

Could be. Or at least parts of it.

Those familiar with this story and with sailing ships point to the technical knowledge of barque (three masted) schooners displayed by the old man as evidence he had served aboard a ship like that or knew his way around one.

Now what makes the story plausible is that while Great Lakes historians have no proof of a ship named the *Erie Board of Trade* on the Great Lakes, there was a schooner with a rather similar name—the *Chicago Board of Trade*—during the years in which the story is set. Further, events in the ghost story and what befell the *Chicago Board of Trade* are similar in some details.

This *Chicago Board of Trade* was launched at Manitowoc, Wisconsin, in 1863, making it about ten years old at the time of the old sailor's events. She carried grain and other cargo on Lakes Huron and Erie, same as the *Erie*. Her home port was Bay City, Michigan.

In July 1874 the schooner then under the command of Captain Thomas Fountain was bound for Buffalo, New York, with 28,500 bushels of shelled corn when it struck bottom and scraped over rocks on the lower reaches of the Detroit River, near Malden. The ship continued on for some time with all crew manning the pumps. The crew discovered three feet of water below and could not pump it out fast enough. All hands took to the lifeboats. The ship sank bow first in ten fathoms (sixty feet) of water some twenty-five miles distant from Cleveland.

All the crew and Captain Fountain made it to Fairport, Ohio, a Lake Erie harbor settlement. The schooner itself was a "total loss—$19,000 for the hull and $42,000 for the cargo of wheat."

But suspicions arose that the schooner had been scuttled. Within a month, a Buffalo, New York, business newspaper was reporting the ship "went down under rather peculiar circumstances." The ship's insurers contracted with a salvage company to raise the hull and tow it to Buffalo to launch an investigation. The raising apparently had to wait until the following spring. By March 16, 1875, the Chicago Inter Ocean newspaper was reporting that the *Board of Trade* had been "scuttled and sunk intentionally" to obtain the insurance.

It was not until August 1875 that divers and two tugs raised the schooner's hull and took it to dry dock. Attention turned immediately to "holes in the water closet pipe" as an initial cause of its sinking. Accident or deliberate damage? The question remained open until it was reported that Captain Fountain "had run away." At that point it seemed, as one newspaper reported, "the statement that the vessel was sunk by foul play has some confirmation."

A trial was apparently held, as was done in the ghost story, but unfortunately a transcript of the proceedings has not surfaced to show if the death of a crewman occurred prior to the ship's sinking.

But unlike the ghost story, the *Chicago Board of Trade* had a second life. The hull was bought for $700 by Henry A. Hawgood, a shipowner in Cleveland, who "took her up the lake and rebuilt her." The ship was listed as a Great Lakes merchant vessel as late as 1884.

The trail of a Great Lakes ship with the name of *Board of Trade* seems to end there, at least for for the time being. We are left to wonder if the old sailor perhaps changed the ship's name in his telling and added a few fictional details to make it a more chilling yarn. Is there a red-haired Scotsman who figures prominently in the trial testimony? The answer to that might depend on whether you believe in ghosts or not . . .

Man on the Beach

Deer Park

Captain Truedell was a dreamer. Throughout his decadeslong career in the old Great Lakes Life-Saving Service, including twenty years commanding the station at Grand Marais, Michigan, the captain always dreamed of the important things in his life before they happened. His mother had the gift of prescience and passed it on to him.

The most chilling example of the captain's strange ability to see into the future occurred during his second year in the Life-Saving Service, while he was stationed at Deer Park, Michigan. Once a busy lumber port, Deer Park was little more than a ghost town by 1892.

Truedell usually slept from eight in the evening until shortly before he was called for his watch at midnight. On the night of April 30, 1892, however, Truedell had a particularly fitful sleep. In fact, a dream was playing and replaying and so lifelike that when he eventually awoke he was soaked with perspiration.

In the dream, Truedell was standing on the beach near the station as a storm rose across the lake. Out of the mist walked a man, well dressed and obviously cultivated. As the stranger passed Truedell, he reached out, as if to shake the captain's hand.

Truedell grasped his hand, cold and wet to the touch. The stranger then turned to look directly into Truedell's face and walked into the surf, vanishing under the turbulent waters.

His watch that night was quiet and uneventful. Although a gale continued to blow in from the northwest, the men at the Life-Saving Station had received no distress signals.

At breakfast the next morning, the men joked about Truedell's dream, claiming that his quiet duty was evidence that this time his precognition was wrong.

But early in the afternoon, a soaking-wet, dazed sailor straggled into the station. His ship had gone down in the gale, and only he survived as far as he knew. His name was Harry Stewart, the wheelman.

143

His ship, the *Western Reserve*, belonged to a millionaire, Peter Minch. At that time it was the biggest ship on the lakes, a sturdy three hundred feet long. Minch was so confident of the *Western Reserve* that he took his family aboard for a pleasure trip from the Soo Locks to Two Harbors, Minnesota, where the ship was to take on a load of iron ore.

When the storm had hit, however, Minch ordered Stewart to continue sailing around Whitefish Point and Point Iroquois against the captain's advice. The pounding gale buckled the decks; the ship snapped in two, sending the crew, Minch, and his family into a steel lifeboat and smaller, wooden yawl. The lifeboat sank, but its occupants were able to scramble aboard the yawl.

Early on the morning of May 1, the yawl capsized in the surf, fifteen miles west of Deer Point. Only wheelman Harry Stewart lived.

True to Captain Truedell's dream, the *Western Reserve* had sunk at about nine o'clock the previous evening, just at the time the captain was beginning to "see" the disaster in his sleep.

After listening to Stewart's story, Captain Truedell was assigned to patrol the beach in a westerly direction, searching for any other possible survivors. He soon found the body of a well-dressed man lying face down in the sand. Truedell hesitated a moment before he rolled the body over. The man's hand—wet and cold—brushed against his own.

Could it be?

He looked at the dead man's face to be certain.

It was.

Redemption

Detroit

An old woman named Marie Louise Kennette lived alone in a little house on the river road to Springwells. She was rude, unkempt, and loved only her money and a violin, a family heirloom. A shoemaker by trade, she was so miserly that she spent her evenings wandering the streets so she would not have to spend money on heating or lighting her home and often begged food from neighbors so as not to fritter away her hoarded sums on groceries.

But early in what would turn out to be her own last year on earth, 1868, those who knew her noticed a change of behavior—she began to take better care of her personal appearance, often stayed home at night reading by the kerosene lamp, and spoke pleasantly to those whom she met on the roadway.

The reason for Marie's "redemption" constitutes one of the oldest ghost stories in Detroit.

A number of years earlier, Marie had decided to make a little extra money by taking in a boarder. Clarissa Jordan was an elderly lady who regularly attended mass and prayed several times a day. Marie laughed at her piousness, as her own church brethren had ostracized her for her many eccentricities.

Clarissa tried to reform Marie. She attempted to persuade her to attend church more regularly and, after that failed, sought to scare Marie with ghost stories showing the presence of supernatural forces in human lives.

There was, for example, her story of old Grand-mère Duchêne, who sat at her spinning wheel for weeks after she died. The droning of the wheel nearly drove her son insane until he bought fifty masses for the repose of her soul.

Clarissa spoke also of the *feu follet*, or the will-o'-the-wisp, sent to the door of a girl at Grosse Isle while her lover was trapped in a swamp. The mysterious light led her to him, and he was rescued.

And remember French hunter Sebastian's ghost boat, Clarissa solemnly added, which ascends the Straits of Mackinac once every seven years to keep the Frenchman's promise to his betrothed that he would always return to her—dead or alive.

"Bah!" Marie hooted at Clarissa's tall tales. "I don't believe in your silly stories, or your purgatory or your hell . . . which you can go to at once for all I care! But I will make a bargain with you—if you die first, come back to me right here. Should I die before *you* then I will return. We will then know if there is any other world but our own!"

Sometime after this conversation, the women had an argument in which Marie swore never to speak to the lodger again. But, she added, their agreement to return from the dead was still to be upheld.

For the rest of their time together in the house, the two women avoided each other. Instructions or messages were written on scraps of paper and left for the other to find. They ate in different rooms. If by chance one saw the other coming down the hallway, she would duck through the nearest door. To the outsider, it appeared as if each woman existed in a different dimension, unable to see, hear, or communicate with the other.

Clarissa Jordan died early one winter. One evening not long after, Marie was out visiting, so as to spare the expense of heat and light in the early darkness. A young neighbor boy spotted her and asked why she had left the lights on in her house. He knew of her miserliness and was surprised. Marie returned home at once, but when she got there the lights were off.

Marie's kerosene lamps were reported shining over several subsequent evenings, but she never quite returned in time to catch the "culprit." The stout cane she held in her hand was always poised, ready to strike down the intruder.

Determined to put an end to the problem, Marie left the house at her usual time one day but then sneaked back in minutes later, quietly climbed the stairs, and hid under the covers of her own bed. Moments later, a light blinked on downstairs in the sitting room. But, instead of remaining where it was, the glowing orb ascended the staircase. It was phosphorescent and seemed to shimmer as it moved down the hall, through the door, and into Marie's bedroom. The glow gradually took the form of her old, pious lodger, Clarissa Jordan.

"I know you!" Marie cried out. "Come no nearer! I believe! I believe!"

Until her death a year or so later Marie Louise Kennett grew softer, kinder, and more neighborly. She even stopped her miserly walks at night. However, she also aged very rapidly.

The sight of the ghost of her old lodger, it is said, had a most profound effect on her.

The Lynching

Menominee

One of the most gruesome legends in all of American history was spawned in the Upper Peninsula lumber town of Menominee, on the shores of Green Bay, a few miles north of the Wisconsin border.

On September 26, 1881, a pair of thugs known as the McDonald boys stabbed to death Billy Kittson. The next day, a crazed mob broke into the jail holding the killers and subjected them to "timber justice" so grotesque that it almost strains credulity, were it not so well documented.

The sadistic carnage also gave rise to the grimly accurate foretelling that each vigilante would die "with his boots on."

The McDonald boys were actually two cousins, although they were closer than most brothers. Their surnames were different, but everyone called them the McDonalds. The tall, slim one was Big Mac, born a McDougall. His shorter cousin was known, naturally enough, as Little Mac.

They had reputations as mean, deadly knife fighters, especially when they had been drinking, which was most of the time. It was the wise citizen who gave this ornery pair a wide berth.

By most accounts, the trouble began after the 1881 spring lumber drive. The McDonalds got into a fight in Pine River and ended up stabbing Sheriff Ruprecht as he tried to break it up. The sheriff recovered and deputized two-hundred-pound muscleman George Kittson, Billy's half brother, to track down and arrest the pair. He did, and the McDonalds spent the next several months in jail.

They were released on September 24 and drifted down to Menominee, swearing vengeance on George Kittson. They both found work at the Bay Shore Lumber Company.

The Kittson family was fairly prominent, if not highly respectable, in the pioneer lumber town. There were three boys—George, Norman, and Billy—all sons of an Englishman who had fled the catastrophic Wisconsin

Peshtigo fire in 1871. He moved to Menominee shortly thereafter to become its second permanent settler. Billy, the youngest boy, was a rough character known to like whiskey and women, and not always in that order. Norman was cut from the same cloth.

On the afternoon of September 26, the McDonalds left work at the Bay Shore Company and headed for the Montreal House, a seedy saloon in the west side neighborhood known as Frenchtown, where Norman Kittson bartended.

The more the McDonalds drank, the more belligerent they became. They warned Norman that his brother George was a dead man. To back up the threat, they drew knives. Eventually they staggered out of the bar and headed for the Frenchtown whorehouse ensconced behind the jack pine near Bellevue Street. Inside, Billy Kittson was drinking whiskey out of a jug with the girls of the house. When the McDonalds barged in, a fight ensued. Billy hit one of the McDonalds over the head with an empty bottle, then headed for the relative safety of the Montreal House. The McDonalds caught up with him in the street outside. Norman Kittson saw the pair closing in on Billy and shouted a warning.

"I'm not afraid of those sonsabitches!" Billy yelled back. Big Mac smashed Billy across the head with a heavy club and then plunged a knife deep into his rib cage as he lay sprawled on the ground. Norman ran to Billy's aid, but Little Mac knocked him away. Billy struggled to his feet, only to be stabbed by Big Mac in the side of the head.

Norman managed to draw a revolver from his coat pocket. He fired twice. Little Mac clutched his leg as he and his cousin fled.

By all rights, Billy Kittson should have fallen right away. But he had drunk so much whiskey that he was oblivious to his mortal wounds. He limped inside the Montreal House, ordered drinks for everyone, and then promptly fell over dead.

Norman's wounds were serious but not fatal. The McDonalds were captured a few hours later at the train depot trying to get out of town and were promptly locked up. Word spread like a fire through virgin pine that young Billy Kittson had been killed and the notorious McDonald boys were responsible. At every tavern and hotel, on each street corner in Menominee, lumbermen talked of little else. Their voices were loud and angry, especially the next day, when it became clear that a hearing on the murder would be postponed. The prosecutor had trouble, for even though the McDonalds were in custody, many witnesses thought fulfilling their civic duty to testify against them might shorten their own lives considerably.

As the liquor flowed, the talk turned to inflicting rough justice on the pair. They had knifed a sheriff, killed the son of a well-known family, and generally created a reign of terror in the city.

Six men were ringleaders. Frank Saucier, a drayman, offered the use of a stout section of timber to batter down the jailhouse door. Bob Stephenson, the superintendent of the Ludington, Wells, and Van Schaick Lumber Company, supplied the rope. Max Forvilly, owner of the Forvilly House on Ludington Street, the gathering place for the mob, constantly replenished the whiskey.

Stephenson headed the mob with Louis Porter and Tom Parent, both timber bosses, and Robert Barclay, an ex-sheriff who ran a livery stable.

Late that afternoon, the half-dozen men, followed by a group of hangers-on, grabbed the ramming timber and marched on the courthouse. Only two deputy sheriffs guarded the McDonalds. One of them, Jack Fryer, challenged the mob, but Louis Porter immediately disarmed him and shoved him aside.

The mob ransacked the jail and found the two McDonalds cowering in a cell. Big Mac pleaded to be allowed to argue against his imminent fate. They ignored his whimpers and threw a rope around his neck.

Louis Porter grabbed Little Mac, but the outlaw pulled a small knife from his boot and stabbed him in the hand. Enraged, Porter grabbed an axe from a man named Laramie and whacked Little Mac, splitting open his skull. He was done for.

Nevertheless, the mob drew ropes tightly around both men's necks and dragged them from the jail. Big Mac was still conscious even as he was pulled by the rope over an iron fence. Witnesses say his neck stretched several inches when his head got caught in the fence.

Down Main Street, the jubilant mob hauled the McDonalds, one already dead and the other on his way. The mob took turns jumping on the bodies, stomping out bloody chunks of flesh with their heavy boots. A few even "rode" them for a distance. The macabre procession took on the appearance of a parade as men, women, and even children joined in.

Church bells peeled and whistles blew. Everyone cheered the spectacle of the McDonald boys getting "just what they deserved."

Near a railroad crossing, the mob strung up the McDonald boys from a tall pole. Big Mac twitched, moaned once or twice, and then died.

Not everyone appreciated the sight of the boys swaying in the breeze at such a prominent location. Some thought the bodies might scare the horses and frighten the women and children. After some arguing, the mob came up with a solution. Why not take the boys back to where the trouble had begun—the Frenchtown whorehouse?

And that is just what they did. They let fall the corpses and dragged them up Bellevue Street. At the church, Father Menard tried to stop them, but they brushed him aside.

The priest glared after them and declared that for these sins each man present would "die with his boots on."

Undeterred, the men dragged their prizes through the front door of the whorehouse and into one of the bedrooms, dumping the bloodied, mangled remains on a bed. They rounded up the girls and, one by one, forced the dozen ladies to climb into bed with the corpses.

When the mob tired of their entertainment, they ran the girls out of the house and burned it to the ground. They left the McDonald boys' remains tied to two small pine trees outside the burning building.

Had the leaders of that mob known what strange fates awaited them, they might have thought more seriously about their own actions and especially Father Menard's curse, almost lost in the hubbub.

First struck was Bob Stephenson, who supplied the rope. A few months after the lynching, Stephenson's lumberyard caught fire. His men refused to run between two piles of lumber and tip them over to save them. Cursing them, Stephenson himself ran between the piles, trying to douse the flames with water buckets. The fire caught him but when he cried out, fumes from his whiskey-sodden breath ignited. His body exploded in flames, from the inside out. He lingered in excruciating pain for three days before he died.

Frank Saucier, who had supplied the battering ram to break down the jail door, died without apparent cause on a train trip from Iron River to Menominee.

Louis Porter, who recovered from the knife wound Little Mac had inflicted on him, came to his end when he went with his men on a log drive. Porter sent them on ahead, saying he was tired and wanted to rest. When the crew returned at the end of the day, they found his body propped against a tree, his arms folded across his chest. No one knows why he died. Some say a poisonous snake bit him.

The list goes on: A man named Dunn was accidentally sliced in half by a head saw in a Green Bay sawmill. Albert Lemieux, a timber cruiser, slashed his own throat midway through a poker game he was losing in a lumber camp late one night. Alfred Beach drowned when his boat capsized.

Some of the men learned of the peculiar deaths of their comrades and vowed they would not die in a similar manner. They would avoid the curse by leaving the region forever.

But the curse was too strong. On his way to a family reunion, ex-sheriff Robert Barclay pulled up at the gathering, jumped out of the wagon, waved, and dropped dead.

And Max Forvilly lost his hotel, his money, and his family. He died on a small farm at Peshtigo Sugar Bush, crazy and penniless.

The Lake Odessa Mystery

Lake Odessa

The old house at the corner of Tupper Lake Street and Sixth Avenue in the small town of Lake Odessa was haunted, of that there was little doubt. But just what or who flitted through its darkened rooms and tromped across the front porch remained a mystery.

Lake Odessa was a quiet village at the turn of the century, slumbering midway between Lansing and Grand Rapids. Dan and Cora Shopbell moved into town after being disillusioned with life on their farm a few miles away. They decided to build a new house on a vacant lot across the street from Cora's parents, George and Delilah Kepner. Uncle Dan, as everyone called him, built the house himself, right down to the cabinetry in the kitchen. As the foundation he used the old cellar that remained from a previous house that had burned many years before.

Uncle Dan took great pride in the dwelling, pouring several inches of concrete into the walls so rodents could not enter, and installed one of the first indoor bathrooms in Lake Odessa. He also crafted most of the furniture by hand.

Soon after Daniel and Cora moved in, they realized something was very wrong. They rarely talked about it with her parents, or her sister and brother-in-law, the Gardiners, who lived with the Kepners across Sixth Avenue. The Shopbells were practical, hardworking people not given to flights of fancy. They found it uncomfortable to discuss any troubles they could not understand. Their niece, Leona Gardiner, learned as a teenager about their experiences in the house, and it is her recollections and investigations that preserved the story of the mystery house.

It was shortly after the Shopbells settled into the house when they began hearing odd noises. If the couple was in the sitting room, a banging came from the back of the house. Daniel ruled out rodents since the concrete prevented their getting into the walls, and there were no tall trees near the house to scrape against it. At other times, the couple was brought out of their chairs by what sounded like a big ball or oversized pumpkin rolling across the porch and then slamming into the front door. But when they opened the door, they found nothing. No ball. No pumpkin.

The odd happenings in their house went far beyond the occasional unexplained sound. An old-fashioned, woodburning stove stood in the sitting room. As Cora and Daniel watched, the stove door sometimes gently swung open and then slammed shut, just as if someone was checking the fire.

They made their decision to move the evening when Daniel, who was sitting in his favorite chair, was picked up—chair and all—held aloft for a few seconds, and then set back down. There was absolutely nothing to explain it.

Although they had only lived in it for a year, the Shopbells sold the house for a negligible sum to Gottlieb and Anna Kussmaul and moved back to their old farm, which they found much less hectic.

Gottlieb was a first-generation American who still spoke with a heavy accent. Stocky in build and strong, with a colorful vocabulary, he was a generous man as well, always ready to come to the assistance of his neighbors. He worked at a local grain elevator, hoisting hundred-pound bags of grain for hours at a time.

Anna, in contrast, was small and refined, a woman who had been educated through the twelfth grade, which was unusual in that era, and later studied music. She taught piano lessons for many years in Lake Odessa. At one time, she and her brother, Byron, a violinist, formed a dance orchestra, which played at local events and practiced in the Kussmauls' sitting room.

The couple had one daughter, Hattie, a pale, thin child who was the delight of her parents. She married young but died in her midtwenties in a severe flu epidemic following World War I.

The family also had a big gray tomcat, Tiger, who was Hattie's special playmate and who seemed to have a mysterious way of walking through solid walls.

During the day, the family let the cat into the house, but at night, Tiger slept in the barn on a pile of straw. Nevertheless, the Gottliebs were often awakened in the early morning hours when the cat walked across the foot of their bed. But before any one of the family could put him outside he would vanish. The next morning there he would be as usual, outside the back door, crying to come in. They never could figure out how he got out.

Little Hattie was the unwilling witness to another strange episode in the old house. Her mother sometimes gave music lessons to a few students in nearby towns. She took the morning Pere Marquette Railroad to her pupils' homes and returned late in the afternoon. Hattie stayed with the Mosey family after school, across Tupper Lake Street, until her mother returned.

One day after school, Hattie decided instead to go on home. She was soon back at the Mosey house, crying that a man was in their bathroom with his foot up on the tub shining his boots.

Mrs. Mosey sent her two sons to investigate and waited on the porch, holding Hattie by the hand. The boys failed in their search. Mrs. Mosey tried to persuade Hattie that it must have been her imagination, but the little girl refused to go back home until her mother came for her.

A later episode seemed to vindicate Hattie. One summer night in 1911, a frantic pounding on the front door awakened the nearby Kepner household. Crying out that her husband was ill, Anna Kussmaul had come to fetch Mrs. Gardiner, a nurse who often stayed with families. Mrs. Gardiner remembered what happened:

I threw on my clothes and ran over with the kerosene lamp in my hand, for the street lights in those days went out at midnight. As soon as I looked at Gottlieb and heard his breathing, I knew what was wrong and called Dr. McLaughlin. . . . We worked over him the rest of the night before the doctor felt it was safe to leave him. He left strict orders not to let Gottleib sleep more than twenty minutes at a time, for fear he might slip into a coma. He was to be roused enough each time to answer a question rationally.

I worked there ten days or maybe two weeks, and I will never forget those nights. It seemed that as soon as Hattie and Anna were asleep, the noises would begin. At first I was scared; then I got mad and would try to find what caused them.

The only way I can describe them is that they sounded like men fighting, or anyway how I imagine it would sound if men were fighting. There were dull, heavy sounds like people wrestling on the floor; dull thumps like blows and grunting sounds. I can't describe it any different. It always came from the back of the house, from the dining room or kitchen, and the minute I would get out of my chair to go and see what it was, it would stop short . . . I never heard a sound while I was up and moving around, taking care of Gottlieb. I always said I wouldn't spend a night alone in that house for a million dollars!

It was not until much later—when Anna Kussmaul described the harrowing night in an interview—that Mrs. Gardiner found out everything that happened the night Gottlieb became sick.

As Mrs. Kussmaul told a newspaper reporter:

It was a stifling hot day in August. Gottlieb came home from work drenched with sweat and exhausted. He said he was too tired to eat supper, but I coaxed him to eat a bowl of bread and milk, then to bathe and go to bed. It had been a terribly muggy day, and it didn't cool off after sunset, as it sometimes does. However, he had fallen asleep almost at once and I could hear him snoring while I washed the supper dishes.

Hattie and I sat on the porch a little while, but it was no cooler out there, so I cleaned Hattie up and put her to bed soon after eight. I was so miserably hot I took off my corset—what horrid, heavy things those old corsets were!—and decided to go to bed myself although it was not yet nine o'clock . . .

Gottlieb was still snoring and I got into bed facing him and lay that way for a few minutes, but soon turned with my face toward the window in hopes I'd get at least a breath of air.

As I turned, I was paralyzed with fear for I clearly saw a man silhouetted in the doorway. He was advancing toward the bed. I was too frightened to make a sound or move until he was right beside the bed, when I jerked the sheet over my head and called, "Gottlieb!"

I got no answer and tried to kick him, but he just kept snoring. I don't know how long it was before I got up the nerve to uncover my head and reach out and pull the string that led from the light bulb down to the head of the bed, where one end of it was tied. When the light came on there was no sign of anyone there, nothing was disturbed, and there was no sound except for my husband's snoring.

I fell asleep at last, but not for long. I awakened to realize that something was wrong. The snoring that I had heard so long did not sound right; it was more than just snoring. I tried to awaken him, but it was impossible to rouse him. I knew then that something was terribly wrong, and that was when I went running for [Mrs. Gardiner].

Gottlieb Kussmaul had suffered a seizure. Although he later recovered, Anna believed that the "man" she saw had been there as a warning not to fall asleep, that her husband was ill.

The Kussmauls stayed in the house until 1946. During all those years they were plagued with odd noises, thumps, groans, and footsteps, but nothing serious enough to warrant them moving away.

What, then, might have caused the disturbances? Was the house haunted?

Could the mysterious events be connected with the previous home that had burned in the late nineteenth century, leaving only the excavated cellar upon which Daniel Shopbell built his home?

There are two versions told of what transpired in that first house, either of which might have produced a ghost or two. The original owner had been a cattle buyer or real estate agent, depending on which version of the events one believes. In both accounts, a stranger appears one day with a good deal of money. In one story he wants to buy cattle, and in the other he is a land speculator from out of state who wants to settle in Lake Odessa. The house owner murders him for the wad of money and shortly thereafter the house burns to the foundation.

The scenario makes sense. Mrs. Gardiner claims she heard the sound of men fighting and a body falling to the floor. Perhaps that man in Anna Kussmaul's bedroom and the mysterious intruder Hattie saw were both the same person—the victim of that killing whose name has been long forgotten to history.

The Spurned Suitor

Gross Isle

The capture of Detroit after the surrender of American General William Hull and his two thousand troops in August 1812 was one of the most humiliating defeats suffered by the American forces in the War of 1812.

What is not so commonly known is that in the days before Hull's final surrender, a series of smaller clashes were taking their toll on both sides. In planning one of those skirmishes, British General Isaac Brock made the decision that troops under the command of Lieutenant Adam Muir would lead an assault on American soldiers at Mongaugon—now Gross Isle— on August 9, 1812. Even with their tough Wyandot Indian allies led by Tecumseh and Walk-in-the-Water, the British knew it would be a dangerous mission from which the young lieutenant and a number of his men might not return.

The night before he led the expedition, Muir was rejected by the woman he loved, and he was killed in battle the next day. The lieutenant's ghost is condemned to wander the quiet woods of Gross Ile.

Stunning Marie McIntosh was the daughter of Angus McIntosh, a Scottish businessman living in British Ontario. She and her family lived in a grand

home near present-day Windsor. Lieutenant Adam Muir had been court-
ing her for quite some time. Their courtship was rather chaste by today's
standards, as was often the case in that era. Their moments together typi-
cally came at formal gatherings or in the presence of their families. To
make matters even more difficult, the lieutenant was exceedingly shy where
women were concerned; he spoke to only a few close confidants of his desire
to marry young Marie.

Marie knew in her heart that the handsome soldier was the man she
wanted to marry, but she grew ever more impatient with his bashfulness
and began to find it quite irritating. She could not tell him of her own
feelings, for that would have been quite unseemly without a formal engagement. Nevertheless, it did not occur to Marie—not yet twenty years of age
herself—that, despite words of marriage never having been exchanged,
Lieutenant Muir would ever doubt her love for him or that she would agree
to a marriage proposal.

If he would only ask.

On the eve of the British raid on Mongaugon, Marie's shy beau faced a
most harrowing assignment, one from which he might not return.

Lieutenant Muir decided he had to tell Marie of his feelings and propose
marriage. He imagined that the warmth of her love would shield him from
harm when the time came.

On the night before battle, August 8, the lieutenant obtained a short
leave from his company and stole away to the McIntoshs' home. Marie
was alone save for her housemaid. He met her in the parlor and spoke
forcefully of his love. Then dropping to bended knee, he asked for her hand
in marriage. He told her of the coming battle, that tomorrow he would
face a perilous assault on the American forces, but that with her assent to
an engagement he could face the enemy with confidence.

What then would have possessed Marie to do what she did?

Was it her immaturity in dealing with matters of the heart?

Or was she truly irritated at Lieutenant Muir's timidity in not making
his intentions clearer before this night? We will never know.

Whatever her motivation, Marie McIntosh turned away from the
lieutenant. She immediately rejected his earnest proposal.

The lieutenant was entirely unprepared for such a stinging rebuke. He
quickly rose to his feet and dashed from the room.

Now it was Marie's turn to be distressed. She was just playing a game to scold him for his timidity. She thought he would linger a few moments in the hallway before returning to press her to marry him. When he did not return, she hurried out to find the front door open and Lieutenant Adam Muir mounting his horse.

She cried out his name, scrambling down the wide porch steps, but he did not hear her as he rode away.

The young housemaid ran to her side.

"He must certainly know that I love him," sobbed Marie. "Men are so stupid, so matter-of-fact. They take months to make up their minds to woo a girl, and if she does not immediately say 'yes' they feel themselves aggrieved and wounded."

The maid nodded sadly and held her mistress close.

Marie had no choice but to await Muir's return from the dangerous mission. She had no knowledge of how long that would be, of course, whether a single day or several.

Nightfall came and there was no sign of the young officer. At her maid's insistence, Marie at last went to bed. The maid drew tight the window shutters and pulled the curtains around the bedstead.

Sleep eluded Marie for many hours. She went over and over the circumstances of that brief encounter with the one man with whom she wanted to spend the rest of her life but had rejected in a fit of pique. How could she have been so foolish! She was filled with so much regret at her thoughtless behavior.

As the morning sun began its ascent above the horizon, Marie fell into a disturbed slumber. She soon woke abruptly to the sound of the door to her chamber being thrown open. Rapid boot steps crossed the floor. Marie drew aside the bed curtain and gasped. She shrank against the pillows. Young Lieutenant Muir stood a few feet away, his face as pale as moonlight. A brutal gash angled across his forehead. Blood that had oozed down his pale cheeks left long, dark stains on his muddy uniform.

"Fear not, my dearest Marie," came a hollow, unfamiliar voice that bore some similarity to the lieutenant's own. "Though the Americans were victorious, they will not long rejoice. England will soon triumph. I was shot through the head, yet I fell in honor. My body lies hidden in a dense thicket. I beg you for one final act of kindness. Rescue it from the wild beasts of the forest so that I may be remembered with an honorable burial. Farewell, my love."

With that he reached out and with a calm borne of death laid his fingers on her right hand. The coldness of that touch, the iciness of the grave itself, sliced through her skin. She fainted against the soft pillow.

The sun was high when Marie finally awoke.

Her first thoughts were of that dream—for is that not what it must have been?

She glanced down. Across the back of her right hand were two deep, dark impressions—scars as if two fingers of a man's hand had burned into her flesh.

She leaped from bed. Calling to her maid, she hastily dressed and ordered that a horse be saddled. Her servants pleaded with her to let one of them accompany her. She ignored them and raced off to General Brock's encampment at Malden.

She was able to find Walk-in-the-Water—the Wyandot British ally who was also an old friend of the McIntoshes—and haltingly told him of her dilemma. She pleaded with him to be taken to the battle site. He reluctantly agreed and together they went by canoe across the Detroit River. Once they reached shore, Marie moved as if in a trance toward a bramble thicket.

"This is where we shall find him," she whispered.

It did not take long. The blood-spattered remains of Lieutenant Muir lay as he had fallen. In the cold light of a new dawn, the fatal bullet wound on his forehead was even more terrible than it had appeared on his ghost the night before. But she had found him. That was all that mattered.

Walk-in-the-Water and several of his men removed the soldier's body to Sandwich, Ontario, where he was buried with military honors.

At the funeral, Marie wore a black glove on her right hand.

Marie McIntosh did marry. Her husband was a decent man who had heard the bittersweet story of Lieutenant Muir and Marie's courtship. They remained childless.

The dark impressions left by Lieutenant Muir's touch stayed with her for the rest of her life—a reminder perhaps that impetuous behavior and careless words can have consequences far greater than we might ever imagine. She wore the black glove to remind her of his love.

On August 9, 1813, and for decades thereafter on that date, Marie dressed in a pair of wood sandals and wrapped herself in plain, black sack-cloth. She went door to door from Windsor to old Sandwich as a mendicant pleading for money or goods for the ill and for the poor. No church or churchman required such atonement for her transgression. She placed the burden of self-sacrifice on herself.

The shaded woods once plentiful in Grosse Isle—what was once Mongaugon—remained the soldier's ghostly home forever after, his bloody form slipping quietly among the ancient oaks toward the soothing river.

Minnesota

The Ghost Wore Plaid

St. Paul

Nancy Bagshaw-Reasoner hoped to make some extra income working part-time at the box office at St. Paul's storied Fitzgerald Theater, the "Fitz" as it is affectionately known. As an actor and producer, Bagshaw-Reasoner loved being around the Twin Cities theatrical community in most any capacity and the Fitz is a venerated Twin Cities live entertainment venue.

One fall afternoon she was on duty in the small, unassuming theater box office off the main lobby. It had been quiet—a few walk-up sales, the odd telephone order. Garrison Keillor's *A Prairie Home Companion* had ended its fall run at the theater some time before and was out on the road. A few special events were scheduled—an author interview, an early holiday staging—but not much else.

The ticket booth is adjacent to the theater's cozy lobby but can be accessed through a separate outside door, around the corner from the box office, when the theater is closed.

As darkness settled across the city, Bagshaw-Reasoner started pulling together statistics on the day's modest sales, her final responsibility before she locked up for the night. The business offices were closed.

She saw someone looking at her through a little-used side window, so she poked her head out the main ticket window, looked down the dimly lit passageway, and called out, "I can help you over here!"

She had caught only a quick glimpse but did note it was a man. He had quickly backed away. She saw he had dark hair and that he appeared to be wearing a dark plaid shirt. His face was hidden in shadow.

She felt a little queasy when no one came around the corner. A minute or two ticked by. She realized that the outside door buzzer had not sounded. It had been installed to alert ticket staff that someone had come in. Other staff had been working that day, but by now they had all gone home. The only way to the ticket booth would be to come through the outside door.

When it was obvious this shadow man, as she now thought of him, was not going to show himself, she thought she must have been mistaken. Maybe it was her reflection in that old window he had used; yet that did not seem probable.

Oh, well, she thought, *that was a little strange . . .*

She turned her attention back to the sales figures.

Suddenly she caught a slight movement outside that same side window. Was this guy back?

Now her unease grew to sharp anxiety. Had someone, somehow, slipped into the theater undetected? Was he now playing games with her? Perhaps intent on doing her harm?

Again, she leaned out the window. "I can help you over here!"

He must be down there, around that corner, she thought. But she was not going down there to find out.

Again Nancy Bagshaw-Reasoner waited.

Her growing uneasiness turned from anxiety to fear. If someone was playing a prank on her, it was not funny.

"I'm closing up the box office!" she yelled out. She waited. Would he show himself again?

This man in the shadows did show himself, but in a manner Bagshaw-Reasoner could never have anticipated.

As she sat back, she detected another slight movement through the side window. The stranger had returned.

The first two times he had been at the window, he dodged away when she looked directly at him. This time she shifted only her eyes to the right to focus on him. He was standing still, watching her. She could see that he was a slightly built man of early middle age with thick, brown hair and prominent sideburns. He wore a dark-brown, plaid shirt. A workman's clothes.

She thought his expression seemed very, very sad. He did not move.

She quickly turned to face him.

The two stared at each other for a few moments, and then, as she remembers the encounter, the stranger moved laterally in a blur, like the Road Runner in a Warner Bros. cartoon.

"It was the scariest thing in the world," Bagshaw-Reasoner said of the man's bizarre vanishing act.

He had not been transparent nor was there anything even vaguely ghostly about him, she said. He looked at her and then *wooosh*, he was gone.

"If I could live through that, I think I can survive anything in the world. I almost had a heart attack."

As she would later learn, Nancy Bagshaw-Reasoner had met Ben, the ghost of the Fitzgerald Theater.

After his sudden disappearance, she slammed closed the ticket window and ran into the business office to hide. She called her husband and pleaded with him to come pick her up. In her fear, she struggled to set the alarm and the motion detector. At one point, the alarm even blinked *motion detected*, which only added to her panic.

She did not tell anyone else about her experience until several weeks later. She and Jude Martin, a supervisor in the business office, were sharing duties one afternoon in the box office. Bagshaw-Reasoner happened to glance out that little-used side window. She screamed. The same man had appeared, though this time he was hazier.

"I saw his face, his dark hair, and I saw his shirt. The rest of him was a blur."

Martin had been elsewhere in the booth waiting for a computer printer job to finish. She was startled by the scream, but she saw nothing.

"It's back again." Bagshaw-Reasoner pointed.

This time when Martin looked out the window she saw a white, translucent figure moving past.

Martin told Bagshaw-Reasoner they might have just seen Ben, the resident ghost of the Fitzgerald Theater. But she assured her that seeing him was not unusual and that he did not seem to be evil or malicious.

Bagshaw-Reasoner was relieved and told Martin about her previous encounter. She had no idea that the theater might be haunted.

"I thought I'd been losing my mind," she said.

When the theater first opened as the Sam S. Shubert Theater in 1910, a tribute by show business tycoon brothers J. J. and Lee Shubert to their late brother, it was one of the most elegant theaters anywhere in the country. It first hosted vaudeville stars and silent films until the rise of talkies in the late 1930s. This theatrical grande dame was renamed the World Theater when live entertainment was eliminated. Later, the theater focused on showing foreign films. Minnesota Public Radio bought the deteriorating building in 1980, and after a few years of extensive remodeling that restored its earlier elegance, the theater became the home of *A Prairie Home Companion*. The World was rechristened in 1996 to honor native son F. Scott Fitzgerald on the centenary of his birth.

For decades, theater employees have said that the ghost of a man called Ben has startled them with sudden appearances or has puzzled them with his trickster behavior. Although old theaters like the Fitz are expected to have a ghost or two, the close encounters people have had with Ben—including Nancy Bagshaw-Reasoner's experience—make this theater a distinctive addition to the roster of haunted playhouses. There is speculation (but scant evidence) that Ben may have been a stagehand whose supposed signature was found on a note hidden in the ceiling during the theater's remodeling; another suggestion is that he was a workman who drank himself to death in the stage door alley adjacent to the theater.

It is difficult to pinpoint just when the stories of Ben the ghost originated. Sightings increased in the 1980s during the theater's renovation, but it seems he has not been as active in more recent years.

Most encounters with Ben have taken place at two theater "hot spots"—the box office and business office complex, and then in the theater itself around a set of upper-level audience box seats.

In the theater's business office near the box office, staffers have had issues with their chairs and blamed trickster Ben.

One member of the business staff had been running envelopes through a postage meter in another part of the complex and returned to find his desk chair missing. A search discovered it behind the gift shop off the lobby. Another person was alone finishing up some ticket accounting in the box office when he left to use the restroom. He returned to discover his chair gone. He found it sitting in the middle of the inner lobby. He said it was like the chair tried to follow him into the restroom.

In the box seating area, sightings usually revolve around audience members or others seeing someone up there. Members of a ballet company spotted a lone man standing next to one of the seats when no one should have been up there. On another occasion Ben may have been prowling about during a production of the British ghost drama *The Woman in Black*. At an invited audience preview of that show, theater staff noticed that at one point many audience members turned their heads nearly in unison to look up at those box seats. When curious staff members later asked several audience members what they were looking at, all of them said they had seen an actor there and supposed a scene was beginning. It was not.

Both Jude Martin and Nancy Bagshaw-Reasoner agreed that seeing Ben was scary, but not in the way one might think. "It's not fear," Martin said. "It's knowing you might get surprised when you least expect it."

Although Bagshaw-Reasoner no longer works at the Fitz, she continues to have one nagging question: "Was he somehow reaching out to me? Here was this sad man looking at me. That was the most dramatic element to it, other than the fact that it scared me to death."

At first she was frightened this intruder meant her harm. She was more terrified when she realized she was not dealing with a flesh and blood being. Even then she thought she ought to make an emergency call to someone, perhaps the police.

"And then when [he] moved like *whooooosh*, I thought, Oh my God this isn't a police issue. Somebody call the Ghostbusters!"

"You never forget it. I can picture it like it happened yesterday. It was such a strange, strange thing."

Now You See Them

Rochester and Becker County

There are several haunted highways in Minnesota, but two stories of supernatural roadside experiences stand out, though they were separated by nearly a century and a half in time.

Legendary stories of women in white haunting American roadways—such as this first story from Rochester—have been told in every state of the Union. Sometimes, however, tales of haunted highways arise from a specific, tragic event, as in the story from Becker County whose roots go back nearly a century and a half.

Stan Sauder was driving south on U.S. Highway 52 coming into Rochester as he does five times a week from his home outside Pine Island to his job at the Mayo Clinic. As usual, he eased into the right-hand exit onto the cloverleaf with Highway 14 so he could connect with eastbound Civic Center Drive. It was about nine thirty in the morning. The weather was clear, nearly perfect on this fall day in 2007.

As he rounded the curve to get on Civic Center Drive, Sauder was startled to see an attractive middle-aged woman with blonde hair standing in the grassy median of the cloverleaf; her arms hung loosely at her sides. She did not move. Her light, white summer dress fluttering in a gentle breeze seemed out of place for the time of year.

The inside of that exit ramp is surrounded on all sides by asphalt—the two-lane exit and four-lane Civic Center Drive. There are no sidewalks or other pedestrian access points that would allow a person on foot to safely reach it on a high-traffic morning like this one.

There is a bike path but still Sauder said one has to climb over fences to get to where she was standing. And she was certainly not dressed for fence climbing or bicycling.

"It was the strangest, most bizarre thing that's ever happened to me," he said. "I thought, *What on earth is this woman doing just standing there?*"

Surprisingly, she made eye contact with him as he carefully rounded the curve, trying at the same time to keep his eyes on her. For what he estimates was over half a minute, the two stared at each other. She followed his progress around the cloverleaf. He took a momentary look for oncoming eastbound traffic on Civic Center Drive before he glanced back to this mystery woman.

She had vanished.

"It's virtually impossible that she crossed the street without getting hit. There's so much traffic," Sauder said. Neither was there anywhere for her to hide.

He did not see any parked vehicle along the road, nor did she look to him to be outwardly upset or distraught.

She seemed, he said, peaceful.

To this day Sauder often takes that exit. And to this day he tries to figure out who this vanishing woman might have been and how she could have gotten there.

"I know that she was there, but what was it I saw? What does it mean?"

Is it possible this was a real person who somehow got into the inner area of a busy highway cloverleaf? Perhaps. Is it probable? Not really.

Although he carefully chooses his words, it is clear Stan Sauder thinks this vision in white was not a living entity.

In the summer of 1989, Norman Reeser was in his car creeping along Becker County Highway 11 on an early foggy morning. He had left his cabin on Pelican Lake in the far northwestern corner of Otter Tail County to make his way to Audubon, about twenty miles to the north.

It was slow going in the heavy fog past Pike's Bay, along Big and Little Cormorant Lakes, and through tiny Lake Center.

Sometime after passing Little Cormorant Lake, as he hunched over the steering wheel squinting to see down the highway, Reeser's attention was suddenly taken by sudden movement along the edge of the woods. A woman and a child—a young boy, it seemed—were walking away from the woods and directly onto the highway only a few yards in front of him. Both of them stared straight ahead, looking neither left nor right.

Reeser slammed on the brakes waiting for the inevitable impact of metal against flesh. He knew it would come; they were now on the road itself. But as Reeser came to a stop, the two figures astonishingly reappeared in the southbound lane walking down through the fog-shrouded ditch and into the woods. They did not look back or acknowledge him in any other way. Reeser could not understand how he avoided hitting them—even at the speed he was traveling, the few yards that separated his car from them was too short a distance to have avoided an impact.

Reeser still was traumatized by the incident when he stopped at a café in Audubon a short time later. He told the waitress about his near miss with the woman and child on County Road 11. A couple of local men sitting nearby overheard what he said and walked over.

The men told Reeser that the two people he had seen were not of real flesh and blood but the ghosts of Deantha Cook and her son Freddie. They were murdered on their farmstead outside Audobon nearly 120 years earlier.

Although it was nearing midnight, John Cook was still wide awake, reading by lamplight in his favorite armchair. His wife, Deantha, lingered nearby finishing some housework. Upstairs, their three children were fast asleep.

The Cook family led an arduous life, eking out a subsistence living on the western Minnesota frontier of the 1870s while still trying to hold on to some sense of civilized normalcy in rough conditions.

John Cook was a Civil War veteran of the Union Navy. After the war, he worked as a government agent on the White Earth Reservation and traded furs with the Ojibwe, which he still did on occasion. He had staked a land claim near the village of Oak Lake, in Becker County's Audubon Township. No doubt he hoped the Northern Pacific depot built in Oak Lake the year before would bring prosperity to the area and by extension to his family.

On his land claim he planted crops and erected a house for his family— his wife and eight-year-old Freddie, seven-year-old Mary, and little John, not quite two.

It was April 26, 1872, and John Cook had reason to be relaxed and in a good mood. Earlier in the day, he had bought a hundred muskrat pelts from an Ojibwe friend. They were now piled in an upstairs corner, awaiting sale to a fur dealer. What he got from their sale would be much-needed cash in hand. As with many farmers, Cook was land rich and cash poor. Little Freddie had gotten so excited by the new pile of valuable soft furs that he ran to tell his aunt Nellie Small, Deantha Cook's sister, who lived with her own family less than a mile away.

Unfortunately, others also heard the news that John Cook had a large cache of valuable pelts soon to bring in a sizable cash fortune.

Sometime before midnight on April 26, John Cook was shot to death in his chair, perhaps by someone standing outside a lighted window. The killers broke down the door and fatally struck Deantha over the head with several hatchet blows. Minutes later the killers clubbed the three children to death as they slept.

The muskrat furs were stolen, and the house was set afire in an attempt to cover up the murders.

Nellie Small's son discovered the still smoldering ruins the next morning when he went over to get some fresh milk. He ran home to tell his mother, who rushed to the grisly scene. Only a few charred timbers remained, still hot to the touch.

Other neighbors soon arrived. They found scattered bits of human remains—children's small teeth, gold fillings, a set of false teeth, and charred bones—barely enough to fill a small bucket. A few of the bones were in the embers; other human remains had fallen into the cellar as the house collapsed in on itself. Shreds of clothing seemed to contain bloodstains.

The Cook family massacre created a sensation in frontier Minnesota.

Deantha's sister knew about the stash of furs and reported that to authorities. An investigation quickly focused attention on an Ojibwe man named Kahkahbesha, who was known as Bobolink. He was eventually charged with the killings and put on trial. After just ninety minutes, a jury found Kahkahbesha guilty and sentenced him to death by hanging. He died in jail under mysterious circumstances before the sentence could be carried out.

Neighbors buried the Cook family's few remains at the old farmstead. A plaque erected in 1923 by the Grand Army of the Republic marks the site.

Little else is left to denote the lives of John and Deantha and little Freddie, Mary, and John Jr. except the story of their terrible departure from this world. There is, however, the legend told by locals in Becker County that their ghosts haunt the woods of Audubon Township. If victims of bloody crimes sometimes rest uneasily in their graves, then surely this is a circumstance when spirits might prowl the countryside.

Norman Reeser's encounter in the summer of 1989 brought the Cook family massacre out of the footnotes of history. Though he did not believe in ghosts, he could not find an explanation for how the woman and boy could have gotten across the road unscathed that did not involve some sort of supernatural intervention.

The Luminescent Attic

Eveleth

On a harsh October day in 1980 in Eveleth, with wind-borne rain tearing leaves from the trees and pasting them to the ground, Tim Mack pulled his car up in front of an old house that had been remodeled into small apartments.

"You wait here," he said to his wife, Jan, and their two young daughters, "while I turn on the lights and take up the luggage."

He tried to sound positive, all the while thinking that he found something oppressive about the place. It had seemed cheerful enough when the landlord showed the second-floor apartment to him days earlier. Darkness came early this time of year, and the house now sat in shadowed gloom. No lights welcomed him. The house seemed desolate.

Mack grabbed two suitcases and climbed the stairs to the front porch. Setting down one suitcase, he slipped the key from his pocket and unlocked the front door. Mack could not find a light switch on the wall so he had to feel his way up the narrow stairway, the suitcases banging against the walls. Near the top of the stairs a light suddenly snapped on. Mack nearly fell back down the stairs. That was when he recalled that the switch for the stair light was inside their new apartment—behind its still-locked door.

After unlocking their door and depositing the suitcases inside the apartment, Mack turned on other lights and went back down to their landlord's apartment. A note on the door read, "Gone fishing for a week. Please make yourselves at home."

Then who turned on the light, he wondered.

As the Macks settled into their new home, Tim tried to forget about the light's mysterious "greeting" and concentrate instead on his new job as advertising manager for the local newspaper, the *Mesabi Daily News*.

Their new apartment, however, continued to distract him as it produced more mysteries.

Some three weeks after they moved in, on a cold November day, the Mack family was watching television in the living room when they heard a crash in the kitchen. Parents and girls rushed en masse to the kitchen to find a drinking glass shattered on the counter. Tim Mack said it was from a wedding set that had survived a number of moves.

Jan Mack was not uneasy, but she never knew what to expect next. Like the night the family came home to find the apartment lights turned on. Jan knew neither she nor any other family member had left them on.

"On that night I wouldn't go up those stairs alone!"

There were other perplexing episodes with the frisky lights. Tim discussed the problem with their landlord, but the man simply shrugged his shoulders. Doubting he would get any real help from him anyway, Tim did not mention the broken glass episode.

"That was just too strange," he said.

Then there was the attic.

The attic of legend is, of course, filled with bats, eerie groans, or perhaps chains being dragged across the floorboards in the night. But the Macks' attic was a quiet, pleasant place, and yet it presented its own quirks. They were using it to store household furnishings until they could move to a larger, more permanent home.

"If I went up there anytime during the day or night," Jan remembered, "there was a translucent light, a warm friendly glow about it. I never felt afraid. It made me feel at peace."

There was a skylight at one end of the attic, but at night, of course, no light filtered through. The streetlights were not bright enough to penetrate the far ends of the attic, and yet that faint luminescence at all hours of the day was always there. It was as if the attic itself was giving off the light. The couple could never determine what caused it.

The Macks also found curious similarities between the Eveleth apartment and their old house in Webster City, Iowa, including attics that had their own mysteries about them.

In Iowa, the Macks discovered what they called "witches shoes" in their attic, which they described as narrow, old, ankle-height, black, leather shoes with sharply pointed toes. Pieces of old newspapers had been stuffed inside them to keep their shape. They were so tiny that the Macks' young girls could not get them on.

Their Eveleth attic did not conceal old shoes, but one day Tim Mack did find one of his guns lying on the attic floor. It was the top rifle from his gun rack, which he kept in the attic. Neither Jan nor the girls ever touched the guns, of course, and there was no way it could have fallen to where Tim found it.

Their Minnesota and Iowa homes may have also shared hauntings, Tim said. The family believed a friendly spirit lived in their Iowa home. On that first day in Eveleth when the light came quickly on above the stairway, they wondered if the ghost had not perhaps traveled with them.

Jan smiled. "Who knows?" she said. "There are experiences we can't always explain."

The following February the family moved to a manufactured home outside Eveleth. They wanted more space for their growing family. They were much happier after they had moved from the apartment. And, they noted, nothing seemed to have moved with them.

Of their short stay in that Eveleth apartment, Tim pointed out that there was not a single, frightening moment but more of a sense that "something" they could not see kept them company, just as it did in Webster City.

He echoes his wife's sentiments. "I've always felt that there is another world, some other plane. There are things that I don't think anyone could ever explain."

Tim and Jan Mack eventually moved on to southern Minnesota, where they owned several weekly newspapers. Publishing small-town newspapers kept them busy, but they often looked back on their time in Eveleth.

Jan Mack sighed and looked around her husband's cluttered office. "Sometimes I wish we had a friendly spirit around here to help out with things."

But they said they had no reoccurrence of hauntings; their friendly Eveleth spirit, if that is indeed what it was, evidently decided to stay Up North.

Tim Mack grins. "Fishing for walleyes, no doubt."

The Specter Priest

Winona

August 27, 1915. Patrick R. Heffron, bishop of the Winona diocese, was celebrating Mass in the empty chapel of St. Mary's College in Winona, Minnesota. Dust motes danced in a shaft of gray light from a high window. Dawn was the bishop's favorite hour—the day was new and fresh and full of promise. Yet on this day the bishop felt apprehensive. Perhaps it was the heat, already oppressive; his vestments hung heavy upon his shoulders and sweat beaded his forehead.

Bishop Heffron had just raised the chalice when he heard a door latch click behind him. No one ever entered the chapel at this hour. Had a restless student or nun come to join him? He listened for footsteps. There were none. Strange. He spun around and saw Father Lesches, one of the college tutors, dressed in a Prince Albert suit, standing against the back wall. A revolver was in his hand. He raised it and aimed at the bishop.

The first shot struck the bishop in the left thigh. The second tore into the right side of his chest and penetrated his lung. A third bullet shattered the top of the altar.

Bishop Heffron slumped against the altar, a pool of blood spreading beneath his feet. A blood-stained Mass card lay nearby.

The assailant fled, the bishop staggering after him until he collapsed in the chapel doorway. Father Thomas Narmoyle, who was crossing the lawn, rushed to the bishop's side.

Ten minutes later, the Winona police arrested Father Laurence Michael Lesches for assault in the first degree. The priest, located in his room, did not resist arrest. He said he shot Bishop Heffron because the bishop had called him unfit for the religious life and better suited to work on a farm. The revolver lay in an open suitcase and a shotgun was found in the priest's trunk.

At the hospital, officers questioned Bishop Heffron. It was common knowledge that although the bishop and the priest had known each other for seventeen years, they had never gotten along. Bishop Heffron, a visionary committed to education, had single-handedly raised the funds to establish St. Mary's College. He was respected and generally well liked but dealt ruthlessly with associates who flouted his orders or failed, in some way, to meet his standards.

Father Laurence Michael Lesches never met those standards. An arrogant, abrasive man in whom the arts of diplomacy and negotiation were wholly lacking, he had few friends.

Bishop Heffron, in recounting his last meeting with Father Lesches, told the investigators that the priest had pleaded again for a parish of his own, saying that at age fifty-five he should have the security of settling in one place instead of being transferred from one parish to another.

"But I told him that he was too emotionally unstable to handle such an assignment," explained the bishop. "I have believed that for years and again I suggested that he consider farm work, which would not require close, personal relationships."

On December 1, 1915, Winona judge George W. Granger called his court to order. The proceedings of the State of Minnesota v. L. M. Lesches had begun.

The trial lasted two days.

Bishop Heffron, recovered from his wounds, was the state's chief witness. He testified that Father Lesches was mentally disturbed, unable to distinguish between right and wrong at the moment of the shooting, and unable to judge the effect of his act.

Other witnesses supported the bishop's testimony. Father Thomas Narmoyle testified that he saw Father Lesches running from the chapel on the morning of August 27 with Bishop Heffron staggering after him. The pistol was entered as evidence in the case.

Court-appointed defense attorneys also pleaded their client's disturbed mental condition. And Dr. Arthur Sweeny, the priest's personal physician and final witness for the defense, stated that Father Lesches was a paranoiac and a potentially dangerous man to be at large.

The jury returned its verdict in less than an hour: acquittal on grounds of insanity, with the recommendation that the defendant be committed to a mental institution.

Father Lesches was transported to the State Hospital for the Dangerously Insane in St. Peter. Embittered by his confinement, he nevertheless began to trust his physicians and to cooperate with them in his care.

Several years later, the doctors pronounced the priest in sound mental and physical health and recommended his release. But Bishop Francis W. Kelley, successor to Bishop Heffron, refused to sign the necessary papers.

Father Lesches languished in the state hospital and died there of a heart condition on January 10, 1943. He was eighty-four years old and had been hospitalized for twenty-nine years. His remains were returned to Winona and buried in St. Mary's Cemetery, two and a half miles from the campus.

Twelve years before Father Lesches's death, his presence on the campus was recalled by a strange event.

On May 15, 1931, a nun entered the room of Father Edward W. Lynch in order to clean it. She found the priest sprawled across the bed—dead. The bed and the body simulated a cross, the bed forming the vertical part and the body the horizontal beam. The corpse, lying face upward, was charred all over. The priest's Bible was also burned. Nothing else in the room had caught fire, not even the bedsheets.

The Winona coroner determined that the priest had died early that morning. Father Lynch had been lying in bed reading. Apparently he reached up to turn off his faulty bed light and ten volts of electricity in the light killed him instantly. But experts said the voltage was not enough to completely char the body.

Father Lynch was a close friend of Bishop Heffron and an enemy of Father Lesches. The two priests had lived together in St. Mary's Hall. They had had numerous arguments, and on one occasion, Father Lesches predicted Father Lynch would go to hell because of his interest in athletics.

Close examination of Father Lynch's charred Bible revealed a single passage that was not burned: "And the Lord shall come again to the sounding of trumpets." This was a verse that Father Lesches had once repeated to Father Lynch.

Had Father Lesches put a curse on his enemy because he was the bishop's friend? The priest's death remains mysterious and unexplained.

In that same year, a priest living on the campus died in a fire. And three other priests were killed in an airplane crash.

In 1921 a new dormitory on St. Mary's campus was named Heffron Hall to honor Bishop Patrick R. Heffron. The bishop died of cancer six years later.

Since shortly after Father Lesches's death in 1943, students living in Heffron Hall have reported strange, late-night footsteps and rappings, unusual drafts, and cold spots on the third floor. Papers lift from the hall bulletin board when no breeze is stirring, and students sometimes suffer identical nightmares on the same night.

One night in 1945, Mike O'Malley, a third-floor resident, was walking along the dimly lit corridor to his room. Hearing footsteps behind him, he turned around.

No one was there. He hurried to his room, pushed open the door, and slammed it shut. The footsteps stopped outside the door. Someone knocked. Mike opened the door. A dark-cloaked figure stood there, his face hidden by shadows.

The student thought it was a resident priest. "What do you want, Father?"

The only response was a deep groan. And then three words: "I want you."

Mike slugged the figure in the jaw. He broke every bone in his hand. His roommate, who claimed to have seen the visitor's face, said it was made of clay.

School disciplinary records noted that a student had broken his hand in a fight in the cafeteria. But no one on campus was known to have suffered a broken jaw.

More than twenty years later, a student on the fourth floor of Heffron Hall started to walk down the staircase to the third floor but felt restrained by an invisible force.

Once several staff members of *Nexus*, a weekly student publication at St. Mary's, launched an investigation into the purported incidents at Heffron Hall. Photographers, researchers, and witnesses were brought in to work under the direction of Robert Kairis, an instructor of history and advisor to the *Nexus* staff.

The team spent two nights on the third floor of the hall, using high-speed cameras with infrared film to record changes in temperature, equipment to measure changes in heat and pressure, and tape recorders, in the company of Kairis and other faculty members.

Just before two o'clock each morning, the instruments showed a drop of ten to fifteen degrees in the seven-hundred-foot-long corridor; the temperature dropped perceptibly—every one hundred feet. Natural causes, such as open doors and windows, were ruled out.

Cold spots are known to occur in structures purportedly occupied or visited by ghosts. Does this prove Heffron Hall is haunted? Which of the priests could be haunting the building?

It is often believed that the spirits of persons who have led troubled lives cannot rest. Of the three priests—Bishop Heffron, Father Lynch, and Father Lesches—only the latter suffered a life of bitter frustration.

In addition, the footsteps were not heard until after Father Lesches's death.

He died between one thirty and two o'clock in the morning, about the time the temperature in Heffron Hall starts to drop. He always used a black, gold-headed cane when he was out walking, which could explain the rappings students have heard.

The legends that have grown up around the ghosts of Heffron Hall are nearly impossible to verify; indeed, the bulk appear to have little if any basis in fact. Yet they continue to circulate on campus. Each has enough touch of the authentic to appreciate why they will not fade away anytime soon.

Mrs. Moriarity Comes Calling

St. Paul

Dick Gibbons sat back in the comfortable armchair of his small study off the living room in his tidy St. Paul home and picked up the novel he was reading. An English teacher by profession, Dick thought that here among his book collection was the perfect place to spend time with the fictional characters he tried to bring to life in the classroom. This room, this private place of his own, was one of the unique features that first persuaded Dick and his wife, Valjean, to buy the well-kept, two-story, brick house on Goodrich Avenue a few months earlier.

He liked nothing better than to settle into his favorite chair and read, as on this particular spring evening. His yellow Labrador was snoring contentedly on the floor beside him. Unexpectedly, since there was no sound save for the occasional car passing on the street outside, the dog raised her head and whined. Dick glanced down and saw her staring at something in the living room that adjoined the study. When she growled again, Dick put down the book and led her into the next room.

Dick remembers well what he saw there.

"The rocking chair was going back and forth as if someone were having a good time. I suddenly felt clammy and very nervous, like all the blood was rushing to my head."

Dick did not trust his eyes at first. The light from his reading lamp in the library barely penetrated the darkened living room. He reached around the corner and switched on the overhead chandelier. The chair was still moving. He looked at his watch and timed the chair's movements. It rocked for another one minute and fifteen seconds and then abruptly stopped.

Dick had no idea how long it had been moving before he noticed it. He took the dog by the collar and tried to lead her to the chair, but she dug her claws into the carpeting, stiffened her legs, and stayed right where she was. She never took her eyes from the rocker.

A few seconds later, the dog's gaze moved across the room as if following something with her eyes. Then she bolted from Dick's grasp and trotted into the dining room and on toward the kitchen. At the foot of a stairway leading to the second floor, she stopped, sniffed, and looked up. Dick followed her gaze up the stairs but could make out nothing unusual.

That eerie experience marked Dick Gibbons's first brush with the supernatural. He later confided, "The rocking chair episode changed me from a mocking skeptic to a believer."

Dick's wife, Valjean, would also change her views. One afternoon six weeks after her husband's strange night, Valjean was home alone, finishing a painting project. She went down into the cellar to fetch her can of paint. The lid was stuck fast. She pried the top all the way around but could not loosen it.

Finally, she decided to get a bigger screwdriver from a toolbox in the kitchen. When she got back to the cellar the lid from the paint can was gone. The can itself had not been moved. She never found the lid.

In late summer of that same year, Valjean again found herself at home by herself when a crash of breaking glass from the old cellar sent her running down there. Two stacks of storm windows were piled on the floor. Dick had propped the windows against a wall at the beginning of the summer. Now they had fallen—in the opposite direction from the way they were stacked. The window glass was cracked in only two of them.

Dick and Valjean were not the only ones who found there was something odd about the house. They had a difficult time finding babysitters. None of the available teens on the block ever seemed to be available.

Dick Gibbons suspected it was because they thought their house was haunted.

The couple started to research the home's history, hoping to find a clue to the mysterious events. A family named Moriarity had built the house during World War I and it had remained in the family until the Gibbonses bought it. Neighbors said old Mrs. Moriarity lived alone for some time before moving to a nursing home. Apparently she claimed to have awakened one night to find a man staring down at her. She thought it was a ghost. Skeptics claimed the elderly woman had either dreamed or imagined the incident. A few people said a burglar had broken in.

The Gibbonses never found out just who their uninvited guest was. They concluded it must have been a member of the Moriarity family who resented "outsiders" in the house. Or perhaps Mrs. Moriarity just wanted to see what kind of people had bought her house.

In any event, if the ghost was indeed a member of the Moriarity family, it must have been satisfied—the peculiar incidents ended as quickly as they had begun.

The Invisible Homesteader

Monticello

On storm-filled nights when the wind was high, Bob Jameson roamed the darkened rooms of his Monticello farmhouse.

"C'mon, Tobias," he shouted when no other living soul seemed to be present. "Scare the hell out of me!"

But Tobias took no orders from the living. He was a ghost. That is what Bob and his wife, Marion, came to believe. And so did the townspeople. Tobias Gilmore Mealey, familiarly known as T. G., built the Jamesons' house in 1855. Bob and Marion said he never left the premises.

The Jamesons never *saw* Tobias exactly, but they heard him on plenty of occasions. "He's a pleasant old fellow," observed Marion, not the least bit dismayed at his antics. "He was here first."

Bob and Marion Jameson bought their house in 1965 and for ten years witnessed a number of odd incidents—footsteps pacing the upstairs rooms when they were empty, beds shaking by themselves, lights turning on by unseen hands, loud knocks and persistent raps shaking doors and windows.

The white frame Mealey house straddled a hilltop at the end of a winding road off East Broadway in the little Mississippi River town of Monticello. There, Tobias, an early city father, and his wife, Catherine, raised their five children.

The old Mealey place was in a shambles when the Jamesons first saw it. Vacant for years, it was ravaged by vandals and neglect. Poison ivy vines grew everywhere; in the winter, ice formed on the basement floor; and skunk families took up residence each fall. Yet beneath the dilapidation, Bob and Marion sensed the charm of a comfortable old house and began its restoration.

The couple, longtime Minneapolis antique dealers, moved to Monticello after losing their Twin Cities home to an urban renewal project. Bob accepted a position as librarian at the Veterans Administration hospital in nearby St. Cloud, while Marion became the Wright County historian. The Jamesons moved their antique business with them and amusingly dubbed their new home "Chaos Castle."

Bob was the first to discover that there was something more than a little bit odd with their "castle."

He went upstairs one evening to begin work on a bedroom. His two puppies, Homer and Roy, trotted by his side. But once inside the room, they whimpered and then crawled under the bed.

A moment later, the dogs yelped as if they had been pinched, crawled out with their tails between their legs, and then plunged back downstairs. Another family dog dashed out of that same bedroom on another occasion and did not stop running until he scooted under a car parked several blocks away.

On another occasion Bob was sitting in a downstairs room recording jazz LP records onto audiotapes. He was using two microphones for the job when, suddenly, footsteps reverberated across the bare floor of that same bedroom directly overhead. Bob figured Marion was cleaning up there, and called to her to be quieter. The footfalls only got louder. Shutting off his equipment, Bob went into the hallway and yelled: "Hey, Marion, either quiet down or put on some slippers!"

There was no response. He started up the staircase and the footfalls ceased. A short time later Marion came into the room where Bob was working. She had been out back all evening working in one of their outbuildings.

The couple had still not identified Tobias Mealey as their resident ghost. But it was not long before their son, David, joined them in solving the mystery. The owner of a construction business in Minneapolis, David Jameson usually visited his parents overnight and slept in a bedroom at the top of the stairs. Well after midnight during one visit, Marion was going back to bed after a trip to the bathroom when she saw David standing at the top of the stairs, swinging his Navy lantern in great arcs to illuminate the walls, the stairs, and the doorway to his room. She thought he was walking in his sleep.

But David was far from asleep.

"There's something in that room, Mom," he shouted.

Something had shaken his bed violently enough to wake him up.

"I thought I dreamed it," he told his mother, "but then after I got back to sleep someone knocked twice from outside my window. I got up and couldn't see anything. I went back to sleep, but then the bed shook again and something knocked again at the window."

Meanwhile, various lights in the Jameson house developed wills of their own.

Marion often remained downstairs reading in a comfortable chair after Bob had gone to bed. On one particular evening she asked Bob to leave the light on for her at the foot of the stairs. She had been reading for some time before she heard Bob come back down the stairs, flip off the light, and walk back up again. She thought he was trying to tell her it was time to go to bed. She resented his attitude and marched up the steps to tell him so. She pushed open the bedroom door.

But Bob was sound asleep. She shook him by the shoulder. He rolled over and opened his eyes. She told him what happened. He assured her that he had never been out of bed.

Similarly, the living room lights blinked on and off for no apparent reason. At first, Marion again accused Bob of being the culprit. But after he vehemently denied it, they called in an electrician. The man spent an entire morning checking every light in the house and could find nothing wrong with any of them. But as the man walked toward the door to leave, all the lights came on at once.

"How'd you do that?" Bob asked.

"I wish I knew," the electrician said, shaking his head.

The house had an old-fashioned parlor in which Bob sometimes smelled frankincense. The odor filled the room and drifted into the hallway. Bob later learned that Tobias Mealey had his wake in that very room when he died in 1905. Perhaps Bob was smelling the lingering odor of incense that had perfumed the room where the corpse had lain.

But not all the phenomena occurred inside the house. Late one fall evening when Bob was alone in the house, he heard a creaking noise from outside, like that of an ox cart. It was coming along the old dirt road outside their house, which was really just a faint trail through the pasture that had been a section of the old Territorial Road from St. Anthony (Minneapolis) to North Dakota.

Bob went to the window and peered out but saw nothing amiss. Then he heard bells like those on harnesses. They were clear and distinct, yet receding into the distance. On another evening when Bob was alone, he saw a ball of light several feet in diameter go by the front door, turn a corner, and float past a first-floor window. At first he thought it was St. Elmo's fire (a bluish glow seen sometimes before and during electrical storms) but decided it was too large for that. He was never able to determine what it was.

Although the Jamesons were never frightened by these experiences, they wanted to discuss them with the previous residents of the house.

Marion contacted Jeanette Sebey, who, with her husband, Carl, had bought the house in 1947 and lived in it until Carl's death. It turns out the Sebeys had some peculiar incidents as well. The two women corresponded at length and were intrigued by the similarities.

Six weeks after the Sebeys moved into the house in 1947, Jeanette claimed that she was ready to move out.

On a sunny May morning, Jeanette and her mother were waiting for a crew from Northern States Power Company to install the poles and make the electrical connections. Loud thumping and banging suddenly shook the house.

Jeanette suspected the workmen were putting up their ladders. But no one had arrived yet.

After Jeanette got back inside, she and her mother heard heavy pieces of furniture being dragged across the floor of a bedroom at the top of the stairs. The commotion was so strong it literally shook the walls.

When Jeanette told her husband the story, he laughed that it was old

Tobias cavorting around. According to local gossip, "T. G." was a "lecherous old goat" who chased the cleaning woman all over the house.

When friends of the Sebeys arrived from Minneapolis to spend the night, they were assigned the haunted bedroom at the top of the stairs. The two couples stayed up late visiting around the fireplace. Suddenly, they heard the scraping of furniture overhead as if heavy chests were being pushed across the bare floor. The guests laughed and congratulated Carl on his skill in rigging a room to sound "exactly like a haunted house." But they passed the night without any further incident.

On another occasion, the Sebeys were working in their front yard, burning out the stump of a large elm tree that had blown down the previous year. With a hot fire going, they decided to have a wiener roast and enjoy a picnic supper. The couple had just sat down on the lawn to eat when someone banged on the kitchen door around the corner of the house from where they were. The Sebeys' dog raised her hackles, barked, and ran toward it.

Carl started for the rear of the house and met the dog racing back with her tail between her legs. She dived over a grassy bank and hid. Carl saw no one.

The couple had just settled down again to eat when they again heard the distant knock. As a joke, Carl hollered, "T. G., you old goat, if it's you, knock twice!"

There were two knocks.

Marion Jameson also corresponded with relatives of Tobias Mealey. She shared with them some of the strange incidents in the house. Up until then, the Jamesons always thought that Mr. Mealey's middle name was Godfrey. But in 1975 his granddaughter wrote and told them that his middle name was Gilmore. She said that maybe all the troubles sprang from the fact that the Jamesons were calling him by the wrong name.

If the Jamesons would call the old gentleman by his correct name, then he might go in peace and stop bothering them, Tobias's granddaughter said in her letter. They started calling him by his full name of Tobias Gilmore Mealey.

At about the same time, the Jamesons jacked up the center of the house and replaced the old horsehair and plaster ceiling in the living room. "The ceiling we tore out is right underneath that bedroom where we had the problems," Marion observed.

After that the Jamesons had no more manifestations of any kind.

Whether it was following the advice in the relative's letter or completing the repairs on the house that eventually drove Tobias away is unknown, of course. Maybe he appreciated the dignity of being called by his correct name. Or perhaps he simply wanted the Jamesons to replace the dangerous ceiling and fix the sagging timbers.

The Phantom Miner

Crosby

Fourteen-year-old Frank Hrvatin Jr. would never forget that date— February 5, 1924.

On that day's blustery morning, he shivered as he removed his street clothes and climbed into his slicker and waterproof boots in the dry house of the Milford manganese mine. A high water table in the area kept the mines wet most of the time, even in midwinter. Young Frank did not mind; he was glad to be working instead of going to school. He toiled at the 175-foot level, shoveling the dirt that remained after timbermen erected the cribbing in newly opened drifts.

At the bottom of the two-hundred-foot shaft, Clinton Harris, the skip tender, operated the electric hoist that dumped iron ore from the ore cars into the bucket, or skip, which was then raised to the surface, emptied, and sent back down.

Two skips were in use, each counterbalancing the other. Harris was substituting that day for Harvey Rice, the regular skip tender, who had called in sick.

Just after three o'clock that afternoon, a crew of miners blasted a cut near Foley's Pond, which abutted a portion of the mine. A terrific wind rushed through the mine, knocking down many of the men. Suddenly, the electric lights went out. Someone tripped the circuit breaker, the lights came on briefly, then they went off again. And then on and off again two more times.

Young Frank Hrvatin was the first to hear the roar of water and to see it spilling down a tunnel.

"The lake is coming in! The lake is coming in!" he screamed, running for a ladder and some safety.

Frank spotted old Matt Kangas, a veteran miner, and helped him along. He scampered as hard as he could to keep up with Hrvatin, but by the time he reached the ladder, the old man could barely climb. Hrvatin got behind Kangas, jumped between the old man's legs, and boosted him up rung by rung.

The last man up the ladder was soaked to the waist and encased in mud when he staggered to safety. Some of the miners were slammed against the walls of the mine tunnels and crushed to death by the terrific impact of rushing air; others, caught by the wall of water, drowned. In fifteen minutes it was all over. Of the fifty men on the shift, only seven lived.

Clinton Harris, the skip tender, died at the foot of the shaft. He apparently could have escaped but chose to remain at his post. Standing next to the ladder, Harris pulled on the whistle cord in order to warn miners on the upper levels that water was coming in.

For four and a half hours, after silt had closed the shaft, the bell he tended rang incessantly. Whether Harris's body had caught in the rope or whether he had tied it off to himself was never known. Workmen from the engine room finally disconnected the bell, silencing the last voice from deep in the mine.

The Milford survivors fell exhausted and gasping on the frozen ground, where men from the mine office tended them as best they could. Young Frank Hrvatin stood by the shaft for hours, staring down into the rising black, churning water. Frank Sr. was somewhere below—alive or dead, his son did not know.

Within minutes word of the disaster was out. The village siren in nearby Crosby blew for hours, as did locomotive whistles, summoning families to the mine. Some residents stood on the shore of Foley's Pond and watched with horror as the water level went down, the ice on the surface sinking further still as the water beneath poured into the mine.

Others gathered silently by the entrance to the shaft, aware but unwilling to admit that those miners who had not escaped were dead. Clusters of new widows eased their pain by linking arms, their bright shawls shielding their heads and faces from the biting wind and thin, sharp flakes of snow.

By midnight, mine-clearing operations were underway. In the subzero temperature, men took turns operating the giant pumps that sucked out twelve thousand gallons of water and slime each minute. Yet water continued to pour in, filling the small drifts and crossworkings in the tunnels. The Crow Wing County mine inspector said he doubted that most of the bodies would ever be found.

For a while it seemed he might be right. Pumping crews worked for twelve days to drain Foley's Pond; it took some three months to drain the mine. Then mud had to be shoveled by hand from the clogged mine drifts before the bodies of the victims could be retrieved. Nine months later the bodies were finally brought out. The Milford mine collapse was the worst disaster to that date on Minnesota's iron range.

True to their strong and independent nature, many miners signed up to go back underground when the Milford reopened. Manganese was in great demand by the steel industry and mine owners guaranteed steady work to every man who wanted it. Most did. And, of course, in almost every case, mining was the only job the men of Milford knew.

But not a miner on the entire Cuyuna Range that opening day was prepared for what they saw in the bowels of the Milford mine. Not only was there the lingering stench of decomposed flesh, but there was also something even more shocking. At the base of the shaft—at the two-hundred-foot level—the men's carbide lamps shone upon the translucent form of Clinton Harris. The ghost's bony fingers clutched the side rail of the ladder, its vacant eyes gazing upward. The whistle cord was still knotted around his waist.

The miners staggered back. Then the phantom whistle screamed through the dark, winding tunnels.

The terrified men did not look back as they scrambled up the ladder to the surface.

Not a single one of them ever reentered the Milford mine.

A House on Summit Avenue

St. Paul

Howling shattered the midnight air, trembled in the frozen treetops, and then subsided. Again. And again. A man parted the velvet drapes at his window and peered out. The house next door hulked in darkness, the bone-chilling cries coming from somewhere within. The neighbor called the St. Paul Police Department.

Patrolman Jerry Dolan and his partner sped to the splendid Romanesque-style mansion on Summit Avenue, a boulevard of grand old homes.

The officers parked their squad car and ran the spotlight slowly over the red sandstone walls of the darkened house, revealing nothing out of the ordinary. The patrolmen left their car, went to the back door of the house, and knocked. No one answered so they pushed it open. Standing on the threshold, they swept the room with their lights. Two steps led down into a combination utility-laundry room whose ceiling was webbed with clotheslines.

In a far corner crouched a young man, black hair disheveled and eyes wild with fright. He wore only boxer undershorts. He crossed his arms over his bare chest and shivered uncontrollably.

The officers leaped toward him. Just then the howling rose again.

"I could feel my hair stand on end," Officer Dolan said, recalling that February night.

A quick search revealed no other occupant in the house, but there was no time for a thorough investigation.

"I have seen death!" the young man cowering in the corner cried over and over again.

The patrolmen wrapped him in blankets and rushed to the hospital. The examining physician told the officers the man was in deep shock but showed no signs of being physically injured. Dolan learned later that he was a university student caring for the house in the absence of the owner. The howling and the comments about seeing "death" were never explained.

Chauncey W. Griggs, a wholesale grocery tycoon, built the mansion in 1883. Its twenty-four rooms are highceilinged and cavernous, the dark woodwork casting an aura of gloom on the sunniest day. Griggs, however, did not stay long in the house. He grew restless in his business and sought greater challenges. After four years, he sold his home and moved to the west coast, where he established lumber and transportation companies.

Since it was built, the house has been used variously as a private residence and as an apartment house. It once housed an art school. It is reputed to be the most haunted house in St. Paul. At times it seemed to change hands so often that one observer remarked, "It's like a hot potato."

Over the years, families moved in, spent thousands of dollars on furnishings and the hiring of servants, but left within a year or two. Official records do not disclose the reasons for the rapid turnover. It could have been the enormous expense of maintaining a stone fortress lacking in many twenty-first-century conveniences.

The tales of the hauntings in the house can be traced to its earliest years. In 1915 a young maid, despondent over a love affair, purportedly hanged herself near the fourth-floor landing. Since her death, the maid's presence has been strongly felt by many people, including those who know nothing of the history of the house. Visitors have sometimes fallen on the stairs near that top landing, or felt an uneasy sense of foreboding while climbing the staircase. The ghostly maid, however, is not alone. Apparently she shares the house with other apparitions.

The ghost of a gardener named Charles Wade is believed to return to the house to consult books in the library. When he lived, he kept the grounds in immaculate condition.

Roma Harris, a St. Paul spiritualist-medium, once visited the house and "saw," clairvoyantly, a general in a blue uniform with gold trim. Griggs was an officer during the Civil War.

Roma also felt the shadowy presence of a teenage girl named Amy who had often played the piano in the house. It is unclear whether Amy lived in the house at one time or was a frequent visitor. The psychic said the girl died young.

"There has been much sorrow here, a lot of suffering," Roma said.

Most of the stories lack written documentation but the tales persist. Footsteps resound on empty staircases. Doors mysteriously open and close. Rasping coughs come from behind closed doors of unoccupied rooms. Light bulbs shatter. Heavy drapes rustle when no one is near them.

In 1939 the mansion was donated to the St. Paul Gallery and School of Art by the Roger B. Shephard family. A skylight was installed on the upper floor and painting classes were offered to the public. But teachers and students felt uneasy in the house. They sensed presences walking among them or stopping to peer over their shoulders as if to study the works on their easels.

Malcolm Lein, who directed the gallery from 1947 to 1964, told a newsman that he personally never saw or heard anything unusual in the mansion, but he could not discount the reports of others.

"These people were sound, educated, and well read," Lein said. "Yet many had the feeling of some kind of supernatural or unknown thing in the building."

In the early 1950s, Dr. Delmar Kolb, a military intelligence officer in World War II, joined the teaching staff. He was a lawyer as well as an artist. At first he lived in the quiet and comfortable carriage house behind the mansion. Sometime later he moved into a front basement apartment in the house. It was far from comfortable.

"One night I felt two fingers on my forehead," Kolb said. "I was in a cold sweat. I reached for the light, but when I turned it on there was a blue flash and then the room was dark."

Two nights later, Kolb opened a kitchen cupboard door to get a paper bag. The bag leaped off the shelf.

"It took three hops across the floor and stopped," he said. "I thought there was a mouse inside."

Kolb went on to bed but was awakened soon after by the presence of a thin man in a black suit and top hat standing at the foot of the bed. At first Kolb thought it was a costumed intruder until he watched spellbound as the figure disappeared into a solid brick wall.

Kolb left St. Paul in 1959 and two college students moved into his apartment. In the middle of the first night, one young man awoke. Usually a sound sleeper, he had no idea of what had roused him. He did not see or hear anything in the room until he looked up. The head of a child floated in the air above his bed.

Around the same time, another student had moved into an apartment in the rear of the building. He too was shaken out of a deep sleep one night. This time the head of a man floated back and forth across the ceiling of the room. He claimed that the apparition moved in a controlled fashion, staring down at him the entire time.

Was it Chauncey Griggs making another check of his old homestead? Charles Wade, the gardener, returned? Or was it pure imagination?

The St. Paul Gallery and School of Art occupied the mansion for twenty-five years. Then a new arts and sciences center was built and the mansion put up for sale. In 1964 a publisher of occult books bought the house to use as both his office and home.

Carl L. Weschke ordered painting and repair work done before he moved in, and often stopped by the house to check on progress. According to reports, one day he found a window open on an upper floor and closed it. The next day it was open. Again he closed it. After repeatedly finding the window open, Weschke had it nailed shut.

On a number of occasions after Weschke moved into the house, he heard footsteps padding through the hallways and up and down the staircases and doors slamming shut. He always sensed a restless presence, he told an interviewer, but was not afraid because he believed in some kind of world beyond the one in which we live.

One fall afternoon in 1967, he was working in his library. Needing a break, he pushed his chair away from his desk and got up. In the doorway stood a man he had never seen before. He wore a dark suit. His face was long and thin and his hair bushy white.

A lady once called Weschke to tell him she had worked in the house as a girl and had seen the ghost of a young woman in the fourth-floor hallway. The butler at the time had also seen the apparition, she said.

Two veteran reporters from the St. Paul *Pioneer Press* arranged to spend a night in the house to gather material for a series of articles they were producing on ghosts in 1969. The journalists considered the old mansion one of the most famous haunted places in the Twin Cities.

Weschke welcomed staff writers Don Giese and Bill Farmer and photographer Flynn Ell and briefed them on the official history of the house. As the visitors sat with their host in his study, they noticed one of the

191

owner's three cats, a Siamese, crouched on its master's desk, staring up at the ceiling.

After a tour, the newsmen decided to stay in the large top-floor room with its vast skylight, just off the back landing where the maid is said to have committed suicide fiftyfour years earlier, and where some of the supernatural activity seemed to be centered.

Weschke retired to his second-floor bedroom with its private bath and said he would not be leaving his quarters.

Photographer Ell set up two cameras. One was loaded with regular film and fitted with a wide-angle lens; the other held infrared film that would record heat changes if anything invisible to the human eye appeared. Giese and Farmer turned on their tape recorder. Then the three men sat in a circle beneath the one shaded light in the room. Beyond the doorway a bright light illuminated the hallway and the top of the staircase.

Within a short time, all three men were overcome by feelings of what they termed distress.

Giese and Farmer later wrote:

As newsmen we have each been in hundreds of situations that held far greater risks of possible physical danger.

There was no sign of danger in that room. We had no reason to feel apprehensive. Yet each of us soon reported feelings of general uneasiness— a definite sense of discomfort we couldn't define. Each was especially anxious about the hall—brightly illuminated—and the staircase leading to the floors below.

They never heard anything approach them, but suddenly one of Weschke's cats appeared in the room and went directly to reporter Giese. He stroked her back. Then she walked to the doorway, twitched her tail, and looked back into the room. Giese walked toward her.

The cat moved on, toward the top of the stairs, and again looked back, as if urging Giese to follow. He did. But when the cat went on down to the first landing, Giese could not follow. Standing under the bright light of the hallway and peering over the railing at the top of the staircase, he was overcome by fear. He stepped back into the room.

Ell went out into the hallway. He returned.

Farmer went into the hallway. He returned.

All three men agreed that nothing could induce them at that point to go down the staircase.

At twenty minutes past one in the morning, all three men heard five distinct thumps just beyond the doorway, like heavy footsteps. The men sat listening, waiting, eyes fixed on the lighted hall. They did not hear or see anything more.

Shortly after 3:00 a.m., the stairs groaned under the weight of someone walking up them. But then whoever it was stopped. Giese went alone into the hallway and stared down over the railing to the landings below. He saw nothing, but when he returned to the room he told Farmer and Ell that he knew *someone* had been on those stairs.

Five minutes later the stairs creaked again. Then silence.

This time the intrepid reporters and their photographer decided enough was enough. They packed up their equipment and left by the back door.

Giese and Farmer wrote: "We all agreed on one thing. There is no prize on earth that could get us to spend a single night in that great stone house that seems to speak in sounds we cannot explain or understand."

For well over a century people have reported those mysterious sounds and unreal presences in Chauncey Griggs's old mansion on Summit Avenue—the maid who climbs to an invisible noose on the fourth-floor landing, the snoopy gardener who riffles the pages of books in the library, and the thin man in a black suit who quietly slips in and out of locked rooms.

All may have been legends and rumors, but for those who say they came face-to-face with one or more of them, it is a reality they would just as soon forget.

The Levitation of Archie Collins

Minneapolis

Most persons reported to police as missing are eventually located. Either they turn up on their own or are found by a search party, alive or dead. But

193

sometimes a person simply disappears for no apparent reason. It is as if the person disappeared into thin air. .

That is exactly what happened with a magician known as Herman the Hypnotist and one Archie Collins in old Minneapolis. In front of several hundred persons, they vanished from a theater stage never to be seen again. Or so it is claimed.

The year was 1872. Minneapolis was celebrating its incorporation as a city. Gas lampposts were decked with red, white, and blue bunting; the streets reverberated with the cadences of marching bands; and residents keen on revelry partied late into the night.

In a field south of the city, Copson's Traveling Theater pitched its tent for a week-long schedule of performances. Actors roamed the city streets, delivering handbills and hawking the delights of the repertory tent show.

The ballyhoo was not needed. This type of frontier theater was extremely popular throughout the Midwest, and Copson's well-known troupe had a loyal following. Ephraim T. Copson Jr., whose grandfather had brought the company from New York to the Upper Midwest in 1847, ran the outfit. From early spring until late fall, it played villages in Minnesota, Wisconsin, and the Lake Superior coast of Michigan.

On opening night, playgoers from all parts of Minneapolis began arriving early at the tent theater. Three one-act plays were to be presented, with specialty acts in between. During the second intermission, Herman the Hypnotist entertained. Herman, a German actor whose surname was Aikmann, was billed as a performer of amazing feats. He had only recently joined the troupe.

The crowd, eager and expectant, jostled one another in line at the ticket office. Inside the tent, the canvas chairs in front and the rows of benches toward the rear filled quickly. Children sucked indolently on sticks of candy while their parents munched peanuts and popcorn. Heat from the oil lamps intensified the oppressive and pungent odors of food and damp, trodden grass, but few people seemed uncomfortable. Minutes before curtain time, the show sold out and late arrivals were turned away.

On the raised platform at the front of the tent, the first play began. Spectators cheered their favorite performers and soon the unfolding drama absorbed everyone.

When the play was over, the first intermission entertainment began, a fat lady who did acrobatics on top of a donkey. It inspired gales of crude laughter.

The second play received even more enthusiastic response than the first; the thunderous applause perhaps based less on merit and execution than on the anticipation of seeing Herman the Hypnotist, whose amazing abilities were already being talked about on the show circuit.

However, earlier in the evening Herman had been taken ill and in the show-must-go-on style, another entertainer had agreed to repeat her act. She stood backstage, waiting to go on, when Herman suddenly appeared, rudely bumped her aside, and swept past. He neither spoke nor acknowledged her presence.

Meanwhile, on stage a giant firecracker exploded in a bang and cloud of acrid smoke. Out of it Herman appeared. Tall and slim, clad in funereal black, he resembled an animated exclamation mark. His dark eyes flashed in a powdered face the color of chalk.

Fingering his string tie, the hypnotist strode to one side of the platform and called for a volunteer. Men nudged one another in the audience, but no one stepped forward.

"I must have a volunteer," repeated Herman, his words edged with contempt. "I cannot do my act until someone joins me. It is harmless. No one will get hurt."

He surveyed the audience and finally a girl seated in the third row got up and climbed the steps to the makeshift stage.

The hypnotist bowed and directed the girl to a chair in the center of the stage. "You will relax and go to sleep. Then you will do exactly what I tell you."

The girl had other things in mind. She leered up at the actor and made a coarse suggestion.

He glared at her.

Suddenly a huge ball of sticky taffy soared through the air and landed on the girl's head. Herman spun on his heels.

"Who did that?" he screamed in rage.

People stared at their shoe tops. No one spoke.

When the hypnotist stopped trembling, he waved the girl off. Facing the audience again, he sneered, "Maybe the clown who threw the candy would care to assist me."

Now many sets of eyes settled on Archie Collins, who sat in the center of the front row. Catching the cue, the hypnotist began taunting the young man.

Collins blushed and squirmed in his seat as his friends around him called out, "Archie! Archie!" The chanting grew louder and feet began stomping.

Finally he could stand it no longer. Archie leaped to the stage and sat in the chair vacated by the girl.

Murmurs of speculation rippled through the audience. Collins, while a likeable and well-meaning fellow, was a daredevil with a strong will. Surely a poor candidate to be hypnotized. Yet, in less than a minute, the young man's eyes were closing and he was nodding as the hypnotist droned on: "You are now asleep. Sound asleep. You will do anything I say." He leaned close to Collins.

"Remember that. Anything."

Collins sat rigid in the chair.

"Now, rise, rise like a puppet on a string!"

Herman the Hypnotist's voice trembled with excitement and he stood on tiptoe to emphasize his command.

The audience gasped as Archie Collins rose and seemed to hang in midair.

"Rise! Rise!!" shouted the hypnotist. "Rise!!!"

The audience gasped as Collins floated out over the front row of chairs.

"It's a trick! Cut him down!" called a man in the rear of the tent. No one seconded the demand. Most of the playgoers sat numb, electrified, staring openmouthed as Collins floated higher and higher like a leaf carried by the wind.

Then someone shouted, "Hey! Look at the hypnotist!"

Herman now had the appearance of a skeleton—a crazy, crooked smile on his skull and long, white bones shining eerily. Was it a trick of the primitive gas lighting used in nineteenth-century theaters?

Slowly the skeleton levitated a foot or two above the stage floor, then disappeared completely.

A man stood up and screamed, "Look!" All faces turned upward.

Overhead, Archie Collins's prone body smashed into the top of the tent. The impact spun him around, revealing his battered face. When he hit the roof a second time, the canvas split and Archie Collins vanished into the night sky.

The audience sat mute; parents hugged their children, wide-eyed with wonder. Finally shuffling feet broke the silence as the bewildered spectators streamed from the theater. The last play never went on.

One of the show's officials went directly to Archie Collins's home to report the young man's disappearance.

The family was stunned, his mother nearly hysterical with grief. How could her son simply have been spirited away by some unseen force, in some unknown manner?

Police launched an investigation.

At the theater site, all was confusion. Actors and actresses, some still in costume, milled around or stood talking quietly in small groups. Knots of spectators lingered in the shadows at the outer edges of the field.

The theater's owner, Ephraim Copson, visibly shaken by the events of the evening, told the police that whoever had walked on stage as Herman the Hypnotist was in fact not Aikmann. Earlier that evening, Copson said, Ulrich Aikmann, Herman's son, reported that his father had been bothered by food poisoning and would be unable to perform. He had spent the evening in bed, cared for by his wife and Al Jones, Copson's personal assistant.

Copson stated further that he himself had summoned a doctor for Aikmann and that he had then asked another entertainer to take Aikmann's place.

Police officers questioned the entertainer at length about the man who bumped into her backstage. The poor woman felt somehow at fault. Choking back sobs, she mentioned the performer's unexpected rudeness but said he had looked enough like Aikmann and dressed like him for her not to otherwise pay attention to him.

Who was the imposter then? And how did he vanish before the eyes of that Minneapolis audience? And where was Archie Collins?

The questions were never answered.

While the truth may never be known in this particular case, there is a possible explanation for the disappearances. A skilled magician well-versed in the use of what were called magic lanterns and limelight, a powerful light that could be directed and focused to create a vast array of optical illusions, used in that era could have faked the disappearance of both magician and subject.

In the late nineteenth century the "Skeleton Act" was very popular in sideshows and traveling theaters. Here's how it worked:

A volunteer stepped into an upright casket placed behind a sheet of glass set at a forty-five degree angle to the stage. The audiences as well as the volunteer were usually unaware of this glass partition. Bright lights concealed from the audience shone upon and in effect blinded the volunteer. At the side of the stage, in total darkness, stood a skeleton in an upright casket placed at right angles to the casket containing the volunteer and to one side of a panel that held a vertical strip of lights.

When, at the same moment, the lights were switched off the volunteer and on the skeleton, the spectators saw the image of the skeleton in its casket reflected in the sheet of glass. It appeared to be exactly where they had seen the volunteer.

A magician, using similar aids with help from an assistant, could have created his own metamorphosis and disappearance from the stage.

Furthermore, a levitation such as that performed on Archie Collins was another common act and could have been achieved by smoke pictures from a magic lantern—a device consisting of a small metal box with a carbide lamp and colored glass slides—hidden at the rear of the stage. With the tent and most of the stage in darkness, fires were lit in braziers at the front of the stage and chemicals added to the fires to cause columns of smoke to rise.

An assistant to the magician projected a series of slides onto the smoke of a young man in various positions, suggesting floating or levitation. As the images flashed by, the movements of the smoke brought them eerily to life. It was to these images that the magician gave his commands.

A stooge planted in the audience could have shouted that Archie was going through the roof while appropriate sound effects simulated the noise of ripping canvas. The audience members, distracted by the sudden appearance of the skeleton and confused by the smoke images, believed they had actually seen Archie vanishing through the roof of the tent.

Records do not indicate whatever became of Archie Collins. Perhaps his life was unhappy and he welcomed the opportunity to make an unforgettable departure. But who had taken Herman the Hypnotist's place? That was never discovered. Were he and Archie in the scheme together? That was widely speculated on.

Whichever if any of these scenarios may be accurate, all of them prove one thing—the hand *is* quicker than the eye.

Missouri

The Hornet Spook Light

Joplin

Twelve miles southwest of Joplin, near the Missouri–Oklahoma state line, a gravel road arrows through a canyon of blackjack oak. This obscure east-west track, not quite four miles in length, lies in Oklahoma, just beyond the former border village of Hornet, Missouri. Known as Spook Light Road, or, as it is called locally, the Devil's Promenade, it is similar to other roadways in the Ozark foothills. Except at night. When darkness falls, a mysterious light appears, bobbing along from west to east. It has been seen frequently from dusk to dawn for over a century. Early pioneers called it the Indian Light, but it is now more commonly known as the Hornet Spook Light.

The ball of fire, varying from baseball-sized to larger than a bushel basket, spins down the center of the road at great speed, rises to treetop level and hovers, then retreats. At other times, it sways from side to side and up and down like a lantern being carried. But no one is ever there to carry it.

Observers say the light is silver, red, or yellow. Sometimes blue or green. It is usually seen as a single glow, but one woman said she saw it "burst like a bubble, scattering sparks in all directions." If chased, the light seems to go out, only to reappear later. One man drove his car directly at the light until it vanished.

Although the mystery light has never been known to harm anyone, some observers claim to have had close personal encounters with it. Early one morning, Gregory Briones was driving nearby when he turned around and saw the Spook Light sitting on the lid of his trunk.

"It throwed off a good bit of light, like an electric bulb close up to you," he told a news reporter. "I took off in one big hurry."

A man walking along the Devil's Promenade said the light swung past him close enough so he could feel its searing heat.

Other people reported seeing the light bob through open windows of automobiles; one car caught fire. On at least two occasions, the light was observed six miles beyond the western end of the Devil's Promenade, near Quapaw, Oklahoma.

Chester McMinn, who farmed near Quapaw, was working his fields late one summer night when the Spook Light appeared overhead, illuminating his acreage with silvered brilliance.

Louise Graham was riding home in a school bus from a carnival at Quapaw when the light appeared outside the rear window of the bus. The brilliant yellow fireball badly frightened her and her schoolmates and forced the driver to pull over. Only then did the light drift away.

Generations of local people believe that the Hornet Spook Light is a ghost, or "ha'nt," in local parlance. There are many legends to account for the queer glow.

One version of the legend involves the Quapaw Native Americans who once called the region their home. It is said that a woman and man of the tribe fell in love, but the girl's greedy father demanded a larger dowry than the young man could afford. Unable to marry with the tribe's blessing and unwilling to separate, the lovers eloped. Their absence was soon discovered and a party of warriors sent in pursuit. Overtaken on a bluff above the Spring River, the couple joined hands and leaped to their deaths.

Shortly afterward, in 1886, the light first appeared; it was thought to be the spirits of the young lovers. It created such a panic in the village of Hornet that many people abandoned their farms and moved away. The light was a hoodoo, they claimed, that brought death.

Another legend claims the Spook Light is the ghost of an Osage chief who was decapitated on the Devil's Promenade. The Spook Light is the torch held high in the chief's hand as he returns to search for his lost head.

A third legend places the origin of the light in the Prohibition era (1920–33). Although the law forbade alcoholic beverages, illegal whiskey sites known as stills pervaded the Ozark hills. With some regularity, federal agents raided the operations, flushing out these so-called moonshiners.

Eventually they caught old Uncle Dick Hunt, purveyor of the finest "corn likker" in the area. It was so fine, in fact, that Uncle Dick refused to pour it into bottles that had contained any other blends. He used bottles of only the best brands or the buyer's own stone jug. But after the Feds raided him and broke up his still several times, Uncle Dick got smart. He mounted the still on the rear of an old spring wagon. Whenever the agents were around, Uncle Dick moved the still to the safety of a nearby cave. The Spook Light is Uncle Dick Hunt's still, jouncing around on the back of the wagon eternally heading for cover.

Over the years, the light has been studied, photographed, and even shot at with high-powered rifles in efforts to identify and explain it.

So what is it in reality?

Marsh gas? Probably not. Winds fail to disperse the fireball as they do conventional marsh gas.

A will-o'-the-wisp? The light is far more intense than the luminescence created by rotting organic matter.

Glowing minerals from the numerous piles of mine tailings in the area? Maybe.

A pocket of natural gas ignited by lightning and once worshipped as a fire god by Indians of the area? Not likely. Natural gas flames and, in time, burns out.

Anomalous lights, such as the Hornet Spook Light, have been reported all over the world for thousands of years. Some experts believe that these lights are electrical atmospheric charges generated by the shifting and grinding of rocks deep below the earth's crust. Although such lights are frequently associated with earthquakes, their presence does not necessarily predict quakes. The distorted electrical field that results from these charges can make the light appear to act in an "intelligent" way, changing direction and altitude and giving chase. And physical encounters with the electrical field can make a person fearful and apprehensive. Sleep difficulties, skin burns, nausea, and temporary blindness may follow.

Joplin, Missouri, just north of the Spook Light area, lies on a great fault line running from east of New Madrid, Missouri, westward into Oklahoma. Four earthquakes during the eighteenth century were followed by a devastating series of quakes that convulsed this area in 1811–12. Strange lights may have accompanied these quakes, but it was not until 1886 that the Hornet Spook Light was first reported. Although the appearance of the light has not been accompanied by any major quake in this century as far as is known, seismologists consider this region of Missouri one of the most unstable areas in the country, and the generation of an electrical atmospheric charge may possibly explain the Spook Light.

Over the past quarter century, a dramatic increase in earthquakes has occurred in an eight-state region, including Missouri, Oklahoma, and southern Kansas. Geologists speculate this escalation in seismic activity is due to a rise in hydraulic fracturing, commonly known as fracking, in the area.

Other teams of investigators who have studied the lights conclude that they are those of automobiles driving east on an old, iconic portion of U.S. Highway 66. This highway is about five miles away in a direct line with the Devil's Promenade but at a slightly lower elevation. A high ridge lies between the two roads. The density and rarity of atmosphere as it rises over the ridge causes the light to bend, creating the eerie effects.

In 2014 a professor from the University of Central Oklahoma conducted an experiment and explained the Spook Light as car headlights from the junction of Highway 137 and E 50 Road outside of Quapaw, Oklahoma.

Old-timers smile and shake their heads. They know the mystery light was seen in the same spot in these woods long before the automobile was invented and the highway built—back in horse and buggy days, they would say.

Whatever the Hornet Spook Light may be—and the debate will no doubt go on—thousands of visitors will continue to visit the area. Cars park bumper to bumper on the narrow gravel road, while drivers wait and watch for that strange light that swings and sways and bobs along up in the night sky.

Sentries in the Night

St. Louis

The snow came, blanketing roofs and mortaring window frames. Inside the house on the hill, Dr. John J. O'Brien lit another lantern and set the dinner table. His wife, Elizabeth, added wood to the cookstove then peered through the kitchen window clouded by steam from the kettle of stew bubbling on the stove. Her husband stood behind her, his full, red beard barely touching the top of her head. Usually the gaslights of St. Louis shone like a jeweled carpet spread far below, but now, beyond the swirl of flakes, no lights were visible. Nor were there any sounds—not the clatter of buggy wheels on the cobblestone street or the call of children at play. Only the ceaseless howling of the wind.

"It's unreal, isn't it?" murmured Elizabeth, looking up into her husband's face. "It's as if we're suspended in time, cut off from all living things."

John detected a quiver of excitement in her voice. He knew that, like a child, she both loved and feared blizzards.

"I'm glad you finished your rounds early today," she added, ladling the stew into bowls and setting out great slabs of freshly baked bread.

Her husband nodded and sat down at the table, the chair creaking beneath his weight. He was truly a massive man with a deep, hearty laugh and a streak of Irish whimsy that people said was his best medicine. Yet tonight no whimsy livened up the doctor's face.

"Elizabeth," he began, "I haven't seen Mrs. Kilpatrick for a long time." He knifed a slab of butter onto his bread.

"I've had her on my mind all day. As you know, she has that weak heart."

Elizabeth's jaw tightened and her cheeks flushed, but John saw in her eyes the same gentle light that had first attracted him to her, when she was Elizabeth Fitzwilliam and he was the stranger passing through town — an Irish physician recently graduated from medical school in Dublin, traveling across America to see the world before settling down to a practice in Australia. But Elizabeth had charmed him; so had St. Louis. The adventurous young doctor-to-be never did get to the South Pacific.

John had known from the beginning that Elizabeth was the only woman with whom he wished to share his life; he sensed that she was proud that his patients' needs came first, and he loved her deeply for it.

Now their eyes met across the table.

"But John, you wouldn't be going to see Mrs. Kilpatrick on a night like this, would you?"

He stared into his empty bowl.

"If I thought for one moment . . ." His voice trailed off.

". . . that she needed me," finished Elizabeth.

She then murmured, "Of course."

The dinner table conversation waned. John's preoccupation distracted him and he fell silent. Finally he rose, went into the living room, and stood by the fireplace. He laid another log on the glowing embers.

Hands clasped before him, he watched fingers of flame encircle the dry wood and bounce the light off the soot-blackened back wall of the firebox. From the corner of his eye, he saw Elizabeth clearing away the dinner dishes. She moved deftly, with that certain resilience that all adaptable women possess.

John went to the kitchen doorway. "I'm going to Mrs. Kilpatrick."

Elizabeth nodded. She knew that would be his decision long before he said it aloud.

He never knew how he had acquired that sixth sense about the condition of his patients, but this inexplicable intuition often meant the difference between life and death. He suspected it was a gift given to most country doctors in that era before the telephone.

Dr. O'Brien pulled on his boots, put on his heavy overcoat, fur-lined cap, and gloves; then wound the long, wool muffler Elizabeth had made for him around his neck. He kissed his wife good-bye and begged her not to wait up.

Trudging to the stable behind the house, he kicked the drifts into snow showers.

Moments later, the horse was hitched to his buggy.

The doctor sat high on the box spring cushion, his medical bag beside him. Glancing back, he barely saw Elizabeth's face framed in the kitchen window, hands cupped to her cheeks, nose pressed against the glass. He knew she would watch the rig until its twin oil lamps vanished in the cold, snowy night.

What Dr. O'Brien did not know is that he was setting forth on the most unusual house call of his life, one that he would never forget.

The wind had picked up, driving the snow with stinging fury against his cheeks. He tried to shield his face with one hand while holding the reins to guide the horse with the other. Perhaps he should have put up the rubber side curtains, but he never liked to use them because they obstructed what little vision he had to the sides.

He hunched forward now on the seat, trying to see where to make his first turn. The Kilpatricks lived several miles away down a maze of side roads. In daylight and good weather the route was not difficult. But now, in the darkness and with swirling snow obstructing nearly everything in sight, even familiar landmarks were obliterated. Dr. O'Brien found it nearly impossible to see junctions with other roads.

Following a bend on the main road, he met the blizzard head on. He could see but a few feet ahead as the horse slowed its walk even further. The oil lamps were useless.

Then the wind seemed to take a momentary pause to catch its breath. At that moment came the faint sound of a barking dog. Dr. John thought he had imagined it. But there it was again, louder, and more distinct. He rose, leaned over the leather dash, and peered through the veil of snow.

That is when he saw them—two giant mastiffs, one on each side of the buggy, slightly ahead of it. Was he nearing the Kilpatricks and did the dogs belong to them? He could not remember; he had never noticed any, but he would not necessarily have seen them if they were kept outside.

If not that, where had they come from?

He had to take a chance; there were no other options. And so he followed them. When the dogs led to the left, Dr. O'Brien turned with them.

When the dogs led right, the rig followed. The doctor lost track of all the turnings, the jigs and the jogs, but he never took his eyes off the barking four-footed guides as they plunged effortlessly through the driving, drifting snow.

After a final turn, Dr. O'Brien saw the Kilpatricks' cozy frame farmhouse covered with snow, its roof rimmed with ice. A lantern's glow shone through a frosted window. He drove the rig beneath an open shed at the side of the house, grabbed his medical kit, and eased himself down from the seat.

He knocked and Mr. Kilpatrick opened the door.

"Oh doctor, it's so fine you came," he said, shaking his guest's hand warmly. "The missus is poorly today and has such trouble breathing. Here, let's dry your clothes by the fire. And warm yourself, please."

Mr. Kilpatrick took Dr. O'Brien's overcoat and spread it over the back of a chair near the hearth and put his boots close by. The doctor warmed his hands, let the ice melt out of his beard, then went into the bedroom to check on his patient.

The woman's pulse was slow and her breathing labored. Dr. O'Brien gave her medicine for her heart and something to put her to sleep. In a short time she breathed easier and drifted off to sleep.

Mr. Kilpatrick insisted that Dr. O'Brien stay for hot coffee and food. Grateful for the chance to relax after the strain of his trip, the doctor pulled a rocking chair closer to the fireplace.

"Tell me, sir, where do you keep your dogs in this weather?"

"Dogs?" echoed the host. "But I have no dogs."

Neither did any of his neighbors.

By four o'clock in the morning, the storm had passed and the landscape bathed in the glow of a full moon.

Dr. O'Brien drove home slowly. At he labored to remember each turn, he watched for the dogs, listened for their barking. But he met no living thing on his trip home that night.

As dawn approached, Dr. O'Brien arrived at the back door of his house. He stomped the snow from his boots and pulled them off. He went inside quietly and hung his outer clothes on the hooks by the stove. His shoulders ached and his head hurt. Perhaps he could coax the living room fire into life and relax awhile before going to bed.

In stocking feet, he padded into the living room and found Elizabeth curled up in her rocker, sound asleep by the cold hearth.

Suddenly aware of her husband's presence, Elizabeth jerked awake. "Coffee first, then tell me," she said quietly.

He never knew how she sensed what he needed. Tonight, after the long, late trip, he wanted to relax his body and unravel his mind. When Elizabeth stood, John took her into his arms and held her close. Then he added a log to the still-hot embers and watched the fire flame up.

John and Elizabeth sat together, drinking and talking until dawn fully washed the windows with gray light. He told her of the sudden appearance of the mastiffs and their unknown origin.

During the next few days, the O'Briens asked everyone they knew about the giant dogs. No one they knew kept such dogs nor knew of anyone who did. The doctor recalled that when he pulled into the Kilpatricks' yard, the dogs were no longer there. At the time he had given it little thought, believing that they had found shelter or that his eyes were overly strained from trying to focus through the blizzard.

But Dr. John J. O'Brien, the practical, down-to-earth country doctor, eventually concluded that—as improbable as it sounded—the mastiffs were not real, that they were ghost dogs that had somehow materialized for the single purpose of guiding him to Mrs. Kilpatrick's bedside.

He could think of no other explanation.

The Midnight Rider

Sand Springs

Before the American Civil War, wagon trains rumbling westward often stopped for the night at a place named Sand Springs, two miles west of Roubidoux Creek, between Rolla and Springfield. Sand Springs was a campground that took its name from a spring of soft lime water that boiled up through the sand and gravel. Near the spring stood a small, abandoned country church where countless freight drivers took shelter at night.

Soon after the Civil War ended, stories circulated that the church was haunted. People said that a phantom horseman rode into the building at midnight. The horse hesitated a moment at the door, then walked slowly down the aisle and stopped at the altar. A whinny was heard, then the dull thud of something striking the floor. Measured hoofbeats retreated up the aisle. At the church door there was a final, chilling human laugh.

Up until the 1930s, when the building was razed, people unsuccessfully went out to Sand Springs late at night trying to locate and follow the ghosts with lanterns and flashlights.

Only a few persons knew the true story of the unearthly drama that was reenacted in the building, a tale of passion, intrigue, and revenge.

In 1848 Wyndham Potter, a wealthy planter from Georgia, settled on a parcel of land near Sand Springs. He had no wife or family, but he brought a large number of slaves with him because Missouri allowed that, including a woman named Jenny and her daughter, Carolyne.

Potter built a handsome house and invited his new neighbors to a house-warming at which Jenny presided as hostess. Her daughter, sixteen-year-old Carolyne, was a slightly built but strong young woman who bore a striking resemblance to Wyndham Potter himself.

Two years later, in 1850, Potter died. He left the house and a trust fund to Jenny and Carolyne, along with their freedom. The rest of his estate, including a small piece of land nearby, went to a nephew, Charles Potter.

Charles soon arrived to take up residence on the land he had inherited. Before long, he began worshipping in the little church near Sand Springs each Sunday with Jenny and Carolyne.

A preacher who was called Elder Maupins often filled the pulpit. He was a formidable figure, nearly six feet tall, strong and muscular with black chin whiskers. He had a gaunt and weary wife and two grown sons. Although most people respected him, few truly liked him. His next-door neighbor, an old woman whom everyone called "Grandmother," thought Elder Maupins was evil and cruel. As an example, she pointed to the occasion when she saw Maupins shoot and kill his sons' dog simply because it refused to come to him.

Grandmother soon noticed that Maupins was becoming a regular visitor at Jenny's home. After others questioned the propriety of such visits,

Grandmother herself confronted Maupins. She demanded to know what he was doing in the woman's home. Saving souls, he told her, as God had chosen him to do.

That explanation satisfied everyone, except Grandmother. Was she the only one who saw the dark looks exchanged between Maupins and Charles Potter in the church? Even Jenny and Carolyne were embarrassed and averted their eyes as Maupins, rising on tiptoe in the pulpit, arms outstretched and trembling, declaimed the evils of sin.

But Elder Maupins was soon taken out of the pulpit when a country preacher was assigned to the Sand Springs church. After that, Maupins seldom attended services.

One day cattle buyers passed through Sand Springs, announcing that horse thieves had raided a neighborhood on the Osage River, escaping with twenty head of mules and horses. A posse raced south after the gang. In the exchange of gunfire one officer was killed and another wounded. Supposedly, the lethal shots were fired by a tall man wearing a high-crowned black hat, a red linsey shirt, and dark pants tucked into his boots; he rode a large sorrel mule. It was an apt description of Maupins and his mule, Judy.

Several days later a detective arrived in Sand Springs to inquire about the ownership of a large sorrel mule. Maupins told his wife he had urgent business in the Boston Mountains. After dark, he fled, taking the mule with him.

At about the same time, Jenny's daughter, Carolyne, vanished. Jenny was awakened the night before Carolyne's disappearance by hoofbeats going past the house. The rider was singing a church hymn as he rode. Thinking he was a neighbor returning home, Jenny drifted back to sleep. In the morning, however, she awoke to find her daughter gone, along with many of her clothes.

The grief-stricken mother was certain that slave runners had abducted her and would sell her into slavery.

When the woman known as Grandmother found out, she said she knew better.

"She's run off with Maupins," she whispered. "When you find him, you'll find her."

Years passed and no word of either Elder Maupins or Carolyne ever reached the community.

The Civil War brought difficult times to the people of Sand Springs as husbands, fathers, and brothers went away to fight, some for the Union, others the Confederacy. Charles Potter himself had joined the Rebels and rode off with the cavalry that very year. Soon the parson of Sand Springs was the only able-bodied man left in the community. The women helped one another as best they could and prayed for the safe return of their men.

Then one Sunday morning in 1863, Elder Maupins showed up and sat in his pew. At the close of the sermon, Maupins leaped to the pulpit. The startled minister stood awkwardly to one side as Maupins announced that his mother had died in the Boston Mountains and he had been busy settling her estate. He said he was shocked to learn of Carolyne's disappearance, which he attributed to slave traders, and asked the congregation to pray that she might be returned safely to her dear mother.

"And let us pray also," he concluded, "for a Union victory!"

Grandmother listened attentively. She called him an excellent liar.

During the rest of that year and well into 1864, Elder Maupins stayed in Sand Springs but was often away on long trips to unknown destinations. Charles Potter survived the war and returned home in 1865.

The reason for Maupins's mysterious trips soon became clear.

Someone in Sand Springs discovered that he had been a member of a bushwhacker gang that raided farms and ranches throughout the Finley Creek hills, spreading death and destruction in their wake. Maupins denied it and viciously denounced the Confederacy. Even staunch Unionists were sickened by his bluster.

The affair took an unexpected turn when Charles Potter sent word to the Sand Springs congregation that on a certain Sunday night when Maupins was preaching, he would ride on his horse down the aisle to the pulpit and by looks alone run the elder out of the church and the community forever.

At the appointed hour, the former Rebel officer, in full-dress gray uniform, mounted his horse and rode to the church. Near the close of the service, Potter rode into the church and made his way slowly down the aisle. He reined his horse to a halt in front of the pulpit. A few people gasped, while others anxiously waited for the fight.

Elder Maupins raised both arms to deliver the benediction.

Charles glared at him.

"May the Lord bless you and keep you . . . ," intoned Maupins.

Shots rang out from beyond an open window. Young Potter toppled dead from his horse, blood streaming from his head.

The riderless horse stood for a moment, then turned and trotted out of the church.

The horrified worshippers did not move or speak. Elder Maupins sank to his knees and asked that they pray for guidance. He had uttered only a few words before he glanced up the aisle to the church door. Then, like a crazed animal, he leaped to his feet and dived through the window from which the shot had been fired.

While the congregation sat in stunned silence, the deacons covered Potter's body. It would remain in the custody of two of the minister's assistants until an inquest could be held the next day.

In the morning, a jury was convened and witnesses were called. But there were no clues and the identity of the murderer could not be learned. However, the jury did unravel the mystery of Elder Maupins's hasty exit from the church when the community's ne'erdo-well testified.

His name was Ginger and he admitted that he had been drunk when he had gotten to the church services and promptly fell asleep in the rear pew.

He was jerked awake by the sound of gunfire. Glancing up, his bleary eyes focused on a black horse with saddle and bridle walking toward him. He thought he was having a nightmare, he said, until he saw Maupins in the pulpit.

Ginger went on to say that after the horse left the church and the elder was kneeling, someone stepped through the door dressed in a man's shirt, pants, and boots. He said it was not a man but a young, light-skinned black woman. She pointed a finger at Maupins and then unleashed a blood-curdling laugh. That is when Maupins dived through the window. Ginger added that as the woman turned to leave he noticed a livid scar on the left side of her face and neck. She glanced down at Charles Potter's body on the floor, then fled.

But still the question remained—who murdered Charles Potter?

Grandmother believed that some of Maupins's raiders had carried out the ambush. Others said Potter could have been killed by a Union sympathizer living in the region.

Or was the killer Carolyne herself?

On the following Sunday, a search party found Maupins's body face down in a cedar glade, his throat slit from ear to ear; only a bloody piece of flesh had kept his head attached to his torso. An exquisitely designed Mexican dagger was buried to its hilt between his shoulder blades. It was impossible to tell how long Maupins had been dead. The searchers concluded that after plunging through the church window, he must have made his way along the stream bank and to the glade where his body was discovered. Curiously, there was neither evidence of a struggle nor any footprints near the body.

After Elder Maupins was buried, Jenny told her neighbors she was selling everything and returning to her family in the South. She took only two saddle horses with her.

But why two horses? One would always be rested, she replied. Soon after, she left early one afternoon headed toward Georgia, riding one horse and leading the other.

A few days following Jenny's departure, a horse trader showed up in Sand Springs. When he heard the story of what had transpired, he said he had passed two black women traveling south on the Wilderness Road. He met them in the Roark Hills, south of the old town of Forsyth. The younger woman was dressed in a man's clothes and heavily armed.

The horse trader said she had a scar on her face.

The ghost rider of Sand Springs made its appearance not long after Jenny and Carolyne began their journey south and continued on for nearly seventy-five years. The old church finally succumbed to the elements, its few remaining walls razed in the 1930s.

The Ghost of Paris

Paris

Did the village of Paris, Missouri, play host for nearly seventy years to the gruesome specter of a woman in black floating along the community's streets? Or was the ghost merely an eccentric old lady who rather enjoyed late evening strolls in the fashionable black clothing of a century or more ago, maybe frightening a gullible Parisian or two at the same time?

Although few know of the city's interesting legend today, earlier generations in that northeast Missouri community passed on the story of this woman in black.

Darcy Ambrose saw the woman first. In the dusk of an October evening, she stood in her front yard calling for her children to come inside. Suddenly, a stranger swept down the street, swathed in black, her wide-brimmed bonnet shielding her face. In her hand she waved a cane. Darcy had never seen the woman before, but she assumed she was a soldier's wife or mother. The Civil War had just ended and relatives swarmed into Paris to greet their men folk home from the battlefields.

The next night the woman in black returned. Darcy and her husband were sitting on the front stoop, talking. The stranger again brandished her cane as she passed, and the couple shrank into the shadows of their little porch. Then, in the bright moonlight, Darcy could have sworn that the woman's feet never touched the ground. Although she looked three-dimensional, she told friends the woman herself was not real.

Soon the tavern on the courthouse square buzzed with talk of the ghost. It had an immediate impact on the community's behavior. Tavern patrons arrived in groups of threes and fours and left the same way. Children, scurrying home from after-supper play, burst into hysterics when the stranger brushed past them; three youngsters said they had heard her long skirts rustling in the wind.

Indian summer lingered that year well into November in that part of Missouri.

So did the ghost.

Frightened residents kept their windows locked, doors bolted, and shades drawn. Travelers abroad at night were wary. In several instances, grown men, meeting the ghost, ran down the middle of the street crying for help. Little else was on the lips of city dwellers but this specter in black. Although the ghost always swung her cane at those she encountered, she never harmed anyone as far as is known.

Even when northwest winds stripped the trees, and the snows came, the woman in black did not leave.

Throughout the winter she glided down the icy streets late at night and sometimes peered into an uncurtained window.

Strangely enough when March arrived, she departed.

During the warm springtime and the long, hot summer of 1866, the people of Paris almost forgot their ghost.

But when the pumpkins ripened in mid-October, she returned and, as before, stayed until spring. No one saw her during the daylight hours. For nearly seventy years the dauntless figure in black roamed the village each winter, frightening everyone who saw her.

Who was she? What did she want?

Si Colborn edited the *Monroe County Appeal* for nearly sixty years before "retiring" at the age of eighty-two to write editorials and columns. Colborn said in an interview that he heard the story when he came to Paris in 1920. His late partner at the newspaper, Jack Blanton, often told the tale, sometimes with variations.

Occasionally the woman did not seem mortal, for instance. She was alleged to have had a face that glowed in the dark, and she floated rather than walked.

Colburn, however, said the woman might have been a Paris spinster spurned when her betrothed ran off with another woman. The spinster was very tall, nearly six feet, angular, and "formidable." Having known the woman, Colborn adds, it is obvious why her husband-to-be thought better of the marriage proposal and left town.

There may be some truth to Colborn's explanation.

The woman was not seen after the mid-1930s, shortly before the real-life spinster's death at the age of ninety.

But an Associated Press news dispatch in November 1934 identified the woman as a Civil War soldier's jilted sweetheart who swore on her death-bed to haunt forever her faithless lover and the entire town of Paris.

Whatever the truth of the Paris ghost, the legend that had been passed down for generations disappeared at about that time. Other means of telling ghost stories—radio broadcasts and motion pictures—were growing in popularity, even in rural America where electricity was sporadic at best. Perhaps the newspaper publicity represented the last gasp of interest in the subject. At any rate, the streets of Paris, Missouri, were safe again, and even the most timid citizen—which seemed to be most of them, as no one ever

215

thought to confront the woman in black and ask for her identity—could walk fearlessly into the night.

The Corporal's Lady

Columbia

Margaret Baker sat in her dormitory room in Senior Hall at Columbia Baptist Female College, staring at the front page of the newspaper until the print blurred before her eyes.

She read the two stories:

> Columbia, Mo. *Isaac Johnson, a Confederate corporal, was executed in this city yesterday. He was arrested as a spy in a dormitory room of the Columbia Baptist Female College by General Henry Halleck, commander of the Union forces occupying the city. The Rebel had been sought for weeks . . .*
>
> Columbia, Mo. *Sarah June Wheeler, a student at the Columbia Baptist Female College, died yesterday in Senior Hall, the dormitory in which she resided. The body was found in the bell tower by classmates. An investigation into Miss Wheeler's death has begun . . .*

Cold, brutal facts—the kind you see every day in the newspaper. Margaret read no further. She knew the story by heart. The only thing she did not know was that these tragic events would be recounted over the years, the tale embellished until it achieved legendary status. Even today, new students at what is now Stephens College hear about the corporal and his lady. And every Halloween at midnight they wonder if the ghost of the lovely Sarah June once again will visit Senior Hall, searching for her Rebel.

In 1862 the Civil War raged throughout the South, into the border states and beyond. Although Missouri had declared for the Union, General

Sterling Price tried to organize a Confederate campaign in the state. Any chance of concerted pro-Southern action ended when he was defeated at Pea Ridge, Arkansas, in March 1862. Yet Missouri remained a state divided where thousands remained Southern sympathizers.

After this decisive Union triumph, General Henry Halleck moved his Union forces into Columbia. The presence of Halleck's Army of Occupation particularly upset Dr. Hubert Williams, president of the Columbia Baptist Female College, and its dean, Miss Clara Armstrong. The administrators feared for the safety of their young females and reminded them constantly not to call out from their windows to the soldiers in the streets.

One evening after dinner, a student named Sarah June Wheeler who was from Independence, Missouri, dashed up to her room in Senior Hall to get badminton racquets for herself and her roommate, Margaret Baker. Rummaging in the closet for the racquets, Sarah did not see the soldier climbing over the sill of her open window until he staggered toward her.

"Please, miss," he began. "Where am I? What is this place?"

His gray uniform was soiled and torn, the rifle in his hands caked with mud.

"A Rebel!" screamed Sarah.

He sprang at her, clasping his hand over her mouth. She struggled to free herself but a moment later he collapsed. Just then Margaret Baker came in and gasped at the sight of the soldier sprawled on the floor beside a trunk.

"Oh my God!" she cried. "Did the South win the war? Hallelujah!"

She leaned out over the windowsill and gave a Rebel shout. Then she slammed the window shut and turned to Sarah.

"Why there's nothin' but damn Yankees out there."

Sarah curled her small hands into fists. She had always tried to be fair, to understand another's viewpoint and never knowingly hurt anyone. But Margaret's allegiance to the Confederacy was too much. Margaret could scarcely be otherwise. She was born and raised in Little Rock, and her father, in lieu of paying his daughter's tuition, sent two of his slaves to the college — Lucy Evans and Elijah Patterson. They cleaned, cooked, served, and worked in the school's laundry.

The young women's innate kindness took over their indecisiveness, and they knelt on either side of the soldier, loosening his uniform to check for injuries. He did not appear to be wounded; at least there was no blood anywhere. Sarah put smelling salts under his nose and the soldier quickly regained consciousness.

No, he was not ill or wounded, he said, only weak from hunger. The girls helped him into a chair. Margaret summoned Lucy and Elijah and ordered them to smuggle a tray of food from the kitchen and to say nothing of the soldier's presence.

After the soldier had eaten, he introduced himself as Corporal Isaac Johnson, Fifth Cavalry, Mississippi section. He had fought at Pea Ridge and had just escaped from Camp Douglas, Illinois, traveling by night and hiding by day. His father had been killed in General Grant's bombardment of Nashville. Isaac was seeking to avenge that death by sneaking into Columbia to kill General Halleck.

Sarah's eyes filled. She understood his bitterness; her own father fighting for the Union had been killed by Robert E. Lee's troops. She was so devastated by the loss that she twice attempted suicide.

Perhaps that is why she agreed with Margaret to hide this man, not that many years older than themselves.

In the coming days, Sarah busied herself in ways her mother never would have approved of. Keeping Isaac safe and secure in her room was a constant strain.

Whenever anyone knocked at the door, Isaac leaped into the closet to hide behind rows of crinoline dresses or rolled under the bed. Sarah was popular, and her many friends liked to congregate in her room because it was the largest and most beautiful room in Senior Hall. It was directly beneath the bell tower.

Although Sarah enjoyed these visits, she feared Isaac would be discovered. Margaret and the slaves had been sworn to secrecy, yet Margaret often spoke thoughtlessly.

Sarah remained with Isaac as much as possible, often feigning a headache at meal times in order to be with him, requesting that a tray be sent up later. Although she had never before talked to a Confederate soldier, they argued bitterly over slavery. Sometimes he would defend his cause, but more often he would smile and sit down at Sarah's piano to play the old songs he had learned growing up in Senatobia, Mississippi. His gray eyes would sweep over the piano keys, then search Sarah's face. When she knew the songs, she sang along.

In the music and in the softness of his eyes, Sarah found a tenderness, a warmth she had never known before in a man. She was only moderately taken aback when he declared his love for her.

One day, Elijah, tired of colluding with Sarah, told her it was her duty to turn in the soldier. But she assured the slave that Isaac meant no harm.

Finally word somehow reached General Halleck that a Rebel soldier was on the loose in Columbia. Knowing the attraction that young pretty girls held for bored soldiers, the general suspected that the Rebel might be hiding at the college. Perhaps even the college administration was providing protective custody, he thought, for Southern sympathies ran high in the city.

Halleck paid a call on President Williams and Dean Armstrong and warned them both that he would shut down the college unless the soldier was captured.

That evening the president gathered his young female students together and delivered the general's ultimatum. His face was pale, his voice strained. The students were stunned.

Sarah was frightened. Had she been betrayed?

Perhaps Margaret's loose tongue revealed Isaac's presence?

Margaret had shouted the Confederate victory yell out the window after all. Had a Union soldier heard the cry and noted the room it came from? How much did General Halleck know?

Sarah urged Isaac to surrender. Escape was hopeless, she said; the city was ringed by Union forces. But Isaac had a better plan. He would flee to Canada disguised in a suit "borrowed" from President Williams's own closet.

The next evening, after the students had gone downstairs to dinner, Elijah crept along the corridor, the president's clothing draped neatly over one arm. Sarah waited in her room. Under the cover of darkness Isaac would be on his way to safety.

But at the close of the dinner hour, throngs of young women barged through Sarah's door, screaming, "Turn him in, Sarah! Turn him in!"

Someone had seen Elijah delivering the clothing to Sarah's room. Sarah's thin shoulders trembled and she slumped against the piano.

Sarah searched the crowd for a friendly face. Margaret, her color ashen, pushed her way through the group and put an arm around her roommate.

"Silence!" Margaret yelled. Her classmates paid no attention.

The clamor rose until President Williams and Dean Armstrong burst in. General Halleck was at their heels.

"This college is closed—absolutely finished!" roared the general. "Now, pack up and leave—everyone!"

Isaac threw open the closet door, faced General Halleck, and introduced himself.

"I am the soldier you are looking for, sir. I beg you to let the students stay. I have been hiding here without their knowledge."

General Halleck stepped forward. "I arrest you as a spy," he said.

"But I am a soldier, sir."

"That may be, but you are attired in civilian clothes."

"What does that mean?" asked Sarah.

"It means the firing squad," replied Halleck.

Three nights later, at twilight, Corporal Isaac Johnson was executed in the street beneath Sarah's window. When the last shots rang out, the tower bell slowly rang. Above its tolling, Sarah thought she heard her lover's voice. It grew louder and louder, telling her to join him in the bell tower.

Sarah rushed out her door and climbed the steps. The air blew fresh and cool against her cheeks. She took the bell cord in her hands.

"I'm coming, Isaac. I'm coming!" she called.

Her lifeless body was found hanging in the tower, the stout bell cord coiled around her neck.

Margaret put aside the newspaper, leaving thumbprints in the ink. She rose from her chair and walked to the window. Stars spangled the sky and a full moon had risen above the treetops, illuminating the cluster of soldiers in the street below. Although the Union troops were bivouacked up on the hill, a night patrol continued to keep guard in the street by Senior Hall. The men's voices rose and fell and now and then broke into laughter.

Margaret lingered for a moment, then turned away. The tower bell began to toll. And the ghost of Sarah June Wheeler, searching for her Rebel, began its ceaseless journey.

Mark Twain, Psychic

St. Louis

The literary father of Tom Sawyer and Huckleberry Finn was a dreamer. How else could one man have created characters so authentic that they have become part of the American experience? The mind of Samuel Clemens, known to all as Mark Twain, roamed continents and centuries to create his fictional narratives.

But Sam Clemens also had nightmares. In one, he foresaw the tragic death of his own brother Henry Clemens.

In 1856, at the age of twenty-one, Sam left Missouri for New Orleans, determined to embark on the next steamer heading to the Southern Hemisphere. He had just finished reading a graphic account of Army Lieutenant William Herndon's 1851 expedition to the Valley of the Amazon, and he dreamed of visiting Peru. Unfortunately for him, but perhaps providential for literary history, no steamboats left New Orleans for that port of call.

With no friends and even less money, Sam turned to a relatively new acquaintance, Captain Horace Bixby, a pilot on the steamer *Paul Jones*, which had brought Sam to New Orleans. Sam had struck up an acquaintance with Bixby on the journey, and the captain had let him take a few turns at the wheel. Now Sam asked his friend to take him on as an apprentice pilot. Bixby agreed—for a fee of five hundred dollars, one hundred of which was to be paid in advance.

Sam steered for Bixby north to St. Louis, where the fledgling apprentice borrowed one hundred dollars from his sister Pamela's husband, William A. Moffett. The balance was to be paid out of Sam's earnings as a cub pilot.

For the next eighteen months, Sam learned the art of piloting a steamboat on the Mississippi River, first with Bixby aboard the *Paul Jones* and later with a pilot named William Brown aboard the *Pennsylvania*.

While apprenticing on the *Pennsylvania*, Sam found a job aboard the steamboat for his brother Henry. It was not nearly as glamorous as life seen from above in the pilothouse and it did not even pay a salary, but Henry was content to be a "mud clerk," a sort of apprentice. The name derived from one of his duties, to secure all the landings, which meant the person ended up in the mud. But there was the promise of promotion, perhaps all the way to first clerk, or purser. Henry signed on early in 1858, his long hours including the time the boat spent in dock at New Orleans or St. Louis, the far ends of its usual Mississippi River run.

Pilots did not have any duties when the steamers lay in port. In St. Louis, Sam stayed with his sister and brotherin-law. Henry usually visited at dusk each evening, returning to the boat later that night. The mud clerk worked from dawn until nightfall seven days a week.

Sam's eerie dream of death came one night before the *Pennsylvania* was scheduled to return to New Orleans. Henry left the family about eleven, more solemn than usual. He shook hands all around, as was the custom. His mother, who was staying with the Moffetts, said good-bye to Henry in the upstairs sitting room. Something made her follow him to the head of the stairs, where she again bade him farewell. Henry's seriousness was unusual, and his mother noticed it.

Sam awoke before dawn the next day with horrifyingly clear pictures from a nightmare he had playing in his mind's eye: his brother was laid out in a metal casket balanced on two chairs in the Moffetts' sitting room. He wore one of Sam's suits. His hands clasped an arrangement of roses to his chest. All the flowers were white, except for one bright red rose in the center.

Sam dressed quickly. Was his brother dead? His dream seemed so real. So real that he avoided the sitting room, where he feared his brother's body lay, and left the house. The cool air bathed his face as he strode down Locust and then onto Fourteenth Street. He suddenly stopped. Henry was not dead, he realized. Of course, it had all been a bad dream, a nightmare. He sprinted back to the house, ran up the stairs, and burst into the sitting room. There was no casket. Although he still felt a chill about what he dreamt, Sam's joy was profound. Yet he could not shake his memory of the dream, even on what turned out to be an uneventful trip downriver from St. Louis to New Orleans.

On that trip, Sam Clemens had an argument with his master, Mr. Brown, that led to his dismissal from the *Pennsylvania* on June 5, 1858.

Fortunately Sam had a backup job in New Orleans for the times when he was forced into idleness between river trips. He worked as night watchman on the freight dock, his pay three dollars for each twelve-hour shift. Henry often joined him on his rounds.

A few days later, the *Pennsylvania* left the port of New Orleans for St. Louis with Henry on board. Sam remained behind.

On June 13, 1858, near Ship Island, a few miles below Memphis, the *Pennsylvania*'s boilers exploded, killing over 250 passengers and crew and seriously injuring three dozen people, including Henry Clemens.

Remarkably, Clemens's loss of his job aboard the steamboat may have saved the life of this future American author.

Sam was on another steamer about a day behind. At the towns they stopped in as they traveled north, he began hearing the news of the explosion aboard the Pennsylvania. But there was little news of the survivors, including, of, course Henry Clemens.

Once he reached Memphis, Sam Clemens worriedly searched for Henry. He finally found him on a mattress in a large Memphis warehouse, which had become a makeshift hospital and morgue. Around him were the burned and maimed survivors of the explosion, the screams of the dying echoing off the high ceilings. Henry had inhaled scalding steam during the explosion and was among the most critically injured. Doctors and nurses, forced to pay more attention to those they thought would live, told Sam that Henry's scorched lungs gave him little chance of survival.

One of them, a Dr. Peyton, however, promised Sam he would take a special interest in Henry and try to save him. Miraculously, Henry responded to treatment. Within a week Henry Clemens was pronounced out of danger. However, Peyton warned Sam that his brother still needed much rest and must stay where he was. While Sam sat with his brother one evening, the cries of the injured were particularly disturbing to Henry. Dr. Peyton ordered a small amount of morphine for Henry to help him sleep.

Henry did not live to see the next sunrise.

The young physician on duty, whether due to a misunderstanding of Dr. Peyton's instructions or the lack of measuring devices, administered too much morphine. Young Henry Clemens died within a few hours.

His body was carried into what was called the "dead room" and placed in the only metal coffin available, a gift from some wealthy Memphis women. That is where Sam found him. At once the dream he had weeks before in St. Louis came back to him in perfect detail. Henry even was dressed in one of the suits Sam had given him. As Sam stood near the casket, an elderly woman walked in and placed a bouquet of roses in the dead boy's hands. They were white—with a single red rose at the center.

Sam Clemens took passage accompanying his brother's body back to St. Louis. When the boat docked, he set off for his brotherin-law's office, hoping to find him there, as the business day had just begun. Sam missed him, however, and by the time he got back to the boat, Moffett had already been there, recovered the body, and had it sent on to his own house.

Sam raced ahead, wanting to save his mother the trauma of viewing Henry's morphine-twisted face. Undertakers made little effort to make corpses presentable in that era; wakes and funerals were often held in the home.

He arrived just in time to forestall the unloading while he went inside to comfort his mother. Upstairs in the sitting room, he found two chairs spaced a coffin's length apart, waiting to receive their burden. If he had arrived a few minutes later, the casket would have been positioned on them, the final detail of his prophetic dream fulfilled.

This premonition of death stayed with Samuel Clemens for the rest of his life. Even as a very old man, more than fifty years after Henry's ghastly death, he could still remember every detail of the nightmare—and its tragic, real-life counterpart.

Forever Mine

Kirksville

Henry Burchard and his wife, Harriet, were inseparable, she saw to that. She thought her farmer-husband was "too handsome for his own good," as she put it. Harriet saved him from the lures of prettier women by accompanying him everywhere he went. Henry reacted with amused tolerance, although sometimes he complained that he could not even go out on the back stoop to cut a plug of tobacco without Harriet's banging through the door after him.

Henry had never been unfaithful to his wife. She simply was born a jealous woman. He did have the conversational habit of looking a person directly in the eye, and women usually responded warmly to such attention. He believed it was common courtesy, although an oversensitive husband observing his own wife speaking to Henry might have had other words for it.

Just after the couple celebrated their thirtieth wedding anniversary, Harriet Burchard got sick and died of consumption. Henry was shocked and saddened by his wife's death, but he recalled her words, "Man was not meant to live alone."

So five months after Harriet's death, Henry married Catherine Webster, a pretty young widow whom he and Harriet had known for several years. After the death of her husband in a farm accident, Catherine had rented out the farm and moved to town, where she lived on her rental income and some small savings.

Three weeks after her marriage to Henry, Catherine was home alone when a tremendous crash that sounded like large rocks clattering across the metal roof shook the very foundation of the house. Catherine dashed outside. Sure enough, rocks of all sizes lay strewn everywhere. Where had they come from?

The nearest neighbor was half a mile away down the dirt road. Catherine gathered up her long skirts and picked her way across the rocks and around the farmhouse. She saw no one.

Then, to her amazement, the rocks at her feet rose slowly into the cloudless sky, hovered above the rooftop, and cascaded over the shingles again.

The poor woman, too frightened to move, stood rigid, her hands shielding her face.

That night when Henry arrived home from work in town, Catherine related what had happened. He told her it was nonsense, just her imagination, that she was just tired and overwrought from the excitement of the wedding. They went outside to look, but the rocks had disappeared. Only clumps of coarse grass edged the foundation. Catherine was more alarmed than ever.

The next night, while the couple slept, their sheets and blankets were snatched away. Shivering in his nightshirt, Henry leaped up to find them heaped on the floor at the foot of the bed. Catherine had slept through it.

Henry put the bedding back on the bed and crawled in. No sooner had he fallen asleep than he was again awakened to find the covers on the floor. Catherine still lay unmoving, her eyes closed, her long hair spread like a fan across her silk pillow. Henry thought it unlikely that she had kicked off the bedding, unless, of course, she was punishing him for not believing her story of the rocks.

He remade the bed with Catherine in it, taking care this time to tuck in the quilts quite tightly. Now, they could not easily be thrown off.

Eventually, Henry got back to sleep, only to awaken a third time, when his pillow was ripped out from under his head. He found it on the floor. He got up and lit a lantern just as Catherine's pillow flew out from beneath her head and landed at Henry's feet. Her head fell back against the mattress and she woke up, screaming.

Henry stared, speechless and powerless to prevent this mayhem. What had jerked the pillows from under their heads? Putting down the lantern, he sat on the edge of the bed and took his wife in his arms.

She looked up at him, sleep still in her eyes, apparently unaware of what had been going on.

"But Henry, why are you up?"

He would not frighten her. "You were restless," he began. "I thought maybe you were having a nightmare. You . . . you . . . threw your pillow on the floor." He handed it to her.

"I don't remember," she murmured.

"No," he sighed. "But now it's very late and we both need sleep." Henry tucked the covers tightly around his wife, extinguished the lantern, and crawled back into bed.

Daylight could come none too soon, Henry thought as he drifted off to sleep.

The mysterious events of that night recurred and Henry, who was not able to explain them, tried to forget. Yet he always woke up when the bedding and his pillow were jerked from the bed. Catherine, on the other hand, usually slept on. He envied her for that.

Then came the night Henry would never forget. Unable to sleep, he was in bed reading by dim lamplight. Catherine slept soundly beside him. Suddenly, a piece of the bedding rolled back. A handwritten message was scrawled on the underside of the white coverlet:

"These things shall continue forever."

The handwriting was that of his first wife, Harriet Burchard.

The Curious Visitors

Ste. Genevieve

Night was coming on as Jules Felix Valle lay back against his bed pillows. He was in the process of recuperating from difficult surgery to remove one of his eyes, which he had injured many years before in a boxing match. Jules was surprisingly upbeat about the loss. He thought that he had much to be grateful for.

Along with his wife, Anne-Marie, who was nearly thirty years his junior, Jules lived in one of Ste. Genevieve's most historic homes—the circa 1806 Creole-French inspired Guibourd House at One North Fourth Street. Jules had retired from business in St. Louis and bought the charming home in 1935. The couple devoted long hours to restoring the interior to its original state, filling the rooms with seventeenth- and eighteenth-century antiques. The home's elegant gardens enclosed by century-old brick walls were being returned to their original grandeur. Jules's roots in the community ran long and deep—he was a descendant of François Vallé, the first civil and military commander of Ste. Genevieve.

On this night, a light breeze coming in through an open window carried the sweet, heavy fragrance of honeysuckle from the verdant gardens.

He was nearly asleep when he felt a tap on his shoulder. Careful not to disturb his bandages, he turned to see what it was his wife wanted.

Instead of seeing Anne-Marie bending down to speak with him, Jules faced three small old men dressed in heavy woolen shirts hovering beside his bed, nodding and smiling at him but not making any sound at all. They looked rather like French voyageurs. And they were floating there because their bodies ended, simply faded away, at their waistlines. He saw right through them and to the wallpaper on the far side of the room.

Jules found that he was not a bit frightened, really only perplexed as to who these incomplete visitors might be and why they were standing next to his bed on that summer night in 1939, about four years after he and Anne-Marie moved into the Guibourd House.

For lack of a sensible answer, he smiled back at them, perfectly willing to accept that they very well might be the ghosts of earlier house tenants come back to pay a visit.

When Jules told his wife the next morning about the three men, the couple suspected that their sudden appearance probably was intertwined somehow with the long and colorful history of their home and that of Ste. Genevieve itself, the oldest town in Missouri.

Creole families from present-day Illinois crossed the Mississippi River in 1750 to establish farms in the rich bottomlands, and a settlement that would become Ste. Genevieve was soon established. In 1763 the Treaty of Paris assigned the territory west of the Mississippi River to Spain. Ste. Genevieve became a reluctant outpost of the Spanish empire. A garrison was established, but regular troops were stationed there only at intervals. Then in 1803, Ste. Genevieve and all of Missouri was acquired by the United States in the Louisiana Purchase. In 1812 the village was included as part of the Missouri Territory.

La Maison de Guibourd, or the Guibourd House, dates to about 1806, and perhaps earlier. The belief is that Jacques Dubreuil Guibourd, a native of Angers, France, built it. Guibourd ended up in the French colony of Saint Domingue (now Haiti) working as a secretary to a wealthy planter. During the slave insurrection there in August 1791, Guibourd was saved from certain death by his valet, Moros, who sealed Guibourd inside a large keg that was then carried on board a ship bound for France.

Guibourd arrived back in Europe only to face the perils arising from the French Revolution. Somehow he made his way across the Atlantic to Philadelphia, where he met French merchants from the village of Ste.

Genevieve who were there to buy supplies. Delighted to find men with whom he could communicate, Guibourd decided to accompany them back to Ste. Genevieve. The records are not clear, but it seems Guibourd (and his valet Moros too, apparently) lost his possessions and what money he had either when his ship to America capsized or they were robbed somewhere on his way to Missouri. At any rate, he arrived in Ste. Genevieve penniless but within a few years was able to regain his fortune enough to build the home that still bears his name, establish a business, and start a family. He loved the little French community from the moment he saw it.

Guibourd married Ursula Barbeau, daughter of the commander at Prairie du Rocher, the French fort across the river, and the sister of Jules Valle's great-grandfather. The house remained in the Guibourd family until it was sold in 1906 to Clovis Boyer.

Jules and Anne-Marie Valle knew little of the Guibourd or Boyer families. They did recall that two of Guibourd's descendants had been associated with tragedies in the house. A woman named Miss Victorine, whom everyone called Miss Vickie, died in the bedroom occupied by Anne-Marie. One of Miss Vickie's brothers, a doctor, committed suicide in the house following a bank failure.

After Jules Valle's eye operation and the appearance of the three little men, Anne-Marie looked further into the possibility that their house was haunted and invited her friend, who also happened to be a psychic, to visit them. Anne-Marie was intrigued with the house's long history, the two tragedies associated with it, and Jules's visitors.

The psychic's name was Elizabeth Heins. The first order of business, she said, would be to take a walking tour around the property. She concluded that Spanish had been spoken there. The Valles thought it likely as the location of the house made it not inconceivable that Spanish civilians or soldiers might have been quartered there during the town's brief time under the Spanish flag.

Perhaps the men Jules saw were not French voyageurs at all but Spanish *viajeros.*

Anne-Marie was not concerned by her husband's story because she had felt presences throughout the house ever since they moved in. The little men were only the most recent in a long line of eerie episodes.

For instance, Anne-Marie once employed Dora Williams, a conscientious maid with a delightful personality who soon developed a close bond with Anne-Marie. Dora went quietly about her work each day, and at night returned to her private quarters, which were upstairs in the rear portion of the house; this area had originally been the slave quarters.

Dora passed away unexpectedly. Soon after her death, Anne-Marie heard footfalls overhead and knew instinctively they were Dora's. She heard them only once, but various other housekeepers who worked in the house in the years to follow noticed them as well.

The Valles owned several dogs over their nearly forty years there. The canines seemed keenly aware that an extra presence might be about. Dusky the Scottish terrier sometimes cowered with fear and whined and scratched to get outdoors. While that may not seem unusual for a dog, Anne-Marie found it to be out of character for this terrier, normally not afraid of anything or anyone. She thought maybe he encountered the home's animal spirits.

Then there was a dog they owned called Jamie, a playful collie who acted as if he were seeing another dog in the house. That happened as he stood at the living room door and growled softly, as he always did when strange dogs got too close. Yet his tail hung straight down, wagging slowly to signal friendship.

There may have been a reason for the collie's behavior. Before acquiring Jamie, Anne-Marie owned another collie called Peter, who died of old age. She thought it might be his ghost that Jamie saw. The idea was bolstered because a family friend who had been extremely fond of Peter was a houseguest not long after the dog died. Jamie first behaved strangely when the guest visited that time. Anne-Marie thought that Jamie was seeing the ghost of Peter, who had come back, she thought, to say hello.

Despite all that went on during the Valles' tenancy, Anne-Marie was never truly frightened until one early March night in 1949. Jules had died of a heart ailment at the age of sixty-six two months earlier. Anne-Marie was living in the house alone. On that March night, she was jolted out of bed by loud banging and crashing coming from Jules's old bedroom. It was as if heavy furniture was being picked up and heaved against the walls; the whole house shook under the impact. Then Anne-Marie heard what seemed to be buckets of glass being poured on the polished bare wooden floor of his bedroom. She thought surely every lamp and picture had been smashed yet knew instinctively that was not possible.

"Listen to me, whoever or whatever you are!" Anne-Marie called out, pulling the blankets up to her chin. "You are not going to frighten me! You are not going to drive me from my home! Now, get out!"

The commotion stopped, and she went back to sleep. The fresh day brought great relief. The bedroom furnishings were all intact; not one piece had been moved. A quick search showed nothing in the house had been disturbed.

What had Anne-Marie Valle heard?

Poltergeists were intending to take over the house. She always maintained that if she had succumbed to fear, they would have done just that.

Anne-Marie Valle lived in the house until her own death in 1971. Jules left his entire estate to her. She is said to have never been happy in Ste. Genevieve, but the terms of her wealthy husband's will required that she remain in her adopted town.

After Anne-Marie's death, the house was donated to the Foundation for Restoration of Ste. Genevieve to be turned into a museum, which it has been for nearly fifty years.

But the uncanny at the Jacques Guibourd Historic House, as it is now known, did not end with Mrs. Valle's death.

Kristine Basler, a Ste. Genevieve native, was a manager at the house about a decade later. Although Basler did not live in the house, the ghosts that frequented Jules and Anne-Marie Valle let her know they were still around in the most unusual circumstances.

On an especially cold December afternoon, Basler was in the cellar fleshing deer hides. To flesh a hide is to clean it of all remaining flesh; it is done on what's called a fleshing beam. She was working on hides that would then be made into buckskin worn by some of the reenactors at the Jour de Fête, a celebration held the second full weekend of August each year to commemorate the early French settlement days.

Basler had just finished cleaning her fifth hide when she heard music coming from upstairs—a classical baroque tune played on what sounded like a piano or a harpsichord.

The same piece was played over and over several times. Basler said it was like a child practicing for a recital.

She got up and walked toward the front of the house, but the music stopped abruptly. Basler resumed her work.

Suddenly, a man's voice shouted, "Hey!"

This time Basler dashed upstairs, looked around, and took a quick peek out the front window toward the street. She confirmed that no one else was in the house or outside nearby.

Everything was in order. The sidewalks and streets were empty. Later she learned that the Boyer family who owned the house before the Valles were musical, and the mother was said to be a pianist.

About a year later, Basler moved into the two-story rear portion of the house that was originally the slaves' quarters. After she was settled in, she acquired an original RCA Victrola that turned on and off by itself while the heavy discs spun faster and faster when she attempted to play them. The vibrations shook even a nearby box of the heavy records. The phenomenon generally stopped as abruptly as it had started.

Anne-Marie Valle had owned a Victrola at one time.

Basler said that at certain times and in certain places she believed the house gave off "bad vibes." She felt ill at ease in Jules's bedroom; if it was after dark she did not go in at all. She knew that some thought there might be poltergeists, so she had never slept in Anne-Marie's bed. She tried sleeping in the attic, which had housed the former slave and maid's quarters, but she scrambled back down into her own bed a couple of hours into the experiment because she felt too uncomfortable there.

Like many houses alleged to be haunted, the Guibourd House also displayed electrical problems.

One night a bulb in the dining room chandelier blinked off while Basler was sitting in the room. Thinking the bulb was loose, she got up to tighten it. Before she even touched the bulb, it lit up and the bulb next to it went out.

Sometimes an illuminated light seemed to quickly blink somewhere just out of her range of sight. Yet she is not entirely certain it was just a light flickering.

"It was more like a shadow passing by," she said. Much the same might be said of all the ghosts at the Guibourd House.

Nebraska

Miss Anna

Hastings

Hastings, Nebraska, is a pleasant city of some twenty-five thousand residents. Within its city limits, one finds Hastings College, some half-dozen tree-shaded parks, the site of the Adams County Fair, and the Hastings Museum, noteworthy for a fine natural history collection, frontier memorabilia, and a small planetarium. The town is situated in the south-central part of the state, about twenty miles south of Interstate 80.

The people of Hastings are not given to pretension or hyperbole, thus their belief in events of an alleged supernatural origin is not intense, if it is there at all.

The story of Burton Nelson, a lifelong resident of Hastings who described himself as the "fairly stable" father of four sons, is even more remarkable because of this general local skepticism. He may have been the only man in Hastings to have seen a ghost *and* been willing to talk about it.

One day in 1962, Burton Nelson awoke in the early morning hours to a thunderstorm. His wife slept next to him. He was surprised to see a woman standing in their room next to their infant's crib. She was turned away from him and yet he could see she was patting the baby's back.

She was quite distinct with a "white misty form." Just like a real person. Except for one thing. Nelson could see right through her to the wall behind.

She turned her head toward him and smiled. He smiled back.

Nelson was not afraid. When the woman looked at him, her wan smile somehow made him understand that she was not there to harm anyone.

And then most extraordinarily of all, this sad woman seemed to start communicating with Nelson but not in an audible way. It was like he could read her thoughts.

It was in this way that Burton learned she had lived in this very house during the 1930s and loved babies, but she herself had never married. Her greatest regret was not having any children of her own. Her name was Anna C. Peterson and she had worked at Mary Lanning Hospital in Hastings.

"It never entered my mind to be scared or to wake up my wife next to me, that's the crazy part of it," said Nelson.

"She was a quiet, private, lonely woman who loved babies," he said, and that was all he learned about Miss Anna, as he called her, though he got the feeling she had either taken her own life or died in less than happy circumstances.

She was a "nice-looking lady," Nelson thought, probably in her late thirties or early forties. She was of medium height with a stocky build but not overweight. Her brown hair was done up in a bun. She had on a green uniform with dark stockings and heavy, black, oxford-type shoes.

"She smiled and seemed to radiate kindness and love," said Nelson. "I felt comfortable with her. In fact I thought that if anything was ever to go wrong in that house she would be the first to tell me."

But the ghost never actually *said* a single word, nor did Burton Nelson initiate a conversation of any sort.

The next morning, Nelson thought it had all been some sort of weird dream and told his wife all about it. The more they hashed over the details—and there were many—the more they realized it was not a dream. He recalled a passing car on the rain-slicked street, for instance, and the ticking of an alarm clock.

Nelson decided to keep a pencil and paper in the kitchen to record the event should Miss Anna show up again. He would be certain he was not dreaming, as he would have to walk through the living room and into the kitchen to get to his writing material.

He did not have to wait long.

No more than a week after her first visit, something woke up Nelson at about the same hour of the morning. It was raining outside. Miss Anna was standing by the crib, once again stroking the baby's back.

The baby had been restless earlier in the evening.

"It was obvious to me that she was trying to soothe him back to sleep," Nelson said.

He climbed out of bed and went to the kitchen table to write in his journal all that was happening and how he felt about it. When he got back to the bedroom, Miss Anna was gone, and the baby was sleeping soundly.

Burton Nelson never saw Miss Anna again, but his quest to discover her identity had just begun.

The Nelson family moved to another house shortly after Miss Anna's final appearance. Burton Nelson pushed the incidents to the back of his mind for several years, but he could not help wondering if there was any connection between the woman who had "identified" herself as Anna C. Peterson and an actual woman who may have lived, and perhaps died, in Hastings, maybe even in the very house to which she seemed attached.

Nelson decided to start a search for her at the Adams County Historical Society. He told the librarians he was doing family research because he thought they might be suspicious of someone looking up a ghost's lineage.

He began by scanning city directories for her name, beginning with those from the early twentieth century. His efforts were soon rewarded.

He found an Anna C. Peterson listed in a 1930s city directory. She had lived in the Nelsons' former house between the years of 1935 and 1937, though it is possible she had lived there longer, as city directories were only published every two years in that era. The information he could find on her was spotty. She changed addresses several times. Nelson did not find a telephone listing for her, indicating perhaps that she rented rooms and shared a telephone with others.

During the 1920s, Anna's occupations were listed variously as a store clerk, laundress, and finally a mangle operator at the Mary Lanning Hospital laundry. A mangle is the machine commercial launderers use to press clothes after they have been cleaned.

Nelson could not find any trace of Anna in city records after 1939 nor could he locate an obituary for her. He looked through city cemetery records but found no grave listed. He assumes she may have been from another small town in Nebraska and, if she had died in Hastings, might have been buried in her hometown.

Nelson went to the Mary Lanning Hospital personnel office to inquire about employment records dating to the 1920s and 1930s only to be told they had been thrown out years before. However, Nelson was in for a stroke of luck when he was told of a retired hospital employee who had worked at Mary Lanning during the years Anna Peterson had been employed there.

"She remembered Miss Peterson quite well," said Burton Nelson. "Anna was a quiet, shy, reserved person who worked right alongside this retired employee."

The retired laundry woman described Anna in almost the same detail as Nelson had seen her on those late-night visits, right down to the green uniform, dark stockings, and black shoes. Her hair was long but she kept it up in a bun for safety around the laundry room machinery.

Nelson then asked if the retired hospital worker remembered when Anna died.

The woman thought it had been in the late 1930s when she was still fairly young, but no one seemed to want to talk about it, she told Nelson.

"Something was not quite right, but yet she couldn't tell me exactly what," said Nelson. "I asked if she might have taken her own life, but she said she couldn't really say for sure. I got the feeling she knew more than she was ever going to tell me."

The old lady told Nelson that the thought of Anna C. Peterson dying young and childless still made her sad.

Where Miss Anna came from, and where she died, remains a mystery. Apparently she never married, or at least there is no record of her taking a husband. It was obvious to Nelson that she had affection for babies. Today Miss Anna might well have become a single parent by adopting a child. In the 1930s, of course, that would have been virtually unheard of for an unmarried woman who would have been considered a spinster without prospects after she reached a certain age.

Why did Miss Anna's ghost linger in the Nelsons' home? Could her affection for their baby have hinted about something in her past, perhaps the detail her former coworker held back when she talked about Anna's life? Could she have become pregnant out of wedlock? No man wanted to call her his wife, but that would not have stopped someone from taking advantage of a trusting and genial disposition. If someone did father her baby, then what? There is no record of her ever having married. Did she move far away and have the child? Did she, or her baby, die in childbirth? Did something else happen to baby and mother? Or was it simply her unfulfilled desire for children that brought her back to her old home?

This woman who led such a seemingly simple life left many complicated questions unanswered.

Terror of Omaha Heights

Omaha

Irish coffee laced with gossip. That is what an invitation from Bridget O'Hanlon always implied, and Henrietta Hale was looking forward to a pleasant afternoon with her friend. She had no way of knowing how terrifying the visit would turn out to be.

Dried leaves crackled underfoot and the wind tugged at her shawl as Henrietta hurried along the streets of Omaha Heights on that November day. Bridget saw her friend coming down the street and threw open the door.

"Sure, and begorra, Henny, you're looking fit! Do come in!" Bridget said, helping Henrietta with her shawl and bonnet. Then Bridget added abruptly, "Now I've got some work to finish, but I won't be long." With that she turned and slipped back up the staircase.

Henrietta knew Bridget as well-meaning but distracted, often leaving her guests to fend for themselves for an hour or more while she finished a chore in another part of the house. Casual acquaintances thought her rude, but Henrietta and her other close friends learned to be tolerant of her eccentric, sometimes disconcerting ways.

Henrietta went directly to the sitting room at the rear of the house and settled into a Morris chair by the windows. No sooner had she sat down than she heard a knock at the front door. Was another visitor expected? Bridget had not mentioned it.

She listened a moment for Bridget's steps on the stairs. When she did not hear her friend coming down, she went to the door herself. No one was there. She closed the door, but before she could lift her hand from the knob, the knocking outside came again, more insistent than before. Henrietta opened it a second time.

She looked up and down the street, which, at this hour, was deserted. Unable to account for the sounds, she shut the door and returned to the sitting room.

A moment later, the pounding on the front door shook the walls of the house.

Quite upset by now with these nonsensical interruptions, Henrietta bolted from the chair and peered cautiously around the doorjamb before stepping into the hallway. This time the front door stood wide open; a few leaves even had blown in and lay on the carpet. At the same time, she heard heavy footsteps behind her coming from the sitting room where she had just been. When she turned to close the front door, it slammed shut on its own.

Then the cacophony began—footfalls seemed to reverberate from nearly every room, the front parlor, the kitchen, the bedrooms. Everywhere there were the sounds of tramping feet. The dining room chairs rose and crashed against the walls, and agonizing groans and cries rose from the cellar under the kitchen.

Henrietta Hale stood trembling in the hallway.

Portraits in heavy frames on the wall opposite her fell to the floor, spraying shards of glass into the air. Terrified, fearing the imminent collapse of the house, she screamed and fled out the back door. She hiked up her long skirts and ran for her life. Fiendish yells from inside the house followed her as she raced down the street and to the safety of her own home.

That evening Bridget O'Hanlon and her husband, John, called on

Henrietta. Bridget carried a pot of Irish coffee and her apologies to her friend.

She confessed that she, too, heard the commotion that afternoon but had been too frightened to come downstairs. And when the walls started to shake, she had hidden under the bed until her husband got home. Henrietta was none too pleased to have been abandoned to fend for herself.

John O'Hanlon apologized and picked up the events then and said he knew the source of the terrifying ordeal Henrietta had gone through.

Five years earlier, when repairs were being made on the house, a human skeleton was discovered in the cellar. It was suspected that a peddler had been murdered, his remains dumped in a makeshift grave beneath the kitchen. Shortly after the body was found, the household disturbances began. Few families remained long in the house.

When the O'Hanlons bought the house, John hired Eddie Warner, a painter, to do some redecorating. Warner worked half a day, and then quit because of the strange noises. His successor, Frank Hitchcock, did not stay much longer than a day.

Bridget said she and John would be moving out of the house the next day. Although they had heard raps on the front door and footsteps on the stairs now and then, recent events like that which had transpired that afternoon had become more terrifying.

John and Bridget O'Hanlon invited Henrietta Hale back for a farewell cup of Irish coffee the next day, but she had scarcely recovered from her ordeal.

She sent her regrets.

Beware the Soddy

Phelps County

Late one summer evening, two farmers were heading home from a board meeting at Phelps Center. Both men had spent the daylight hours cultivating corn on their own farms, and now they nursed their weariness in silence on the rough wagon seat. The owner of the wagon had left his double-shovel plow in the wagon box. It clattered from side to side as the wagon bounced over ruts along the trail.

On a lonely lane half a mile south of the present-day village of Funk, an empty sod house on an abandoned farm sat forlornly by the side of the road. Its owner had been driven out by the devastating grasshopper plague of 1874. As the men's farm wagon crawled past the empty farmstead, the two farmers thought they heard screams coming from within the soddy. Their hair stood on end.

Their two horses spooked, then snapped their traces and bolted. The wagon ripped loose and flew at an angle so fast that the wheels nearly tore from the axles. The men were hurled into a field but were able to get up and limp home. The horses had beaten them there and paced nervously outside the barn.

In the morning, neighbors found the wagon in a ditch with the rear wheels crushed. The plow was located behind the soddy. The two farmers never could explain the weird cries or their harrowing experience, but the no-nonsense people of the area did not question their story. They knew the farmers were not given to wild tales.

As word of the haunted soddy spread—and few doubted that this was what the men had encountered—no one traveled that lane again after dark. Even during daylight hours people usually took another route to avoid it.

Nothing much else happened until a few years later when a bachelor named Larson rented the abandoned farm and moved into the soddy. A pleasant man with a ready smile and a firm handshake, he made friends quickly. Neighbors warned Larson that the soddy was haunted.

"I can live with ghosts," Larson chuckled. "They might even be welcome companions on long winter evenings."

Larson worked the farm with diligence, planting, cultivating, and harvesting each crop in its time. He ignored the stories of the haunted soddy and got to work fixing up the place. He replaced the rotted leather hinges on the door, squared the rough window frames, and sealed up cracks in the earthen blocks. The rhythm of the seasons ordered Larson's life in a calm and predictable fashion. He was making that old soddy into a real nice home.

Then one summer night he had the strangest dream.

He was running across a barren expanse of prairie, a herd of wild mustangs thundering after him. There was no tree to climb, no shack to duck into. He screamed, but only the wind answered. Just before the horses caught up to him he caught his boot in a prairie dog hole and fell. He was certain the weight of the wild animals would crush him.

At that moment, Larson awoke in a cold sweat in his own bed. He could not recall a nightmare more vivid or frightening; he felt absolutely paralyzed. Sitting up on the edge of his bed, he rubbed life back into his arms and legs.

But at that moment, he heard the galloping horses again, only this time they seemed directly outside, thundering toward the soddy. His nightmare had come to life. The walls and floor vibrated as the beasts whinnied and circled.

Larson, steadying himself on tables and chairs, carefully made his way to the door and cracked it open. A full moon hung in the sky and a soft breeze murmured in the cottonwoods. He stepped cautiously out onto the grass stubble.

There were no horses outside the soddy, no hoofprints.

Larson wondered if he was losing his mind. How could he have imagined something so very vivid?

The next night he stayed up, drinking coffee and pacing the floor—waiting for the horses. Again they came. He could not see them, but he heard them stomping around the soddy. Again he cracked open the door before opening it fully. There was nothing in sight to account for the commotion.

Night after night the horses returned. Night after night Larson woke at their noisy arrival. Bur then a new sound filled the house, a low cooing like that of mourning doves. He never heard it in the daytime, only at night when he tried to sleep. It almost sounded like it was coming from within the earthen walls. And so he rapped and he probed but he found the walls solid and still no apparent source for any of the racket now nearly overwhelming his sensibilities.

A night's sleep was becoming impossible. A new dimension was added to the tumult. At night he would wake up to find all his bedding piled up on the floor; during the day doors between rooms were thrown open and banged shut by something unseen. Larson's eyes grew puffy from

241

sleeplessness and he jumped whenever a bird sang in the treetop. He was neglecting his crops and animals. His neighbors meeting him in the village noted the change that had come over him. *Is there anything wrong?* they inquired. He shook his head.

By the start of the next planting season Larson had fled. Weeds and shrubs took over the fields behind the soddy.

The next—and last—tenant was also a bachelor. His name was Nels, a giant of a man afraid of neither men nor beasts, real or imagined. He liked nothing better than to sit in the gathering dusk and play his violin after a long day of fieldwork. When he first moved in, a couple of neighbors stopped by to warn him of what happened to farmer Larson and the weird goings-on in and around the soddy. Nels listened attentively and snapped his red suspenders.

"We drink!" he said with a grin as wide as the Platte River. Sitting in the sun of the open doorway, the three men drank and discussed the crops and the weather.

Before the visitors went home, they knew that once again they had a fine new friend living in the soddy. They hoped Nels would stay and prosper.

Like his predecessor, Nels worked the farm with care and made more improvements in the house. Things went well for the first few months. Then one night, just before crawling into bed, Nels glanced out a window. He caught his breath, rubbed his eyes, and looked again. A huge fire burned in the barnyard, the flames leaping higher than the tallest cottonwood.

Nels felt his stomach tighten and pain shoot down his spine. The barn would go up in flames and with it his stock—a few cows, the team of oxen, and a horse. Then he saw that the flames had not yet reached the front of the barn. Maybe he could get to the barn door and save the horse at least.

He dashed out, his nightshirt flapping in the cool night air, and with both hands he pulled open the heavy barn door. There was no heat from flames; no acrid smoke filled his nostrils. The flames he saw did not crackle.

There was no fire.

Cows, oxen, horse slept contentedly. Nels sagged against the door as he looked around. There was no sign of a fire anywhere.

His eye caught the glitter of a gold piece in the dirt. Where did that come from? What good fortune! He bent over to pick it up, then saw it was nothing but an old, rusted, two-cent piece. He took it back to the house anyway.

Nels brewed a fresh pot of coffee and sat up the remainder of the night pondering the significance of the phenomenon he had witnessed.

He had seen the fire with his own eyes, but how had it disappeared? Why had it not scorched the earth and the barn siding? Perhaps it was not a fire. But then, what was it?

Finally, exhausted and without answers, he eased back into bed and fell asleep.

The mysterious fires continued to erupt every week or two, lighting up the night sky. And each time Nels rushed outside, the flames vanished before his eyes.

Late on a November night, when hoarfrost powdered the corn stubble and winds tore the last fluttering leaves from the trees, Nels became even more apprehensive.

Normally an easy-going, relaxed man, he realized how much he had changed since the fires started. Now there was something new welling up inside him, a feeling he had never felt before, a feeling that seemed against his very nature—the feeling of dread. Nels was lightheaded, and his hands trembled. He decided he was getting sick and went to bed early for several nights in a row.

Early one morning, he was jarred awake by violin music, wild and savage notes pouring out of the corners and walls. Nels struggled out of bed and lit a lantern. On the floor against the far wall his violin stood upright, the bow moving deftly and expertly by itself over the strings.

He started to walk over to it, but a force of some kind held him back. It was as if he were pushing against a solid wall to cross his very own living room.

Dropping onto the edge of the bed, Nels swung his head down between his knees to keep from fainting. The playing continued, swinging from one tune into the next.

Nels did not remember going back to sleep. The last piece he recalled hearing was "The Little Old Sod Shanty on the Claim," a song written in 1871 and popular with Great Plains settlers.

At dawn, Nels stretched himself awake and laughed heartily at his nightmare of the previous evening. It had seemed so real, like the nightmares he used to have as a child.

He got up to make his coffee but stopped short.

His beautiful violin lay on the floor in the same spot where he last remembered seeing it played.

The instrument's case stood open in the corner. Nels felt sick to his stomach. It had not been a nightmare after all.

He put the violin away and locked the case. Then he threaded the key onto a thin piece of leather and draped it around his neck. Now nothing could get at the instrument without breaking the lock or smashing the case.

Or so he thought.

Nels was again awakened that very night by the chilling music. He groped for the metal key on his improvised necklace. It was there, still secure. He knew then that whatever was plaguing him had smashed the case to get at the fiddle.

At dawn's first light, Nels found the violin on the floor. But the case was locked and showed no signs of having been tampered with.

Nels moved out that afternoon. Before he left, he told his neighbors what had happened to him. They all believed him and wished him well.

The soddy and the farmstead were abandoned and fell into ruin.

The Bates House

Dakota City

It was past midnight on that fall evening in 1879 when Benjamin Brill drove his gig toward Dakota City. As he passed the abandoned Bates House Hotel, he saw a glow in a second-story window. Strange, he thought. That place had not been used in many years. Bats and owls were its only tenants.

Brill stopped. As he gazed at the odd light, it wavered and moved from room to room, each window alternating bright and dark as it passed. Its bluish cast was unlike any light the man had ever seen.

He got out of his carriage, picked his way through the brush, and pushed open the heavy front door.

He called out, "Hello!"

Silence.

Again he tried to rouse someone inside. "Hello! Anyone here?"

A staircase loomed before him, its treads broken, and the banister cracked and hanging askew. Once the Bates House had been the pride of Nebraska Territory, the place where the United States District Court met each spring and fall. But time and vandals had erased all evidence of its early grandeur.

Brill shoved bullets into his revolver just to be on the safe side. Then, looking anxiously around him, he carefully picked his way up the staircase. In the hall at the end of the landing burned the ball of blue light he had seen through the window.

From somewhere else arose distant piano music—like sad notes in a minor key. Brill stopped to listen. There was something chilling, otherworldly about it. Like a sudden cold wind, it came from nowhere and yet everywhere and settled into his very bones.

At that moment, a being—for that is the only way he could describe it—swathed in a flowing, white robe crossed the landing. It carried a lamp.

Brill felt his scalp prickle. At first, he thought it was a real person. But then standing at the head of the landing, he watched it sweep in and out of every room on that top floor.

It seemed to be searching for something, moving in rhythm with the sad piano music. Brill, more fascinated than fearful, called to the figure. But it brushed past him, unseeing, intent solely on its own perplexing mission.

The figure slipped into a room near Brill, glided across the floor, and hovered in a corner. Meanwhile in the hallway, the blue light Brill had seen once again appeared, bouncing like a rubber ball up and down the corridor. Each time it reached a point a few feet above the floor, it emitted a sort of wail. Then as if by prearranged signal, the robed person in the room kneeled, then sank prostrate to the floor. The light paused at the doorway, wailing and trembling in the air.

Benjamin Brill stood against the opposite wall. He pulled the revolver from its holster, his finger closing on the trigger.

As the light in the doorway floated into the room, Brill followed and peered around the doorjamb. The ball of light changed into a slender taper. As he watched, it materialized into a being identical in every way to the other, also clothed in a long, white garment. The one who had been prostrate on the floor rose and the two stood side by side. They swept out of the room, past a startled Brill, and on down the hallway.

At the far end of the hall, both figures this time sank to the floor and chanted. The hairs on Brill's neck bristled. When he saw them rise and head down the dark end of the hallway, he turned to follow. But it was too late. They had vanished. He staggered outside.

Benjamin Brill sat in his rig, gazing blankly up at the hotel, a derelict hulk limned by moonlight. He heard no sound from anywhere, not even the whisper of wind in the trees as he snapped the whip and was off. The strange blue orb throbbed behind a sagging windowpane, until it too was gone.

A Strange Interlude

Lincoln

On October 3, 1963, a secretary at Nebraska Wesleyan University in Lincoln who had lived an entirely uneventful life experienced one of the most intriguing cases of psychic phenomena ever reported on a college campus.

Colleen Buterbaugh opened a door and stepped back in time. Although for only less than a minute, she saw the campus as it had looked decades before.

The event transformed her from a peppy, lively, and outgoing wife and mother into a much more somber person, those who knew her said, one who never fully recovered from the ordeal of her experience.

On a bright October morning just before nine o'clock, Colleen Buterbaugh, a secretary to the dean, got up from her desk in Old Main clutching a fistful of telephone messages she had accumulated since the previous day. As was her daily routine this semester, she was to deliver the notes to Dr. Thomas McCourt, a popular and engaging Scottish visiting music professor who was spending the fall on campus. The notes Buterbaugh held were from students asking for appointments, or campus and community groups seeking a dynamic guest speaker about a range of topics from Scottish history to contemporary music.

Classes were changing as Buterbaugh headed for C. C. White Memorial Hall, which housed the fine arts departments, including the school's music department. Once in the building, she went up the half flight of steps to the main floor that held the music office. As with many old college buildings constructed at the turn of the twentieth century, White's first floor was actually several feet above ground level. Another half flight of steps led to a lower level. The wide staircase itself wound the entire height of the three-story building.

Colleen threaded her way through the throng of noisy students as she headed down the hall toward the music office, a two-room complex in the northeast corner of the main floor; music faculty had mailboxes in the outer office. Dr. McCourt had been assigned a desk in an inner workroom that also held a small music library. Along the hall she listened to the pleasant and familiar hubbub—a percussionist beat out a simple marimba melody, several piano students practiced various exercises, and some vocal students worked on their scales. She smiled at the happy sounds, all normal sounds of another weekday morning in the music department.

Colleen Buterbaugh did not expect to find Professor McCourt at his desk. In fact she found that he was rarely at his desk, preferring to linger in the classroom counseling students or scheduling meetings for those who wanted some of his time. By all accounts, Dr. McCourt was a born entertainer in great demand for his knowledgeable lectures. So busy was he that the campus telephone operator directed those trying to find him to Colleen's desk in the dean's office.

A few minutes before nine, Buterbaugh pushed open the door leading into the music office.

She very nearly fainted.

A pungent, musky odor swept up her nostrils, one that she instantly recognized as coming from something very, very old. She shivered at the suddenly cooled air, which hit her as hard as a blast of icy air through an open window on a winter's day.

And there was silence. Absolute and total silence. It was as if she had been struck deaf.

Gone were the noisy students chattering away on the other side of the door.

Gone, too, were the sounds of the marimba and the pianos and the operatic voices she had been listening to as she opened the door.

It was a stillness so disorienting in its completeness that every reminder of what she had seen and heard outside the office door had been erased.

Within seconds, Colleen Buterbaugh had her world turned upside down.

Battling against the sharp odor and rattling cold, Buterbaugh struggled to keep her balance. She reached out to steady herself on a wooden counter directly inside the door, wondering how this, her daily routine, this simple errand of taking messages to the music office was now turning into something . . . well, into something very peculiar.

The furnishings were all familiar but the atmosphere was unlike anything she had encountered—the searing cold and musty odor, but also the sense that time itself had slowed down, that she was watching a scene from long ago play out before her eyes.

As she glanced around, her attention was drawn through a connecting doorway and into the inner office. At the back of the room, Buterbaugh saw a tall, dark-haired woman of indeterminate age. She was in the act of reaching up to a shelf, riffling through what appeared at this distance to be music scores. She had not turned at Buterbaugh's entrance, nor did she acknowledge her in any way. She assiduously continued on with her search for whatever it was that she was looking for.

Buterbaugh could not see the woman's face, as her back was turned toward the connecting door. However, Butterbaugh did think her dress oddly out of date—a white shirtwaist blouse with lace at the collars and cuffs. A dark-brown skirt reached nearly to the floor. Her heavy head of dark hair was done up in a tight bun in back with smaller buns over each ear.

Buterbaugh knew one thing for certain—she had never seen her before.

In those same few seconds that she stared at the woman, Buterbaugh had the impression that suddenly there was someone there with her in the outer office, a man perhaps, and he was sitting at the desk to her left. The problem was that there was no one at all in the chair.

A window overlooking the campus drew Colleen across the room. Perhaps she should not have, for the view of the outside world was not at all what it should have been. The main campus artery of Madison Street was there as it had been since the school's founding in 1887, but she was looking at an avenue of packed earth and not the paved street laid decades before. The newly built Willard sorority house was not in view, as it should have been. She should also have seen a corner of Lucas Library—constructed from 1921 to 1923—but it was not there either.

The tall, graceful trees were barely visible through the window. Instead, she saw young saplings that looked recently planted.

Strangest of all was that despite its being a warm October morning, Buterbaugh had the feeling that what she saw outside the windows was from a midsummer day on which a visitor would find the peaceful slumber of a small college campus.

And then it was gone.

All of it. The woman at the bookshelf vanished, the view out the window returned to normal. The musty smell of old, cold things evaporated.

Gradually the muffled chatter of students rushing to class outside the door returned, as did the marimba music and piano playing. Somewhere a soprano hit a high C.

Colleen rushed from the room and back into the familiar hallway. It was if no time had passed at all.

Bewildered. Confused. Frightened.

Colleen Buterbaugh felt all of these emotions as she quickly retraced her steps back to Dean Sam Dahl's office in Old Main. That is when Karen Norton Cook, the alumni office director, saw her returning to the building. The two women were well acquainted with one another.

Cook knew something was wrong as soon as she saw her friend.

"I wondered what was wrong with her because she was as white as a sheet. She looked like she'd seen a ghost," Cook recalled, adding that she appeared to be "lost in her own thoughts."

Cook did not speak to her and finished her errands before returning to her office. She did not realize how perceptive she had been in identifying the cause of her friend's odd behavior. But Cook soon pieced together Buterbaugh's story.

Shortly after Cook saw her, Colleen Buterbaugh was back at her desk in Dean Dahl's office. She tried to type but ended up just shuffling papers and trying to figure out what had happened to her.

According to Cook, it did not take Colleen long to tell Dean Dahl about her experience.

"He wanted to know what was wrong with her," said Cook. "She said she would tell him if he promised not to laugh."

In a voice Dean Dahl later described as agitated, Colleen recounted her experience of only minutes before.

Roger Cognard, a retired professor of English who made a careful study of the Colleen Buterbaugh incident, described the dean as "a nice, gentlemanly, kind person, not given to flights of fancy." Cognard explained, "He supported her story since he knew her to be a woman of calmness and reason. He had no particular reason to doubt her."

The dean and his secretary returned to the music office to see if they could unravel the mystery. However, in the hallway they passed E. Glen Callen, a 1919 graduate of Nebraska Wesleyan who at the time was nearing the end of his career as a professor of political science and sociology.

Dahl and Buterbaugh told him the story. Callen did not flinch. He said the secretary's description of the apparition neatly fit that of Clara Urania Mills, a professor of choral music who was on the faculty from about 1912 until her death.

The circumstances of Professor Mills's death reflect a dedication to teaching not atypical on smaller college campuses. On April 12, 1943, Mills had struggled to campus from her apartment a few blocks away as a late-winter blizzard buffeted Lincoln. Later campus historians speculate that she was somewhat behind schedule and did not want to be late for her class in music composition. She went to her office in C. C. White Hall, sat down in a chair, took off her hat and scarf, and crumpled to the floor, dead of a heart attack while still in her sixties. She had taught on campus for over thirty years. Her office was only a few feet down the hall from the room in which Colleen Buterbaugh saw the mystery woman twenty years later.

Following the chance encounter with Dr. Callen, and a possible identification of the ghost, Colleen went to the alumni office and told her story to Karen Cook. She asked if the office might have a picture of Clara Urania Mills.

Cook knew instinctively to believe what Colleen was telling her. They had a range of years to work with and not a large number of faculty members.

"I don't know if I would have believed her story except that I saw her when she came back into the building and something had happened to her. So I said let's try to look her up in the yearbook."

All the college yearbooks were lined up in a bookcase against the wall. Along the top of the bookshelf were several photographs, including some of former faculty members.

Colleen Butterbaugh gasped and pointed to a group of faculty members in one of the photos, and to one woman in particular in the back row. That was the woman she had seen.

There was only the date 1914 on the back of the photograph. They paged through the 1914 yearbook until they found the same photograph with a list of identifying names.

The person Butterbaugh recognized was Clara Urania Mills.

I have never doubted that Mrs. Buterbaugh saw what she thought she saw. There was no doubt in her mind that she had some sort of [psychic] experience," said Dr. David Mickey, an emeritus professor of history at Nebraska Wesleyan and the author of a three-volume history of the school. He was a faculty member in 1963 and spoke with Buterbaugh about the incident shortly after it took place. He was also a student there in the late 1930s and knew Clara Mills. He said she was a highly regarded faculty member.

"There were some who felt this incident had something to do with a desire to get some attention," said Dr. Mickey, but he stressed that Dean Dahl believed Colleen Buterbaugh's story implicitly.

"It's my understanding that it wasn't an unusual assignment for her to go over there to put messages on McCourt's desk where he would find them later on. But that was the only time that she had anything like this happen."

Roger Cognard was just as perplexed in trying to find any sort of rational explanation, even after studying the incident in depth.

People who knew Buterbaugh, Cognard said, described her as a normal, reasonable person who, as far as anyone knew, had never had an incident similar to this before or after it.

"I guess I would say that something did indeed happen to her. I think she saw something. I don't know what it was, but I suppose it could range all the way from a hallucination to a visit by Clara Mills. I don't discount the possibility, although by nature I am a skeptic," said Cognard.

Cognard was intrigued that the apparition appeared during such an ordinary errand and in the middle of the morning on a busy school day.

"She was doing something very routine and bingo—she's hit with the musty odor, the quiet, the vision, and then it all goes away. From what I know about her I'm sure she thought Dean Dahl would think she was nuts. He didn't and so the story took on a . . . credence," said Cognard.

As Colleen Buterbaugh's story spread in the following weeks and months, newspapers statewide sent reporters to interview her and others on campus. The Associated Press and United Press International reported their own stories. Newspapers, radio, and TV stations nationwide, and even a few overseas, featured Buterbaugh's amazing adventure at the small college.

Representatives of the Menninger Clinic, a psychiatric hospital in To-peka, Kansas, interviewed Buterbaugh.

Cognard said, "She had some psychiatric exams and they wrote a journal article about her. I understand the bottom line was that she was pronounced normal with no history of hallucinations or anything like that."

Karen Cook said, "The Menninger people even took the yearbooks and the pictures. They had her down there I think it was twice. Apparently they decided that she did see something, something did happen to her [in the music office]. I thought, well, I know that because I saw her when she came back into [Old Main]."

Others have suggested that she invented the story or was going through a personal emotional crisis that led her to imagine the entire episode. Some of this doubt is bolstered by the slightly varying versions of the events she seems to have later told interviewers and friends. However, as Buterbaugh herself said, the event lasted perhaps no longer than thirty seconds to a minute so remembering all the specific detail months or years later would be difficult for even the best witness to process.

It has also been suggested that marital discord was among the emotional issues she was dealing with at the time. Whatever the correct story, Colleen Buterbaugh did divorce and move out of state following the incident.

Karen Norton Cook kept up an interest in the case until her retirement. She was considered one of the most knowledgeable about the incident and as such was a primary source for the multitude of people who wanted information. It had brought the college national and international fame, if not precisely the kind they would prefer.

Cook collected newspaper clippings, letters, requests for information, and other material related to the case. Strangely, the neatly catalogued file disappeared about a year before her retirement. Also missing, said Cook, is the bound volume of the campus newspapers that reported the event in late 1963.

Is the ghost of Clara Urania Mills still on the campus?

Although the C. C. White Building was razed years ago and replaced with the Smith-Curtis Administration Building, there are still a few stories of Clara, or someone, haunting the campus.

Professor Cognard said the ghost migrated to Old Main when C. C. White was demolished. There were also accounts that Clara's ghost was seen walking outside her old apartment building a few blocks from campus.

But one fact has never changed. Karen Norton Cook has no reservation whatsoever that her friend Colleen Buterbaugh saw a ghost on that singular October morning.

Ohio

Girl of the Lilacs

Bucyrus

For some men there is only one woman. It is as if love, once bestowed, is spent and cannot be given ever again. Frank Burbank was that kind of man. Ethel Hanley was the woman he loved. She loved him in return. Their devotion to one another transcended death.

One day in late May 1900, Frank Burbank, a surveyor in the Bucyrus office of the Ohio State Highway Commission, was inspecting land a few miles beyond town that the highway commission had arranged to buy. The acreage was part of a farm owned by a Mr. Hanley.

As Burbank and his assistant, Ted Davis, tramped across the fields, Frank felt the heavy heat that was more reminiscent of a July day. Summer had definitely arrived. The daffodils and tulips had already finished blooming and were now replaced by climbing roses and clematis.

Frank led the way up a hill. At the crest, the men paused to catch their breath. Laughing voices came from a white clapboard house a short distance away. The house was bordered by flowers and shrubs. But what caught Frank's eye was a girl, radiant in a white ruffled dress. Hair the color of corn silk spilled over her shoulders, and in her arms she cradled a bouquet of fragrant white lilacs.

It was several moments before Frank saw the photographer with the black cloth draped over his head.

This girl with the lilacs was having her picture taken. A woman stood watching from the doorway of the house and two small children romped playfully at the photographer's feet.

Frank then noticed a rough wooden sign nailed to a nearby tree:

COLD BUTTERMILK SERVED

He turned to Ted Davis.

"Ted, I won't be going back to Bucyrus," he smiled, jerking his thumb at the sign. "I need my daily glass of buttermilk."

Frank never drank buttermilk. Ted knew that. He laughed and reminded his boss that there would be a full moon that night. Then he set off alone back down the path to town.

Mr. and Mrs. Hanley greeted Frank warmly and invited him to stay for dinner. They knew the surveyor by his good reputation. In fact it seemed nearly everyone in the small town knew Frank Burbank to be a hardworking and dependable young man who was saving for further schooling; he planned to become a fully qualified civil engineer.

As Mrs. Hanley bustled around the kitchen, she explained that the photographer had been engaged to take her daughter's graduation picture. The final stitching of the white organdy dress had not been finished, she said, but that would not show in a photograph. There were many other preparations also to be made for the occasion. Mrs. Hanley was cheerful and easygoing, without pretension, and Frank liked her immediately. She put him at ease and so did her daughter, Ethel. At the dinner table Frank could not take his eyes off her and wondered if the others noticed. At the age of twenty-eight he had fallen head over heels in love at first sight.

After the meal Frank offered to help with the dishes, but Mrs. Hanley would not hear of it. Instead he played with Ethel's little brother, Sammy, and the child's orphaned cousin, Addie, who lived with the family.

Later that evening, Frank and Ethel walked down to the meadow and sat on the stone foundation wall of an old hay barn. The rocks held the heat of day and in a number of places wild roses grew, covering the crumbling wall with splashes of pink and red. The lambent light of the rising full moon bleached Ethel's light hair bone white. When she saw that Frank

255

was looking at it, she unpinned the bun and her long locks cascaded across her shoulders and down her back.

The gesture made a statement, wove a spell.

"Frank, when will you be leaving Bucyrus?" Ethel said, breaking the silence. "I mean when will you finish your surveying work here?"

Frank detected the slightest tremor in her voice and chose his words with care. He stood up and faced her.

"I could stay here, Ethel, in Bucyrus, as long as you want me to," he said, reaching down to grasp both of her hands in his.

She smiled up at him. Frank pulled her into his arms.

Frank Burbank accompanied the Hanleys to the graduation exercises a few days later. Ethel, as valedictorian, gave the class oration, and Frank thought she looked lovelier than ever in her white dress with the blue sash. Tucked into the sash was a spray of white lilacs he had given her that afternoon. Lilacs and Ethel. They naturally belonged together, like peaches and cream, moonlight and romance. The thought of one reminded him of the other. Lost in these pleasant thoughts, Frank hardly heard what Ethel was saying up on the small stage. He was certain of only one thing: he was going to marry Ethel Hanley.

The next day Frank asked Ethel's father for his daughter's hand in marriage. He could scarcely conceal his disappointment when her father said no.

"She's only seventeen," the old man said, shaking his head. "That's too young. If you wait two years, until she's nineteen, I assure you I will give my consent. That's how old her mother was when we got married."

He extended his hand to Frank, and the men shook on the promise.

In the fall, Frank Burbank moved to Cincinnati to study engineering. The night before he left Bucyrus, Ethel gave him a copy of her graduation picture. He found a room in a small boardinghouse and worked nights at a newspaper office to earn part of his expenses. The acute loneliness he felt at first was eased by his immersion into his studies and by Ethel's many letters. Frank kept her photograph on his bedside table. Each time he looked at the smiling girl in white he was intoxicated by the memory of the fragrance of the lilacs she held in her hands. It was as if the flowers had come to life within his room.

Meanwhile, Ethel filled her days and weeks to exhaustion so they would pass quickly. She helped with the housework and the care of the younger children. She was a hard worker who also helped with many of the outside farm chores.

She bore her father no grudge for his refusal to permit her marriage. She knew he had acted with her best interests in mind.

Two years later to the day, Frank Burbank returned to Bucyrus, a bona fide engineer. Ethel took the buggy to meet his train. As they drove up the hill toward the Hanley farm, Ethel needed to keep a strong hand on the reins.

"That's a new horse, isn't it?" said Frank.

Ethel laughed. "Yes, and he's so nervous he shies at his own shadow. Don't you, Bill?"

Frank grew uneasy. Skittish horses were always undependable.

The Hanleys rejoiced in Frank's homecoming and set the wedding date for Ethel's birthday, the fifth of June, two weeks away.

The following Sunday afternoon Ethel planned to show Frank a small house that was for sale out on Mansfield Road. Her father had taken the horse out that morning to drive her mother to church in Greggsville. She asked her father if Bill would be too worn out to be hitched up again so soon.

"I don't think so," said her father, "but he's real jittery for being twelve years old. He acts like a two-year-old. Better let Frank drive. And tell him to be careful."

Ethel went upstairs to change into the new dress she had bought to surprise Frank. It was white, of course, with a lace-trimmed ruffle at the waist. She put on a pale-blue straw bonnet with loops of dark-blue satin on the brim. As a final touch she pinned a spray of white lilacs to the ribbon.

Frank caught sight of Ethel starting down the stairway and caught his breath. He thought she was the most beautiful woman he had ever seen. She ran toward him and he swept her up into his arms.

The air was humid and still, the sun warm on their skin, a perfect day for a drive. Spring had been unseasonably long again that year and, in the protracted heat, the flowers had begun to lose color. The snowy apple blossoms had turned brown and the lilacs in the dooryards were starting to fade.

Setting off down the road, Bill trotted along at a steady, comfortable pace. Frank held the reins loosely. Ethel sat beside him on the buggy seat, commenting on the scenery and the houses of people she knew as they passed.

They had not gone far when Frank pulled to the side of the road to permit a fringed-top surrey to pass. A young woman with fiery-red hair and a large, green bow on her saucy bonnet waved from the front seat.

"Hello, Ethel!" the girl called.

Ethel returned the greeting. After the surrey had passed, she turned to Frank.

"That was my friend, Zelia Murdock. You met her at the graduation dance. Remember?"

"I saw only one girl at the dance." Frank grinned and reached to squeeze Ethel's hand. "But a red-haired girl driving a white horse is a good luck omen, I think. Let's make a wish, shall we?"

They both laughed. Frank commented on the newly painted silo on the Hawkes's farm and the nice condition of the Murdock home directly across the road. It was neat and attractive, but he promised Ethel that one day they would have an even finer place.

Just beyond the two farms was Hawkes's Hill, at the bottom of which was a stone bridge spanning a narrow, weed-choked stream.

As Bill started the descent, a boy on a bicycle shot across in front of them from a side road. Frank tightened the reins and pulled up some. Bill shied and snorted anyway, then reared up and leaped forward, snapping the horizontal crossbar of the buggy to which the harness traces were attached.

Wild with fright, the horse plunged down the hill, sending the careening buggy slamming against a bridge parapet. Ethel was thrown from her seat and struck her head on the bridge abutment. She died instantly.

Frank Burbank left Bucyrus immediately after Ethel's funeral. For three years he moved around the country, working in one city after another, trying in vain to shake his grief. He carried in his mind the picture of his beloved lying crumpled in his arms at the foot of Hawkes's Hill.

Then one day in Winnipeg, Manitoba, he decided that he was done living such a nomadic life. He wrote to his former boss, Will Taylor, in

Bucyrus. Was there an opening in the state highway commission there? If so, he wanted it, whatever the job was.

And so Frank returned. The job he was offered was keeping the books for the commission, hardly worthy of his advanced education, but it was enough. He did occasional surveying and on Sundays took long walks alone in the countryside.

Except for visits to the Hanleys, Frank saw few people socially. Mrs. Hanley often remarked to her husband how much Frank had changed. He never smiled and the light had gone out of his eyes; his whole face seemed immobilized, as if set in concrete.

One day in October, when the maples flamed in the woodlots, Frank walked along the highway's edge. A buggy pulled up beside him and a young woman called out. "Hello there. Aren't you Frank Burbank?"

He looked up at the woman holding the reins and nodded. She smiled down at him. "I'm Zelia Murdock. I'll be happy to give you a ride into Bucyrus."

Frank did not know if she had changed, but he doubted that he would have recognized her had she not introduced herself.

"I'm going to the Hanleys for supper, Miss Murdock," said Frank.

"Get in," she said. "I'll be glad to drive you there."

The waning light gilded wisps of red hair that curled beneath the brim of her bonnet. Frank hopped up beside her and the horse trotted on down the road.

After supper, Frank sat in the kitchen watching the children play and listening to Mrs. Hanley's small talk that once made him feel so comfortable. Now the words seemed harsh and distant, like he was listening from a great distance. Part of the time he sensed that she was questioning him, but his thoughts were elsewhere.

When he left, he stopped at the lilac bush beside the millstone. Snapping off a bare twig, he passed it beneath his nose and sighed.

"The scent of lilacs is strong tonight," said Frank, thinking he was alone.

But from the darkened doorway, Mrs. Hanley saw and heard and was perplexed.

No one was surprised when the marriage of Zelia Murdock and Frank Burbank took place. Zelia was headstrong and always got what she wanted.

In Frank she got a consort with whom she had three children. That was all, though. She did not capture his heart as Ethel had, nor even share his thoughts; she seemed not to care for such depth of intimacy.

Zelia inherited wealth and, with hired help to care for the large house and to look after the two boys and their sister, she devoted her time to various clubs and social pursuits. She organized her life around her own interests. Frank was left to his own devices.

The first thing Frank did upon moving onto the Murdock farm was to plant white lilac bushes. Some he bought from nurseries, some he bought from farmers who were thinning out dooryard hedges, and others he dug up from old, abandoned places. In every free moment he wandered the hills and valley of the Scioto River searching for yet another lilac bush.

On a raw March day filled with strong winds, Frank went to the Hanley farm, where he had offered to help unload fertilizer. By late afternoon the men finished the work and Frank climbed into his buggy to leave for home. As he was about to drive off, he thought he saw a woman standing down by the old hay barn foundation. Frank climbed out of the buggy and tied the reins to a hitching post. He started down the path to see who it could have been at this hour and on such a foul day. He had gone only a few steps when he was overcome by the heady perfume of lilacs.

He turned to look back at the big lilac bush. The branches were bare. When he looked again toward the place where the barn had stood he saw her clearly. A young girl in a white dress and a wide, blue bonnet smiled up at him. He cried out and ran toward her. But the apparition faded, swallowed by the shadows of the coming night. Frank Burbank sat for a long time on the cold stones of the crumbling wall, his head cradled in his arms.

The hunting was good that fall; quail and partridge were especially plentiful. On a November afternoon Frank took his gun and his setter, Sport, out to try his luck. The air was clear and crisp.

When Frank reached a dense thicket at the foot of the hill on which the Hanley farm lay, he whistled for the dog, which had raced on ahead.

The setter came bounding up to him trembling and whining with hackles raised. Frank looked in the direction the dog was staring. A girl in a white dress was coming toward them down the steep hill, from the direction of the Hanley farmhouse. She approached slowly; her feet did not quite seem to touch the ground. The network of branches and twigs that blocked her way never bent to permit her passage; the apparition passed right through them. Then, for just a moment she stood smiling, a luminous figure pierced by sapling twigs.

Frank once asked Mrs. Hanley if she had ever been aware of her daughter's presence.

The woman nodded. "Once I thought I saw her walking down by the ruins of the old hay barn."

Mrs. Hanley sighed and looked away. "But I guess it was just a trick of the moonlight."

When Frank Burbank's daughter, Joan, turned eighteen, Zelia gave a dinner-dance in her honor. Before the guests began to arrive, Frank wandered into the dining room. Joan stood by the bay window. Her father thought she looked radiant in her new apple-green silk gown and told her so.

"Daddy," she began, "something strange is going on in the garden. A woman has been pacing out there by the white lilac hedge. She's young, about my age, and she's wearing a white dress and a broad-brimmed bonnet. She seems to float in and out of the lilacs. At first I thought it was one of my friends playing a trick on me, but when I went out I couldn't find anybody. I'm sure I saw her. I was standing right here watching."

Frank looked out but saw no one.

The doorbell rang and Joan hurried to answer. Frank did not greet the guests. Too many people around often oppressed him, even his own children whom he loved.

No, it was the soft, fragrant air of May that made him restless. At times his restlessness, his loneliness, seemed unbearable. He stared now into nothingness until Zelia came for him.

After dinner, more guests arrived and the dancing began. Frank knew the party would last far into the night for Zelia was an untiring hostess. He slipped unnoticed out the back door and for a while walked aimlessly through the gathering twilight. Then he struck out along the brook that skirted the Hanleys' hill.

Far ahead he saw a light in their kitchen.

261

Before Frank realized how far he had come, he reached the thicket at the base of the hill. He stopped suddenly. A girl in white was dancing on the hillside. With her arms extended, she glided in and out among the trees.

Frank's eyes misted and his heart ached with a young man's desire. Tonight Ethel would not elude him. He sprang forward; the figure floated backward, gesturing for him to follow.

He fought the tangled branches, his eyes riveted on the apparition that kept receding farther up the hillside. He had almost reached her when she raised her arm and tossed something toward him. Whatever it was fell at his feet. He stooped over to pick it up. When he looked again, she was gone.

In his hand he held a spray of fresh lilacs.

H. P. and Son

Cleveland

Cleveland businessman H. P. Lillibridge was at work one morning, dictating a letter, when he saw the image of his son hovering a few feet from his desk, his face covered with blood.

Lillibridge paled and put a hand to his head. It was throbbing. When his secretary asked if he was ill, he said no. But he knew then that his boy, Joe, serving as the captain of a freighter somewhere at sea, had been seriously injured or worse.

Lillibridge hurriedly finished his dictation and went home to lunch.

He picked at his meal uncaringly then took a brisk walk to calm himself. He and his son were very close. They shared the same likes and dislikes, habits and opinions, and often, each knew what the other was thinking and feeling. People often remarked that they seemed more like brothers than father and son. Joe captained a freighter as his father had in his own youth; each man started as a common sailor. Lillibridge wrote to his son regularly, and Joe, who had no time for long letters, kept a daily log that he mailed to his father whenever he was in port.

That afternoon back at his office, H. P. sat at his desk and wrote a detailed account of all he had seen in his vision. Putting the paper in an envelope, he sealed it and addressed it to himself. Then he sent for Willis, the cashier.

"Willis," he began, tapping the envelope against his fingers, "please seal this in a large envelope, address it to yourself, and put it in the safe."

"Yes, sir, of course."

"Right away, please."

"I understand, sir," said Willis, taking the envelope.

But Willis did not understand. He had never before been asked to carry out such an odd assignment. A double-sealed letter in the safe with the money and important company papers?

Willis remarked about the peculiar request to the secretary. She too was perplexed. She told Willis that their boss had seemed confused that morning and she wondered if he had suffered a stroke.

But Willis did as he was told. The envelope was mailed, then received by him and secured in the safe. Days passed and every time Willis opened the safe he saw the large envelope and wondered anew at its contents.

Seven weeks after Lillibridge wrote the letter, Joe Lillibridge's latest log arrived from Melbourne, Australia. H. P. called his brother, who was one of his partners, to his office, then summoned the cashier to bring his sealed letter from the safe.

Willis delivered the envelope, leaving a damp thumbprint in one corner. Standing to one side of the desk, he watched Lillibridge slit the envelope open cleanly with a silver letter opener. Lillibridge shook out the sheets of paper, adjusted his glasses, and began reading in a clear voice to his brother and his cashier.

Weeks earlier, H. P. Lillibridge wrote that he had seen a vision of an uprising on his son's ship during which Joe was struck twice in the head by a piece of iron pipe. Joe was badly injured and bleeding profusely.

Lillibridge put aside the letter, then turned to his son's log. Lillibridge's brother and the cashier paled as they listened to Joe's account of a mutiny aboard his ship; it paralleled the father's account in nearly every detail except that Joe survived his serious injuries. Allowing for time and date differences, the father had "seen" his son's apparition at the exact time of the mutiny.

Four years later, Joe Lillibridge died of sunstroke in the South Seas. But his close association with his father extended beyond the grave. H. P. Lillibridge said he frequently received messages directly from Joe and often saw his ghost. On one occasion the apparition warned his father to avoid an unsafe business deal. He heeded the advice, which had proven to be prescient.

H. P. and Joe Lillibridge remained "close," until H. P.'s own death many years later. It made him certain that the bonds between parents and children can remain close even beyond death.

An Invitation

Willis

The hobo was not sure how many miles he had ridden in the boxcar before he decided to go back. He did not know exactly why, but there was something in young Sam's face that disturbed him, something that communicated an unspoken need. The man recalled that he had been about Sam's age when his own father had died. So when the engineer slowed the train at a rural crossing, he jumped off and hitchhiked from the middle of nowhere back to Willis, Ohio.

On the trip back, he wearily reflected on the bizarre events of the day before. It seemed as if it was all part of a dream, yet as he processed the entire evening's events, he realized that everything had indeed taken place.

During a driving rainstorm the previous night, the hobo had crawled off a freight train in the now-vanished village of Willis. Shivering in a light jacket and thin pants, he sloshed through the deserted rail yard. Suddenly, someone spoke to him. "It's sure a bad night."

The hobo looked up to see a man wearing a slicker with a rain hat pulled low over his forehead.

"You got a place to stay?" asked the man. "If you don't you'd better come home with me for the night."

The hobo thanked him and then followed him down the street. Neither of them spoke. After walking two blocks, the man in the slicker turned and walked up to the porch of a house. Stepping aside, he told the stranger to go on in.

He did as he was directed. A woman and her two children were preparing dinner in the kitchen. Giving the tramp a quick smile, she indicated a chair just inside the back door.

"My name is Sarah and this is my daughter, Lucy, and my boy, Sam," she said. "Lucy, set another place at the table for the nice man."

When the hobo sat down, he felt the water drain out of his cracked and weathered shoes; he hoped no one would notice the puddles on the floor. He glanced nervously toward the door. Where was the man who had invited him?

"Sorry for the water, ma'am. I ain't meanin' to make work for ya," said the tramp. "A nice gentleman brought me here. He said to go on in. Looked like he went around the other side of the house."

The woman nodded.

"Yes, I know. We don't eat fancy, but we can always feed an extra." She smiled, stirring some extra carrots and onions into the stew simmering on the stovetop. Neither she nor her children seemed scared or disturbed at the sudden appearance of a disheveled hobo turning up on their doorstep.

The stranger sat quietly and observed the young family finish the dinner preparations. He took in the mouthwatering smells and realized only then just how hungry he was. The only sound to be heard was that of the skillet sizzling in a wreath of smoke.

"Where you headed?" asked Sarah.

"Out west. Have to find me a job," he volunteered.

"Doing what?"

The hobo's cheeks reddened. "Whatever I can git."

Lucy clattered the plates and silverware onto the table while her little brother, Sam, carefully set out the bread and butter and pulled up the chairs. The hobo kept his eyes fixed on the door. What had happened to the man who had brought him here? He told him he would join him in a few minutes. In the silence, the hobo noticed something else rather odd— there were only four place settings. Was the other fellow not going to join them?

Sarah noticed the visitor's agitation. As they ate, she spoke openly to the hobo.

"It was my husband brought you here. He likes to wander around the rail yard on stormy nights. Most times he brings a tramp or two home with him. But don't be nervous—it's fine that you're here. Tell me if you want more to eat."

The stranger stared into his lap, his fingers rolling the paper napkin into a tight, damp ball. He had followed a man down the street and now that man had disappeared. The hobo heard the snap of wood in the kitchen range.

When he looked up, he saw young Sam's eyes upon him, eyes that seemed too old for such a small and somber face.

After the meal was finished, Sarah orchestrated the cleanup, with the hobo chipping in. Once everything was put away, she called to Sam. "Son, show our guest to the spare room."

The tramp liked the sound of the term "our guest." No one had ever called him that before.

The room he was taken to was spotlessly clean and the bed comfortable. Yet for some reason he could not sleep. As he was just dozing off, he heard footsteps coming down the hall. They stopped at his door. A minute later he heard whoever it was walking back down the hallway. The hobo thought it might be one of the children, and he rolled over in bed.

But then sometime later came a knock on the door so hard that that he was shaken from his sleep. He got up and cracked open the door but saw no one. The pounding came again. This time he threw open the door. No one was there; the corridor was empty. But just as he was shutting the door, he felt something cold and wet brush past him. He did not sleep the rest of the night.

In the morning, a warm sun shone. The hobo was boneweary from lack of rest. He got dressed and made his way downstairs. He thanked Sarah and set off for the depot. He reached the tracks as a westbound freight rumbled in. The tramp spotted an empty boxcar with a partially opened door. He was just about to leap aboard when he heard a small voice behind him.

"Here's your cap, mister."

The hobo turned around. Sam, squinting into the sunlight, held the old, sweat-stained black watch cap.

"Thanks, kid."

The train was picking up speed. Another open boxcar came into view. Sam just stood there, watching.

"I've been meanin' to ask you something, kid," the hobo shouted above the din of the moving train. "But if it ain't none of my business, you tell me."

Sam remained motionless.

"I was wonderin' why your old man never came back last night. Maybe he come home late and I missed him?"

Sam's eyes widened. He spoke steadily and without emotion. "My father's dead, mister. He was killed in an accident in this here rail yard almost six years ago."

The hobo nodded. As the train moved away, he returned Sam's friendly wave.

"So long, kid! And tell your old man thanks . . . ," he bellowed as he leaped aboard the last boxcar.

Franklin Castle

Cleveland

Hannes Tiedemann and his wife, Luise, realized their lifelong dream back in 1881—the construction of their turreted home at 4308 Franklin Boulevard NW in Cleveland. The "castle," as they called it, had been planned and built exactly to their specifications. The Tiedemanns were overjoyed.

Some local residents claim that the old couple liked their house so much that they never left, even after their deaths.

Bizarre stories of psychic disturbances have been told for over a century about this mansion on "Millionaire's Row." Scores of newspaper articles and television programs have documented its haunted history.

What do the stories contend? That doors fly off their hinges without being touched, lights go on and off by themselves, chandeliers slowly swing when the air is still. Mirrors fog for no apparent reason, and voices murmur in empty rooms. From time to time a woman in black is seen peering out a narrow window in the front tower room. A little girl—perhaps the Tiedemanns' daughter Emma—begs visiting children to come play with her. She died of diabetes at the age of fifteen, a decade after the family moved in.

The history of the so-called Franklin Castle is a mixture of fact and legend, blurred by incomplete or missing records. It is known, however, that the Hannes Tiedemann family built it and lived there for nearly thirty-three years, that Hannes built his fortune from wholesale grocery and liquor businesses, and that in his later years he became a bank executive.

It is also a house touched by immense sorrow.

In addition to his daughter dying there in 1881, Hannes Tiedemann's eighty-four-year-old mother, Wiebeka, died in the house the same year. She might be the woman in black passersby see on occasion staring out one of the upper-floor windows. Two years later, three more children in the family died. Their father claimed they had been ill, but neighbors suspected there was more to the deaths than that.

The grief-stricken Luise Tiedemann busied herself with her house, adding secret passageways, hidden rooms, and turrets and gargoyles that made the house appear very much like a gothic haunted castle. Luise even added a huge ballroom on the fourth floor.

After Luise's death, Tiedemann sold the place to a family named Mulhauser, remarried, and moved elsewhere. He died in 1908, outliving every member of his immediate family.

In 1913 the Mulhauser family sold the castle to the German Socialist Party, which used it for meetings and parties. The Socialists owned it for fifty-five years, but for most of that time the house was considered unoccupied.

A Cleveland nurse recalled caring for an attorney who supposedly lived at 4308 Franklin Boulevard in the early 1930s. She remembered being terrified by the late-night sound of a small child's crying. The servants refused to talk about it, dismissing the cries as the mews of a desperate cat. But forty years later, the nurse told a reporter that she would "never set foot in that house again."

In 1968 Mrs. James C. Romano bought the Tiedemann castle and she, her husband, and their six children moved in. Mrs. Romano always admired the huge stone house and planned to open a restaurant in it. She quickly changed her mind.

On the day they moved in, their two young sets of twins went upstairs to play. Soon they came down to ask if they could take a cookie up to their friend—a little girl in a long dress. She was crying. This happened a number of times, but every time Mrs. Romano looked for an extra child she found none but her own.

Mrs. Romano sometimes heard organ music, although there was no organ in the house. In bed late at night, there was the heavy tramping of footsteps as if an army platoon was marching back and forth on the third floor, originally a ballroom, where her two grown sons by a previous marriage slept. Sometimes, when no one was up there, she still heard voices and the clink of glasses. She finally refused to set foot on both the third and fourth floors when she was alone, and she forbade her children from playing up there.

Mrs. Romano's fears about the third floor may have been well founded.

Barbara Dreimiller, a Cleveland writer, had a chilling experience there. During a visit, she and three friends had just reached the third floor when they saw a vaporous object, like a blanket of fog, drifting ahead of them.

The friends hung back, but Dreimiller bravely walked toward it. Before she could reach it, she seemed to grow faint. Her friends pulled her free of the sickening cloud just before she passed out. They found no source for the vapor.

One Halloween, the telephone awakened Mrs. Romano at midnight. She picked up the receiver and heard, "Can I sleep with you tonight?"

The voice, she recalled, was deep and hollow as though it "came from the grave." She screamed and dropped the phone. After that incident she vowed never to answer the phone when she was alone in the house.

"A week later," said Mrs. Romano, "I woke up from a deep sleep and found myself in the middle of the floor screaming so loud I lost my voice. And someone was screaming right along with me."

James Romano, who was an electrician by trade, rewired the entire house. Yet light bulbs burned out in a week's time and fixtures burst into flames.

Mrs. Romano consulted a Catholic priest.

He told her she was possessed, at times, by the spirit of Luise Tiedemann and that it was the ghost of little Emma Tiedemann who slammed doors and raced up and down the stairs. The priest felt there were many evil entities in the house and advised the family to leave.

Mrs. Romano's grown sons needed no urging. They moved out after something pulled the covers off their beds in the third-floor bedroom.

James Romano remained calm and philosophical about the house.

"When you buy a castle, you get the ghosts. It's Halloween at our place 365 days a year."

His wife never adopted such a casual attitude. She felt certain the house held dark, brooding secrets. She was too upset to try to learn what they were.

"It isn't something to mess with," she said.

Eventually she became physically ill and admitted the house was getting the best of her. In September 1974 the Romanos sold the place to Samuel Muscarello.

The new owner planned to turn it into a Universal Christian Church and, to raise money, opened the house to tours.

A Cleveland radio disc jockey and a photographer emerged from their tour visibly shaken.

The radio announcer would not discuss his experience, but he turned down an offer of three hundred dollars to spend the night in the castle.

For his part, the photographer said he was sitting downstairs with the owner when he heard a woman's voice call his name.

He ran up the stairs but found no one. The only other people in the house were two floors higher and their voices could not be heard.

John Webster, a Cleveland broadcast executive, told psychic investigators Richard Winer and Nancy Osborn Ishmael that when he visited the castle to gather material for a special program on its hauntings, a large tape recorder was torn from his shoulder and thrown down the stairs, smashing into pieces.

During the visit of a television news cameraman, a hanging lamp turned in a slow circle. Ted Ocepec did not think vibrations from outside caused it.

"I just don't know," he said, "but there's something in that house."

Even owner Muscarello grew uneasy. He heard strange sounds and discovered articles taken from one place and put down in another. His plans for the church did not work out and he sold the castle.

In 1978 former Cleveland Police Chief Richard D. Hongisto and his wife, Elizabeth, bought the property. They thought the twenty-room home, with its beautifully carved paneling and original wood plank floors, would be a perfect place to live, easily spacious enough for the large parties they liked to give.

Yet less than a year later the Hongistos abruptly sold the mansion to George Mirceta, a buyer who was unaware of its haunted reputation. He had bought the Gothic castle for its solid construction and architectural whimsy.

Mirceta lived alone in the house during the week and conducted tours on weekends. At the end of each two-hour tour, he passed out cards and asked the visitors to jot down phenomena they had observed—some reported seeing a woman in black in the tower room; others saw a woman in white. Still others complained of becoming temporarily paralyzed or of finding themselves babbling incoherently.

Mirceta told reporters that he heard babies crying and saw chandeliers swaying. Still, he claimed to be unafraid—he would not live there, he said, if the castle was haunted. "There has to be a logical explanation for everything."

Franklin Castle has continued to change tenancy and ownership. Most recently the castle, which is listed on the National Register of Historic Places, was purchased by a European artist with the stated intention of turning it into a multiple-family dwelling. In 2015 a ghost hunting expedition from a cable television channel spent several hours there. Included in their report was a claim that they heard a disembodied voice.

"*Get out!*" it cried.

The Ethereal Innkeepers

Granville

Shutters bang on windless nights. Stairs creak. Floorboards groan. At first, Mary Stevens Sweet thinks the noises are the natural complaints of the rambling, old house settling down for the night. It is the late 1920s and Sweet has just taken over the management of the historic Buxton Inn in Granville, Ohio.

Several weeks later, Sweet senses a presence on an upstairs outside balcony early in the morning, peering over the railing to the lilac bushes below. In the evening, something follows her into the ballroom where once the night was filled with fiddle music and the rhythmic beat of dancing feet performing an old quadrille.

Before long, Buxton Inn guests say they are being awakened to find a forlorn figure leaning against their bedpost. The flowered wallpaper makes it obvious the unannounced guest is quite transparent.

Other guests are startled when they spread their hands to the fire on the hearth and see a pair of pale, indistinct hands warming themselves beside their own.

There is no doubt in Mary Sweet's mind now. This inn is haunted.

The Buxton Inn was built in 1812 by pioneer Orrin Granger, a Massachusetts native who moved to Ohio to seek a better life for his family. Originally, the inn served as a post office and stagecoach stop. Drivers cooked their meals in the massive open fireplace in the basement and bedded down there on straw pallets. Through the years throngs of travelers of all sorts crowded the old inn, leaving the residue of their memories and emotions imprinted on the structure. Identifying a ghost might be difficult given such circumstances.

In the Buxton Inn, identification came relatively soon, in an unexpected way. Fred Sweet, Mary's son, woke up hungry one night, so he crept downstairs to raid the pantry. He reached for the pie shelf, but it was empty. A ghost stood in the larder, devouring the last wedge of apple pie.

Sensing the young man's disappointment, the ghost drew up two chairs and in a thin, reedy voice introduced himself as Orrin Granger, the builder. The apparition then regaled Fred with tales of the olden days when carriages rolled along the Granville Pike and stopped at the Buxton Inn for fresh cider and rashers of bacon.

The friendly ghost confided that it approved of the way Mary Stevens Sweet was running the place, retaining the authentic nineteenth-century atmosphere and blending it with new, attractive furnishings and tasteful food.

"No need for me to hang around any longer," said Granger. With a wave of his hand and a gentle smile, he was gone.

Years later, a psychic glimpsed the ghost of Orrin Granger again in the house. She described a gray-haired gentleman who looked like a country squire. He wore knee breeches and white stockings and was dressed in blue.

In 1972 Orville and Audrey Orr purchased the Buxton Inn. The Orrs had heard tales of a ghostly lady in blue haunting the old hotel but were determined not to forfeit the purchase because of a "spook" wandering the premises.

Orr, a soft-spoken former minister, spent two years restoring the inn to its original state, even to the vivid-pink clapboard siding. During that time he hired several young carpenters to finish work on the house. One summer evening as they packed their tools for the day, Orr told them the stories he had heard about a lady in blue and how she had frightened unsuspecting guests. The workmen laughed and said they did not believe in ghosts. Proof. That is what they demanded. Proof.

That was not long in coming.

One day an attractive young woman in a blue dress opened the second-floor stairway door, walked across the back balcony, and started down the steps. Then she evaporated before the workmen's eyes. Proof they wanted, proof they got.

The blue lady repeated her visit the next day and every evening thereafter, promptly at six o'clock. The workmen made sure they were finished before then.

Who is this woman?

She is generally believed to be Ethel Houston "Bonnie" Bounell, the establishment's vivacious innkeeper from 1934 until her death in 1960.

Bonnie was an immensely popular woman whose elegant looks lent an air of sophistication to the bucolic Buxton Inn. In her earlier years she had been a singer of light opera. Those who had known her remembered her hats and her lovely pastel dresses.

In fact, blue was Bonnie's favorite color.

More specific information hinting at the ghost's identity came later from a Cincinnati medium, Mayree Braun, and a founding member of the Parapsychology Forum of Cincinnati, who once toured the house. Although the Buxton Inn was unfamiliar to her and she knew nothing of its history, Braun reached some startling conclusions.

She described seeing, clairvoyantly, a woman in blue, from modern times, accompanying her and Audrey Orr from room to room. The psychic said the woman was beautifully attired, had once been on the stage, and obviously liked hats. Mrs. Braun also remarked that the spirit was pleased with the restoration work the new owners were doing, especially the work done in the ballroom. The medium seems to have unknowingly described Bonnie Bounell.

While medium Mayree Braun had identified this "lady in blue" as Bounell, another medium, Peggy Little, a Columbus area psychic and member of the British Spiritualist Church, said the ghost of a lady she had seen in the inn was wearing blue clothing of a much older fashion. Although unable to see the bodice of the gown, she did see a floor-length, blue-gray skirt and heard the rustling of its folds as the wearer swept across the floor. Peggy Little also saw a white cap on the woman's head. She thought it might be Mrs. Orrin Granger, the wife of the original owner of the inn. Or was it Bonnie in another elegant gown?

Orr himself witnessed unexplained incidents in the house. During the long renovation period, he often heard footfalls on the stairs and the slamming of doors in upstairs rooms when no other human being was around. Sometimes he even heard what sounded like coins being dropped on the pegged wooden floors.

Orr had never been scared of the presence, but once he did lose his patience. He had spent an entire evening alone in the inn and was preparing to leave when someone opened the front door, walked upstairs and across the second-floor balcony, opened the back door, and proceeded down the back outside staircase. An incredulous Orr determined no one had entered. All the doors were bolted and every window latched. The Buxton Inn was secure. Or was it? Tired and somewhat exasperated, Orr shouted at his "guest," "If you want this place you can just have it." Later he rethought the offer.

On many occasions he encountered a shadowy male figure in various parts of the house. Orr finally decided that this was probably the ghost of Major Buxton, the inn operator from 1865 until 1905, and the person for whom it was named. The ghost of Major Buxton seemed quite harmless.

"When we first purchased the building, employees would even set a place for the major at the table," said Orr. "One waitress claims to have seen the major sitting in a rocking chair before the fireplace."

The Grangers, Bonnie Bounell, and Major Buxton may be the most prominent ghosts who haunt the Buxton Inn. But some say that there are other "visitors" whose identities may never be known.

In the Tavern, located in the original basement of the house, stage drivers cooked and bedded down long ago. There, psychics observed many spirits, especially between nine thirty and eleven thirty at night when the energy level in the inn slows down.

Peggy Little saw ghosts congregate on the stairs during the evening hours. "It's almost as if they were a wall of feeling," she told one reporter.

Newspaper photographer Gordon Kuster Jr., of Granville, might agree. Kuster, visiting the inn in 1979, observed a pitcher fly off a table and crash to the floor.

There is something about the Buxton Inn that seems to attract and retain its old caretakers. In 2014 Orville and Audrey Orr sold the Buxton Inn to a group of investors intent on preserving the building and restoring the inn and the restaurant to its long-ago splendor. Guests continue to report odd experiences at the historic inn, especially in room number 9, where they say they smell perfume and wake up to the feeling of a cat snuggling up against them at night. It seems that the ghosts of Bonnie Buenell and her feline companion remain very much in residence at the Buxton Inn.

The Pirate's Mistress

Scioto River Valley

The bottomlands of the Scioto River valley in central Ohio are rimmed by forested cliffs lush with undergrowth. Many years ago travelers reported seeing the ghost of a lithe, young girl gliding among the trees. At night they heard screams coming from the vicinity of a ruined mansion, followed by silence, another shriek, and then stillness.

Some said the ghost was the spirit of the little Spanish girl that John Robinson was alleged to have murdered. At least they thought he had killed her. Authorities never did find her remains.

John Robinson entered this wild, inhospitable Ohio country in 1825. He arrived at the village of Delaware, Ohio, with a party of trappers. The village at the time was only a few log huts strung along a portage between the Ohio River and the town of Sandusky on Lake Erie.

Robinson himself was not a trapper, and he was not friendly with any of his traveling companions. He left them without so much as a good-bye or a wave of the hand, stopping for the night at the local tavern, two heavy packs in tow.

The villagers were suspicious. Most foot travelers crossing the wilderness carried the lightest of loads. And while the tavern keeper, the blacksmith, and the stable boy welcomed the stranger and asked about his plans and what assistance he might require, Robinson remained distant.

In the morning, the newcomer rented a saddle horse and set out to explore the local bottomlands and bluffs. In the depths of the nearly im- penetrable forest, Robinson found the retreat he sought, a vast acreage of high-bluff country that afforded a splendid view of the valley below. He took title to the property that night and as soon as the deed was executed, he began designing a mansion grander than any home in Ohio. It was clear he had wealth beyond imagination, but he never revealed where he had gotten his treasure.

Once the plans were ready, Robinson hired an army of stone and brick masons. They blasted from a hillside and cut and laid the rock with utmost precision. Stone by stone, foot by foot, the magnificent building rose in the forest. A master craftsman, Robinson finished the interior himself, carving mantels and cornices and the balustrade for the staircase from virgin oak and embellishing them with intricate patterns of astonishing beauty.

Soon wagons arrived, bringing furnishings imported from Europe— heavy brocade draperies, gilded tables and chairs, desks and chests, trunks filled with linens, silver and dainty bone china. One large leather trunk held easels, canvases, brushes, and oils, while other chests contained books for the library. Such opulence was unheard of in the wilderness of the 1820s.

Indeed Robinson planned for every eventuality, even the most certain of all—behind the house he had built a lavish mausoleum as his final resting place.

When everything was finally finished, Robinson paid his bills in gold pieces. Now the villagers knew the contents of the leaden sacks Robinson had dragged into the tavern. The workmen were dismissed and the new homeowner retired within his house and bolted the doors.

The little community waited for an invitation to the housewarming that never took place. Masons and carpenters who had worked on the house were angered; local officials who had helped Robinson procure the land were puzzled by the rejection. An occasional neighbor who stopped by the mansion to welcome its owner to the area was rudely turned away.

But one day Robinson summoned a workman to make some repairs in the house. The man noticed the walls of the rooms were covered with the owner's paintings, sweeping landscapes of rolling hills and baronial castles and great medieval halls reminiscent of Great Britain. Robinson indicated that he worked at his easel every day from morning to night.

The one painting that astonished the workman the most covered an entire wall of the library. Its setting was the deck of a pirate ship. Dark, heavy-bearded sailors gathered on the stern of the vessel, the officers forward. In the center, the captain struck a swashbuckling pose, sword and pistols at his side, a bold and crafty look on his bronzed face. The workmen recognized the man in the painting immediately—it was Robinson himself. Even in the dim light, the likeness was unmistakable.

Rumors flew. A pirate captain in Delaware County? How could that possibly be? Romantically inclined persons pondered chests overflowing with gold buried on the mansion grounds. And silver. Perhaps even rare jewels and gems. Others thought Robinson must be the black sheep of an aristocratic English family to account for his other paintings with their typical historical English themes.

When Robinson was not painting, he roamed the forest, searching for rare stones and unusual rocks. A neighbor sometimes caught sight of him studying a specimen, turning it over and over in his strong, callused hands.

Then one day local residents glimpsed a most unexpected stranger in the woods near the Robinson mansion—an exotic young girl, small and dainty with hair and eyes as black as the raven's wing and a pale complexion faintly tinged with olive.

In a brocade gown with lace-trimmed sleeves, some said she resembled a Spanish countess. There was a certain nobility in the tilt of her head and the way she moved silently through the light and shadow of the forest. Like Robinson, who had arrived two years earlier, the girl's presence in such a rough landscape was astonishing. Not a single trader had met her on the portage paths.

Rumor had it that the senorita (at least everyone assumed she was not a senora) served as a model for the artist's paintings, that her portrait would be his masterpiece, the crowning achievement of his life's work.

Sometimes, in the waning light of summer afternoons, Robinson and the girl would be glimpsed seated side by side on a stone bench in a clearing at the brow of a hill. But more often the girl was alone, darting like a small bird among the trees, or wandering the willow-fringed banks of the Scioto River.

When the days shortened and the leaves fell, the girl was seen no more. Yet those who lived in the region said she was not silent. They claimed that the girl was dead. Night after night her chilling cries shook the forest and trembled above the valley floor. Word spread that Robinson had beaten her mercilessly when she displeased him and she died from the blows. The settlers were alarmed, but in this age before any organized law enforcement, no one was willing to interfere.

Early snows laced the barren trees and filled the forest. The land lay silent. The great stone Robinson house was silent too. And sinister.

Throughout the long winter, the villagers spoke of Robinson and his companion, of their strange behaviors. Not once that winter had the pair been observed.

With the coming of spring, the snows melted and the river ran full; the trees leafed out and the birds returned. But still no sound came from within the mansion.

John Robinson was nowhere to be found.

Weeds choked the path to the front door, and vines and lichen clung to the damp foundation stones. Over all was an air of desolation.

At last a few hardy farmers banded together and approached the house. They banged on the thick, forbidding oak door. No one came. Using a fallen tree as a battering ram, they crashed through and tumbled inside. There was no sign of life anywhere, only what remained of a furious struggle.

In the library, filled with Robinson's books and paintings, chairs and tables were overturned; the easel lay smashed on the floor. One wall bore the bloodied prints of tiny, slender fingers.

Just above the bloodstains hung the life-sized portrait of the mysterious, albeit nameless Spanish girl.

As the men stared, they later swore the colors of the painting seemed to intensify; her eyes flashed darkly and her lips moved as if to speak. The farmers turned and ran back to the village with their story. By nightfall everyone in and around Delaware knew the mansion now was haunted. The midnight stillness of that night and every night to come was pierced by the mournful cries of the sad senorita.

As the days passed, search parties scoured the woods of John Robinson's estate for some trace of the girl. Only her portrait and a few of her belongings left in the house testified to her life.

Robinson's disappearance was just as mystifying. He left his forest kingdom as stealthily as he had come into it. His hand-carved casket was found in his workshop. Behind the house the mausoleum was filled with snakes.

In time, the neighbors could not resist the temptation anymore and swarmed over the mansion, determined to unearth the fortune they believed Robinson the pirate had taken in plunder and buried there. For months zealous plowmen and woodcutters swung picks, spades, and shovels, overturning stones, uprooting young trees and even undermining the foundation of the very house itself. Others ransacked its interior, tearing out the handsome paneling, pulling down the carved staircase, and stripping the walls bare in their frenzied search for Robinson's ill-gotten gains.

Yet not a single coin was ever found. Time and disregard eventually finished what the treasure hunters had begun, and the mansion was reduced to rubble.

Only the ghost of the young senorita lingers. Legend has it that she still walks the banks of the Scioto River in the twilight of a late, summer evening. And sometimes, in the gathering gloom, a scream, her scream, shatters the stillness and echoes down the valley.

Old Raridan

Jackson and Pike Counties

Whether it is the "elephant's graveyard" or the dying place of the American bison, humans have searched for centuries to locate the sites within each region toward which old and wounded mammals struggle, driven by some instinctual urge during their final days.

In southern Ohio, somewhere within present-day Jackson and Pike Counties, its location lost to time, old-timers told of such a graveyard for the magnificent gray wolf.

The earliest explorers identified this place and called it Great Buzzard's Rock, a high, granite, flat-topped hill. Later generations knew it as Big Rock.

It was the dying place of the wolves.

Bones of hundreds of gray wolves lay strewn across its surface. Buzzards floated in the skies above, waiting for new arrivals.

Until the end of the Revolutionary War, wolves in the region were of little concern to man. There were few people, and the occasional explorer shot a wolf only when it posed a threat. All that changed, however, as civilization edged westward. Pioneers began pushing into the fertile Ohio River Valley, bringing livestock and villages with them.

Wolves were not welcomed in or around frontier settlements. They preyed on livestock as pioneers killed deer for meat, diminishing the herds that were the wolves' primary food source. Settlers slaughtered wolves whenever and wherever they could. Every new settlement pushed the wolves farther and farther westward.

Each wolf pack had its own leader. In about 1796, settlers in what would later become Jackson and Pike Counties when Ohio became a state began to notice that one pack of several dozen wolves in particular followed a magnificent gray wolf.

They called him Old Raridan, the king of wolves.

How he got his name is not known, only that this awesome beast, larger and more powerful than his comrades, often prowled in the distance after a particularly bountiful kill of unsuspecting farm animals. He knew instinctively what the hunters' guns could do and always kept safely out of range.

To avenge the increasingly frequent raids by Old Raridan's pack, groups of a dozen or more hunters would set off after him, their hounds baying in pursuit. Although many wolves and hounds were slain, Raridan always eluded capture. His fatally wounded followers made their painful way to Big Rock, where they died.

Not even the bravest man dared follow a dying wolf to that strange and haunted place. Nor would a tracking hound come within a mile or more.

As Old Raridan's fame grew, so did the number of hunters seeking to put an end to his ways. His time was running out.

Every man wanted to be known as the one who killed the King of the Wolves.

At last, only a few tough old wolves survived, among them Raridan and his mate. The bones of their followers littered Big Rock. Then, sometime in 1801 word spread through the Ohio Valley that only Raridan and his mate still lived. The rest of his pack had moved on westward. Hatred for the old wolf, fanned over many years, became a fury so intense that even godly preachers prayed for his death. People talked of little else. Even women and children took part in the feverish search for Raridan.

Vastly outnumbered, and with the infirmities of old age, Raridan found even his skill and cunning, learned through hundreds of battles, could not save him. An army of men with dozens of hounds now stalked the woods, searching him out.

And then it happened.

Hunters cornered Raridan and his mate in some low hills near the Ohio River. The wolves killed several hounds, but in the process Raridan's loyal mate, the she-wolf, was wounded. Raridan would not leave her behind. Instead, they turned in the direction of Big Rock.

The hounds held to the trail as hours of tracking wore on. For every wound the hounds inflicted on the aged wolves, one of their number lost his life.

Just a mile from Big Rock, the hounds encircled the pair. Raridan let out a howl that froze the marrow in the hunters' bones and snapping and snarling rushed the dogs, slashing in fury inch by bloody inch to reach the foot of the trail leading to Big Rock.

The fight was merciless but Raridan held on, protecting his mortally wounded mate. Then just as suddenly as the baying hounds had been in the center of the fight, they fell back.

Suddenly a shot rang out. The she-wolf dropped, a bullet in her heart. Then a second shot sounded. Old Raridan's right hip exploded in a sickening shower of gray fur, flesh, and bone.

The warrior staggered toward his companion, his life ebbing from a dozen wounds.

He raised his scarred and bloodied head, once majestic and unbowed, and surveyed the men who had destroyed his empire. His stare became a final challenge.

"Here I am, take me!" he seemed to taunt his enemies.

Not more than fifty paces distant, the hunters could easily have finished off their quarry. Yet not one did.

The old wolf turned back toward the trail to his final destination.

"Ooooooowwwwwwwhhhhhoooooo!"

Raridan raised his voice in one last cry.

From the top of Big Rock floated an answer, almost an echo, yet more ethereal. It seemed to give the old wolf new energy, for he gently fastened his powerful jaws around the nape of his mate's neck and dragged her up the trail to the dying place of the wolves.

Old Raridan

Old Raridan is more than a folktale to many who have seen his specter prowling that ancient forest kingdom. When the moon is full, his splendid cry drifts with the wind across Big Rock, where the shadowy form of that giant creature stands defiant against the darkening sky.

Wisconsin

Our Three Ghosts

Pierce County

Doug and Annette O'Brien moved with their two children, one-year-old Nathan and eight-year-old Valerie, into a spacious, century-old house on a quiet street in Pierce County on November 1, 1985. At the time Annette was pregnant with their third child, and they thought it was the perfect house for their growing family.

Within a few months, however, they were having serious reservations. The couple found that eerie and inexplicable events came with their dream home.

All was quiet for about eight months until an especially hot night the following August when their idyllic life changed. Doug decided to go to bed early, leaving Annette and daughter Valerie downstairs. He had had a long, hard day at work and was unusually tired. Adjoining the couple's upstairs master bedroom was a nursery in which four-month-old Trevor was already fast asleep.

Doug was nearly asleep when the baby started fussing. He propped himself up on his elbows and rubbed his eyes. Something made him glance sidelong, toward the open bedroom door. A woman in a long, light-colored dress glided past, toward little Trevor's room.

The baby quieted down immediately. Doug thought the woman must have been Annette, but something did not seem right. He waited a few moments and got up. He looked in on Trevor but the baby had fallen back to sleep. There was no sign of Annette or anyone else. Downstairs, he found his wife and Valerie. Neither one had been upstairs.

Doug and Annette were understandably upset. Who had gone into the infant's room?

Annette took pride in being a calm, easygoing woman. She was not nearly as alarmed by her husband's experience as he was. He had been dreaming, she reasoned. But what if it had not been a dream? A strange woman who seemed to vanish was not something that made either one of them comfortable.

Doug encountered a second mysterious visitor a short time later.

This time he was sitting alone in the living room one evening watching television. A connecting door led from the living room into a downstairs back bedroom. As if out of nowhere, a little blond-headed boy was standing in the doorway. He wore knickers buckled below the knees and a blue shirt. The outfit was clean and neat, definitely not play clothes.

He took a few steps into the room and looked at Doug.

Doug was calmer than might be expected. "I asked him who he was and what he wanted, but he didn't answer."

The child vanished as quickly as he had appeared.

In the morning, Doug told Annette about the boy. She wished she had seen him too.

Another time when Doug was on the couch watching television, a small, bright red ball bounced through the same doorway in which the boy had appeared, and promptly vanished. Perhaps the boy was showing a playful side?

That first-floor back bedroom was one of the centers of the ghostly disturbances they continued to experience.

Doug was the first to reach that conclusion when on a late afternoon he went in that bedroom for a nap and closed the door to the living room.

"Just as I was dozing off there was that lady again," Doug said.

She stood beside the bed wearing a red jacket. Doug stared at her but did not say anything. He could not make out her arms or face yet he knew instinctively it was the same woman he had seen upstairs.

Doug covered his head with a blanket and she went away.

The family's brush with the supernatural took an even odder turn one afternoon when an elderly woman knocked at their front door. She told them her name was Ethel and that her grandparents had once owned the O'Brien house.

Annette and Doug invited her in. Ethel immediately said, "There's a closet in that back bedroom off the living room."

Annette nodded. She said it had been turned into a small nursery and that Trevor was napping in there at the moment.

Their visitor shook her head and paused. "My grandmother used to lock me in the closet and make me pray."

Doug was curious. He wondered to himself if the ghost he had seen might have been Ethel's late grandmother.

They learned more about the history of the house from Ethel on that day, but little else that could identify the causes of a haunting.

Doug worked ten-hour night shifts at a company in Bloomington, Minnesota, a suburb of the Twin Cities. When he started leaving the house at two in the afternoon and getting back home well after midnight, Annette, for the first time, became anxious and ill at ease in the house. What she feared did not come from anything mortal.

"I had all the lights on when I went to bed. I was really terrified. But once I was in bed and my eyes were closed I was fine," she said.

Annette often waited up for Doug because, as she said, "just as long as somebody was downstairs before I went to bed I was all right."

One of the couple's greatest concerns was that the children would be frightened or harmed. Only eight-year-old Valerie had a curious personal experience.

She and a friend were playing in her upstairs bedroom when the door slammed shut.

Valerie thought somebody might be hiding in the hallway and looked around. She even looked in corners where someone could hide. Nothing.

Valerie shrugged and returned to the bedroom. Her friend Abby was not so composed. She told Valerie that she had heard something at the door after it slammed shut and the handle turned.

The girls abandoned their toys and scrambled back down the stairs.

A short time after that, the O'Brien children started having bad dreams—not really nightmares, but scary dreams they could not remember in the morning. Their parents knew then that they needed some help in identifying what might be going on.

At the urging of Annette's sister, the family contacted a Minneapolis psychic named Jacki about visiting their home. She agreed to drive over the next day. The children would not be present.

As long as they live, Doug and Annette O'Brien will never forget Jacki's visit.

Jacki went room to room in search of the spirits. With her were Annette, Doug, and Annette's sister, Susan, the one who had suggested seeking the psychic's help.

"She said we had three spirits—a woman, a young boy, and an old man," Annette recalled. However, only one of their boys would see the man. Doug and Annette would not.

The ghost child had shown himself to Jacki right away. At first she thought he was one of the family's boys, but then he vanished.

The woman was a nanny who would stay in the house for as long as there were children there.

The old man was perhaps the saddest presence that Jacki detected, an alcoholic who died of malnutrition.

The quartet headed for the back bedroom, where Doug had seen the woman in red.

"The psychic said that a little girl was locked in the closet at one time, down on her knees reading a Bible," Annette said. That was nearly an identical description of what their Texas visitor had told them about her own experience.

When the small group got to the master bedroom upstairs, she said that was where the old man had died. And where he still hung out.

"That really scared me," Annette said.

The bedroom was at the front of the house, above a porch. Jacki said there used to be a door from it leading out to a now-vanished balcony and a stairway to the ground. The couple knew about the door as they had replaced it with a window and put a roof over the open porch. Jacki said the old man would sneak out that door at night to go drinking.

In the same room, Jacki seemed to solve another of the hauntings. The O'Briens' bedroom had been Valerie's room when she and Abby saw the door handle turn. Annette speculated that the old man was trying to get in to "shoo the kids out."

The psychic thought the little boy she saw sometimes played in the attic. Each time he went up there he carved his initials on an attic cross-beam. However, the O'Briens had never seen evidence of that.

Jacki claimed the little girl in the closet wanted help for her step-brother, who had been physically abused and denied food. He later died of his injuries and severe malnutrition. But it was all kept very quiet; even the girl did not know what he died of. He was about six or seven years old, but physically no bigger than a three-year-old. His hard, leather shoes were too small and pinched his feet.

The ghost boy is the one that led Jacki upstairs to where the old man once lived. Jacki told the little boy it was time to leave, that it was better on the other side because there were places for him to play.

"What's play?" she said he asked her.

The old man lived in the house at a different time than the child.

"He was not a nice man," Jacki said.

He told her he did not like children because they made noise. She explained to him that the children lived there too and were allowed to make noise. He was not to frighten them.

Jacki said the man was as spiteful after death as he had been in life.

The nanny was a benevolent spirit who did not leave a very strong impression. It is possible that she was the ghost nanny Doug saw tucking in little Trevor

Before Jacki left, the O'Brien children returned home from school. She sat them down and explained that an old man had been giving them the bad dreams, but they did not have to worry anymore. She had put a red aura of protection around each of them. Only spirits with love in their hearts could stay. And the living have superiority over any entity that has passed on. If the family tells a spirit to leave, it must.

Once people realize that, she said, trouble with spirits usually goes away.

Unlike some psychics, Jacki did not drive any of the ghosts out of the house.

"I tell earthbound spirits that they have passed into the next world. They don't have to hang around anymore. Usually they go."

The O'Briens were comforted by Jacki's visit. They sincerely hoped their three ghosts would soon be gone—yet in the spirit world, as in life itself, they knew there were no guarantees.

Everlasting

Shorewood

Bob Lambert really did not want to go upstairs.

The clouds had been lowering all that humid August afternoon, and now the weather bureau had issued a severe storm warning.

He waited. Perhaps the rain would not come. Perhaps it would skip Shorewood and go south. He sat nervously in his lower-floor apartment, occasionally glancing out the window. He just knew he would have to go upstairs. If only Ginny were here. Maybe she could not protect him, but at least she would be around in case anything should happen.

But why should it? After all, ghosts belonged to a bygone era. No one believed in them anymore. Right? Right. But then who or what belonged to those footsteps? For a time Bob thought they could not harm him or Ginny, but now he was not so sure.

"Come on, grow up," he muttered to himself. "It's silly to think that ghosts come out only during thunderstorms."

At the first sign of rain, Bob decided that he would close the windows in the upstairs apartment, just as he had promised the tenants he would do. And nothing would happen.

Shortly after three o'clock, the rain started coming down heavily. Bob had no choice. He started up the staircase, then stopped.

"I'm coming up to close the windows," he shouted, hoping with all his being that nothing answered him back. Farther up the stairs, Bob again paused. "I'm going to shut the kitchen windows first," he called out.

289

If something was around, he did not want to take the chance of surprising it. He hesitated a moment, reflecting on the five years he and Ginny had spent in their Shorewood apartment.

Up until that afternoon, the Lamberts had lived in relative peace with their upstairs "ghost" as if it was another member of the family. But the noises only occurred when no one was home in the upstairs apartment.

The tenants had keys to each other's apartments in case of an emergency. At first, Bob or Ginny would climb the stairs each time the footsteps started in order to check on their source. But the footsteps always stopped before either of them reached the apartment.

The ghost made but one appearance over the years.

Dottie Rosmund, the upstairs renter at the time, was taking a bath. Her husband was out on business for the evening. Suddenly, the air chilled. From the bathroom door, a light, gray mist hovered in the air, the vague outline of a man billowing upward from the cloud. He was staring straight toward Dottie. She watched stricken as the mist evaporated. The Rosmunds soon moved away.

Bob Lambert later discussed the peculiar episodes in the apartment with the woman who owned the building. She told him that one of her sons, who had been raised in that house, was sickly as a child and adult and had been confined for most of his life to a bedroom on the second floor. He died as a young man shortly after his mother moved to a new home. She told Bob that it might be her son's ghost who was prowling the second-floor apartment.

Bob flipped on the apartment lights as the storm built outside. But a few seconds later they dimmed and went off. His flashlight was downstairs and he had no idea where the upstairs tenants kept their flashlights or candles. He would have to make do. Although it was only midafternoon, the dark sky had turned the apartment into layers of deep shadows.

He closed the kitchen windows and started down the long, narrow hallway toward the bathroom. He noticed something palpable in the air, something more than the watery humidity of a typical late, August afternoon. It was a sense of being followed, of knowing that he was not really alone.

The bathroom door was closed; the window inside was probably open. He hesitated. A little voice inside him—and he was never quite sure where it came from—told him not to open that door. A sense of imminent danger swept over him. The tiny hairs stood up on the back of his neck. He could feel the sweat starting to roll down his chest.

He took his hand from the door and carefully backed away. Then, as quickly as he could, he closed the bedroom and living room windows and raced for the staircase. As he passed the hallway, he looked toward the bathroom. Now the door stood wide open. It had been firmly closed a minute before. Had the landlady's son returned?

Bob Lambert did not wait around to find out. He never wanted to visit that apartment again.

Spirit of Rosslynne Manse

Delafield

On the sprawling campus of St. John's Military Academy outside of Delafield, Wisconsin, more than a century ago, a silver shovel turned the first piece of earth for the fourteen-room building that would house the school's president, Dr. Sidney Thomas Smythe, and his family. Rosslynne Manse drew its name from the old Scottish term for a clergyman's home. The house was planned around a massive stone fireplace that Dr. Smythe had seen as a child in his uncle's Scottish home.

After it was built, broad, inviting porches stretched across the front and rear portions of the house, the latter enclosed by pillars wedged atop hand-hewn stone blocks. The Smythe family lived on the first two floors, reserving the large room on the third floor as a sort of clubroom for senior cadets who frequented the house in great numbers. Dr. Smythe insisted on knowing each student personally, and as many as fifteen to thirty cadets dined at the house weekly.

Dr. Smythe was so devoted to the school and its students that he placed a large, leather armchair in front of the huge picture window overlooking the academy grounds so that he could keep an eye on "his" campus.

Although the school sought to shape the strong, moral characters of its young men, the house itself was the site of strange episodes that defied even the president's most rational explanation.

Mrs. Sidney Smythe was sewing in the upstairs hallway on a November evening in 1905. Her two small children, Betty and Charles, were fast asleep. A grandfather clock near the stairway to the second floor chimed eight o'clock, reminding Mrs. Smythe that her husband would soon be coming home and would expect a light meal. She put down her sewing materials, descended the stairs, and started toward the kitchen.

The house had a rather broad entrance hall that extended directly into a living room with two large windows, one facing east, the other south. A rocking chair was situated so that it commanded a view out the south window.

As Mrs. Smythe walked toward the living room, her gaze shifted toward the rocking chair. She was shocked to notice a man, well dressed but quite pale and sickly, sitting in it. Mrs. Smythe backed up a step or two, bumping into the clock. As she reached out to steady herself, she looked back into the living room. The man had vanished.

The next morning Mrs. Smythe told her family about the incident. Even then she coolly took it all in stride, describing the man's appearance, and disappearance, as if the specter had been an old family friend stopping off for a visit.

The Smythes knew that their home was not the first house built on that particular parcel of land. A family named Ashby had owned a house there some time before, but the Smythes did not know anything about the family or what had become of them. Now they wanted to find out, sensing a possible solution to the mystery of the man in the chair.

An answer came the following summer. An elderly gardener, who worked for the Smythes, had also known the Ashbys. One day while he was planting shrubs near the porch, Mrs. Smythe happened to ask him about the Ashbys. The gardener told her a few stories about the family, including the fact that their son-in-law had died of tuberculosis. Mrs. Smythe pressed the gardener for details of the dead man's appearance—they matched in precise detail the figure she had seen in the rocking chair.

Twelve years later, Charles Smythe, by that time twenty years old, also encountered the Ashby's ghostly son-in-law. The rest of the family was attending a function at the school one evening, leaving Charles alone in the house. When they returned, Mrs. Smythe noticed Charles seated in the living room. He did not look well.

At his mother's urging, he recounted what had happened to him earlier that night. He had been upstairs reading when he decided to go downstairs. His dog, Jack, led the way. When he reached the lower landing, he looked toward the window, and there he saw the same man whom his mother had seen. This time he was standing with his feet apart, hands behind his back, facing the window. His face was partially obscured.

Jack the dog marched to the center of the room and uttered a nasty growl. Charles described it as partly a choked snarl, and partly a moan, as if the animal was in terror. He was crouched down, ears laid back, teeth bared, and was staring at the figure by the window.

Charles glanced down for a second toward the dog, but when he looked up, the figure was gone. He searched all around, as the dog tried vainly to pick up a scent; there did not seem to be one.

Betty Smythe, who was upstairs as her brother told their mother about the bizarre event, had noticed the dog sniffing around, going from room to room, whining. He seemed to be searching for something.

Neither Mrs. Smythe, nor her son Charles, sought an explanation for the phenomena they witnessed. And to this day no one knows why the long-gone Ashby's son-in-law, if that is indeed who it was, found it necessary to haunt his former home. There were no other ghost sightings ever reported there.

In 1981 Rosslynne Manse was burned to the ground in a training exercise by the local fire department. Uninhabitable after years of neglect, and too costly to renovate, Rosslynne Manse became a mere memory for the thousands of young men who passed through the gates of St. John's Military Academy. But for others who knew of the peculiar ghost story connected to it, Rosslynne Manse lives on.

Mrs. Pickman Goes Too Far

Milwaukee

On a cold evening at midnight in early December 1913, Max Kubis could not sleep. It was not just the relentless wind slamming against the house, pushing the falling snow into ever deeper drifts, that kept him awake. From somewhere below his second-story bedroom, a faint scraping noise was keeping him awake.

It seemed at first nothing out of the ordinary—perhaps one of the family's numerous cats. The house was locked tight against the Milwaukee winter, after all, and animals become bored during the long months indoors just as their masters do. A frolic late at night was not unusual for the Kubis cats—yet the rhythmic sounds of this disturbance puzzled Max. Felines are sporadic creatures, their activity coming in sudden bursts followed by splendid lethargy. The noises that reached Max's ears seemed human, like someone moving about in the darkness, slippered feet sliding across the oak floors.

Max carefully lifted the blankets and eased out of bed. His wife, Julia, slumbered peacefully over on her side of the four-poster. His feet found the carpet slippers. He threw a robe around his shoulders as the mantel clock downstairs completed its midnight tolling.

His stealth was not necessary. At the instant his hand found the bedroom door, a vicious pounding at the front door roused the entire household. Julia sat up in bed, eyes wide and questioning. The couple's daughters, Helen and Armilla, called out from their bedroom.

Before Max could answer the midnight commotion, however, the front door crashed open and he heard somebody tromp down the hallway and into the kitchen.

By this time, the fearful family found themselves huddled in the upstairs hall, staring down the darkened staircase toward the unseen caller.

"Who's there? What do you want?" Max cried out, his strong voice betraying only the slightest quiver.

After a few seconds of silence, the family moved toward the staircase, flipped on the lights, and made their way down the steps. The little troupe fruitlessly searched high and low. The front door was closed and locked as it had been when they all went to bed.

The Kubis family knew very little about their new house, except that it had been, until her recent death, the lifelong home of Mrs. Alex Pickman. The family had only recently moved back to Wisconsin after a brief residency in Washington State.

Some weeks after the midnight disturbance, on a night when the thermometer hovered well below the freezing mark, Mrs. Kubis climbed out of bed in the early predawn hours to add wood to a bedroom stove. She was halfway across the floor when the distinct image of an elderly woman materialized a few feet away from her. Her hands were held out toward the warmth of the blaze as if trying to ward off the chill.

Could this old woman and the nocturnal prowler be one and the same, perhaps old Mrs. Pickman herself? When Mrs. Kubis described the apparition to a neighbor, she said it matched the former owner, even down to the dowdy housedress the vaporous figure had worn. Furthermore, Mrs. Pickman had told her husband and relatives that she intended to return to her Milwaukee home as a ghost. It seems she may have kept her promise.

Over the following weeks, in the hour between midnight and 1:00 a.m., there were repeat performances of the door opening and closing, footsteps pacing about, and—most disconcerting of all—heavy, labored breathing. That settled it, the neighbors told Mrs. Kubis: Mrs. Pickman had severe asthma.

One night, Mrs. Pickman went too far with the Kubis family. Helen and Armilla were fast asleep when they were jarred awake by the heavy thud of a falling body hitting their bed and then trying to crawl under the sheets. The girls fled screaming into their parents' room, quite convinced that the old lady had jumped into bed with them.

That was enough. The following morning, Max Kubis packed up his family and belongings and moved. In their rush to leave, however, the family left behind their mantel clock. When Julia Kubis returned for it the next day, she found it had stopped—at midnight.

Mr. Sherman Pays a Visit

Plover

Tim and Louise Mulderink always dreamed of owning a restaurant. So it was no surprise when they decided in the early 1980s to buy a historic, 125-year-old house in Plover, Wisconsin, to remodel into a fine dining establishment.

Their task was made all the more challenging because they discovered that not all the deceased owners and residents of the attractive, two-story clapboard dwelling had moved out. As the conversion got underway, someone they could not see opened the doors for them or knocked glasses off the new bar. It might have been someone else who tromped about the upstairs rooms and turned lights on and off.

At first, Tim and Louise were so busy remodeling that they did not really notice the peculiarities. They put in new wiring and plumbing, installed a new roof, and insulated the walls. Tim Mulderink's background in food management and catering was key in the planning, including the conversion of the former garage into a modern, commercial kitchen. Louise, a vivacious, willowy blonde, supervised the interior design of the house-turned-restaurant. The main color scheme of petal pink and burgundy created an elegant ambiance for fine dining.

The Mulderinks named their restaurant the Sherman House to identify it with the famous Sherman House restaurant in Chicago, the couple's hometown. They also wanted to honor Eugene A. Sherman, the most historically significant of the home's previous residents. Eugene Sherman had operated a sawmill and general store in Plover, moving into the house in 1891. Now, nearly a century later, the Sherman House Restaurant was ready for its first guests. The successful grand opening in April pleased Tim and Louise.

Not long afterward, however, the couple found that a crowded dining room would not be their only challenge in what became a rash of exploding drink glasses.

In the first incident, Louise Mulderink was standing behind the polished bar facing a glass-shelved cabinet when one of the drink glasses inside exploded.

"It simply shattered," said Tim. "Louise never touched it. Shards of glass everywhere."

The drink glass had been in the center of a row of glasses. Tim did not think a vibration of some sort had sent it off the shelf, as nothing else moved.

Shortly afterward, two women in the bar ordered drinks. No sooner had the bartender set the first drink down than that glass exploded as well, showering one of the women with liquid and pieces of glass. Fortunately, she was not hurt.

Three witnesses said no one had touched it.

On a Friday night, one of the kitchen helpers experienced a similar incident. A few minutes after he pulled a rack of glasses out of the dishwasher to air dry, there came a loud popping sound.

Tim Mulderink had been standing nearby. "What are you doing, breaking glasses?" he asked.

"I didn't even touch it," said Paul, the kitchen dishwasher, holding a stack of plates he had just removed from an automatic dishwasher.

On another day, during the lunch-hour rush, a fourth glass exploded, throwing shards into the liquor and ice bins.

"The pieces looked like a windshield somebody took a sledge hammer to," said Louise.

By this time, Tim was convinced he had gotten a defective supply of glasses, so he called the company representative, who could not explain to Tim why the glasses had shattered. He said the occasional glass breaks because of a defect, but it is highly improbable for several glasses to do so.

The restaurant opened during its early years at four thirty on Sundays. On one of those Sunday afternoons Louise's father, Charles Grachan, was alone in the house answering the telephone and taking dinner reservations. Someone unlocked the front door and opened it.

"Come in, Mr. Sherman. I'll buy you a drink," Grachan jokingly called out from the next room.

No one came in.

Grachan found the door open just wide enough for a person to slip through. It had been locked.

"Only a few people have a key to that door," he said. "Whoever opened it had to have a key. I heard it click."

But that was not the end of his experiences there. Late one evening, Grachan, Tim, and a friend named Rick were deep in conversation after hours in the bar when the mantel clock on the top shelf behind the bar struck the midnight hour. The men looked up. Each one agreed with the other—it had struck thirteen.

"I've had enough for tonight," said Grachan. He had bought the clock new the previous April and this was the third time it had struck an extra hour. Grachan could find nothing wrong with it.

It was all a bit too much for him. "I'm not scared of anything except something I can't see. I have trouble with that."

Corinne, the restaurant's cleaning lady, had the same opinion. A religious woman who always carried her Bible with her, she reported to work early each morning until the day she quit. "Whatever is in there I can't work there any more," she told the Mulderinks.

Tim shook his head.

"She was scared out of her wits. She would talk about kitchen pots clanging or shadows in the bar; when she was near the entrances she could see shadows going by."

Even though other employees besides Corinne were nervous about working in the house, Tim and Louise Mulderink were not inclined to accept a supernatural basis for the incidents. Tim, especially, looked for logical explanations for everything.

Meanwhile, Louise experienced an episode that changed her mind. For a time it frightened her so badly that she refused to be at the restaurant by herself.

That particular night while another dishwasher finished up in the kitchen, Louise emptied the cash register and took the money upstairs to the office to count and then put in the safe. She kept the office door open. Suddenly, it slammed shut. She opened it back up and took a look down the dim hallway. Returning to her desk, she heard footsteps cross the hall and looked up. That is when she noticed the door to the banquet room opposite the office had swung open. It was always kept closed when nothing was scheduled.

Louise raced downstairs to find the dishwasher. Had he just gone upstairs for some reason? No, he had not left the kitchen.

Louise went back up, cautiously switched on the banquet room lights, and checked around. Nothing was disturbed. By the time she returned to counting the money, the dishwasher was finished and called up the stairs that he was ready to leave.

Louise remembered: "I counted very fast and put everything in the safe, made sure the back [fire escape] door was locked, turned off the light in the office, and made sure all the upstairs lights were off. [We] walked out the door together and he got in his car and left. I got in my car, locked all the doors, and backed the car up. I looked up and the office light was on. I know I'd turned all the lights off and I wasn't about to go back in. So I went home and woke Tim up. I had to tell him what happened."

Neither one returned to the restaurant that night. When they did the following morning, the office light was off.

Louise said her father had a similar experience while filling in at the restaurant when Tim and Louise were out of town. Charles Grachan finished counting the money late one evening, put it in the safe, and turned off all the lights. While walking to his car, he looked up and saw the office light burning. He went back inside and the light was off.

The incidents continued. One Friday night, Tim and Louise and four of the employees were talking in the kitchen when they heard distinct thumping noises overhead.

"Stop talking for a minute!" someone shouted. Heavy footsteps crossed the upstairs hall as if to enter the banquet room.

On a fall night in 1983, Louise witnessed a second disturbing incident. She was upstairs when the fluorescent lights in the office flickered but did not go out. Then Louise heard a tinkling noise. On the back of the office door is a rack holding lightweight metal clothes hangers.

As Louise turned from the safe, she noticed the wire coat hangers swinging back and forth, including one that held Tim's shirt.

"It was as if somebody had brushed past them," she said.

"I went home and told Tim that the ghost was here again," said Louise.

In time, the Mulderinks searched for a possible identity to their ghost . . . or ghosts.

Wendell Nelson, a Portage County historian, provided the couple with background information on the house and its residents. Louise also gathered information from customers familiar with the place. The only person confirmed to have died in the house was a two-day-old infant.

However, all the families who had lived in the house were Methodist teetotalers, especially the Pierce family, who owned it from 1903 until 1945.

James W. Pierce was a Plover grocer. The church deacons and the men's club met in the house, and Mrs. Pierce regularly entertained the ladies' sewing circle.

Louise thought the Pierces might be offended by the transformation of their homestead into a restaurant. Especially after she and Tim unwittingly converted Mr. Pierce's old bedroom into the bar.

"He's probably just having kittens over that," chuckled Louise.

If it is the ghost of James Pierce that roams the house, he might have been there long before its transition into a restaurant. The Mulderinks believe the house has been haunted for at least twenty-five years. The last residents before the Mulderinks, the Sowiaks, who owned it from 1957 to 1982, also witnessed strange phenomena, which a member of the family related to the Mulderinks.

The rear portion of the upstairs banquet room was once a Sowiak son's bedroom. (Tim and Louise removed the wall between two bedrooms to create a private banquet dining space.) The Sowiaks had a fearless yet friendly dog who refused to go upstairs. It would stand at the foot of the stairway and bark and howl. Once, the Sowiak son pushed the dog up a couple of steps, but it came right back down.

The son married and moved to Chicago. Each time he and his wife returned to visit his parents, they slept in his old bedroom. But they got little rest. The couple heard someone come into the room and walk over to the bed. It was as if a parent were coming in late at night to check on a sleeping child. But no one was ever there.

After a few such nocturnal checks, the Sowiaks' daughter-in-law refused to sleep in the room anymore. Her husband stuck it out until one night when something awoke him. He refused to say what had frightened him.

A few sensitive patrons of the Sherman House may have suspected that someone invisible was watching them in the oak-trimmed bar or in one of the comfortable dining rooms. But luckily, since the bar glasses shattered, there were no further incidents involving customers.

They also knew that the front door, secure as it seemed, might open mysteriously at any time, that someone prowled the banquet room upstairs, and that the mantel clock in the bar could not be depended on to chime the correct hour. And that the woman who lived next door might greet Tim and Louise in the morning by asking, "Did you know your office light was on all night?"

Charles Grachan, Louise's father, believed in ghosts and did not worry about who or what might be sharing space with him.

Of the ghost, Grachan said, "He's just a nice, friendly guy."

The Mulderinks eventually sold the Sherman House. The space is now home to the Cottage Café, which capitalizes on the building's haunted history, hosting psychic readings and other paranormal-themed events.

The Nodolf Incident

Platteville

Southwestern Wisconsin abounds with unique geographic formations, such as its deep valleys called coulees, the towering river bluffs, and unique limestone outcroppings. There are pockets of wilderness virtually untouched by the outside world, picturesque villages, and isolated farmhouses recalling a way of life more suitable to the nineteenth century.

The community of Platteville is one of the region's larger cities. It served as an early trading center for the nearby lead miners, the badgers who gave the state its nickname. Today Platteville is a thriving small city that savors its ties to pioneer history.

Just outside of Platteville is a towering rock bluff known as the Platte Mound. Today, the Mound has the distinction of bearing the world's largest *M*, first placed there by students at the Wisconsin Mining School (now the University of Wisconsin–Platteville) in the 1930s. Before there was the *M*, however, the mound had already gained local distinction as being the site of a bizarre incident in the nineteenth century involving a German immigrant family. Those familiar with the case call it "The Nodolf Incident" or simply "the strange night."

In the mid-nineteenth century, Carl Nodolf, a German-born farmer, moved into a sturdy, two-story house on a large swatch of land near the base of the Platte Mound.

Carl had left his bride-to-be in Germany when he immigrated to the United States. Like many other men creating a new life in an unfamiliar land, he wanted a measure of success before he married and raised a family. The deep, rich black soil, the spectacular view of the rolling countryside from the house's windows, and the dramatic mound towering above it would surely appeal to his betrothed as it had to him. No doubt he had simply fallen in love with the region.

Carl prospered and returned to Germany in the late 1860s. When he arrived, he found tragedy—his sweetheart had died in a diphtheria epidemic only a few weeks before his arrival.

Anguish replaced Carl's optimism. Only two of his fiancée's family had survived: her mother and another daughter, sixteen-year-old Louise. Gradually he realized that his dream of a farm and family in Wisconsin could still be fulfilled. He would ask Louise to come with him to America. Louise accepted but did not want to rush into such an important event. She suggested that her mother join them, with the marriage taking place after they arrived in Wisconsin.

So both Louise and her mother accompanied Carl back to Platteville, and Carl and Louise were married soon after. Their first child, a daughter named Minnie Louise, was born three years later. Louie, their first son, was born two years after that.

Louie was two years old and Minnie had just turned five when "the strange night" began. All day a wicked storm moved closer and closer to

the Nodolf farm. Near dusk, the blackened clouds loomed directly overhead and the wind increased to gale proportions.

Carl and Louise tucked their two children into an upstairs bedroom,
then securely locked each bedroom window shutter. Downstairs, Carl
slid the shoulder-high bar across each outside door. They shuttered each
window tightly against the storm.

Still they hesitated to go to bed. Lightning ricocheted across the
night sky. The wind howled more like a November blizzard than a June
thunderstorm. An occasional wolf howled near the house. Too near, Louise
thought.

Shortly after midnight, Carl finally decided the house was secure, and,
with Louise leading the way up the stairs with the lantern, they checked on
the children and tucked the blankets around their shoulders. Only then
were they ready to retire for the night.

A few hours later, a deafening explosion of thunder awoke Louise. At
the same instant, she heard little Minnie's voice crying for help. Louise
quickly lit the lantern and ran into the children's bedroom.

The beds were empty.

By this time Carl was at his wife's side. Together they searched.

"Carl, they must have become frightened and gone downstairs," said
Louisa.

The couple called for the children as they rushed down the stairs. No
voices answered. When they reached the front room, they stopped, straining
to hear.

Between the cracks of thunder and pounding wind, they heard faint
voices—coming from outside the house.

Carl threw off the heavy bar securing the door and swung it open. On
the steps, shivering in their nightwear, stood Minnie and Louie. Carl
scooped them up in his muscular arms.

"Wrap them up," said Louise. "I'll get their dry . . ."

Her husband stopped her.

"Louise, you don't have to get dry clothes. The children aren't wet!"

Despite the heavy downpour, battering even now against the stone-
wall exterior, neither Minnie nor Louie had as much as a drop of rain on
them. It was as if they had been standing in some invisible shell on the

doorstep of the house. Handing the children to Louise, Carl checked each shuttered and locked window and the bolted doors. All were secured from the inside.

"How did they get out there? That is not possible," said Carl, shaking his head.

When their parents asked them what happened, neither child could answer. Stuttering badly, they tried to recall the last few hours but could not. The children stuttered for the rest of their lives, the only two of the eight Nodolf children to do so.

Friends and neighbors offered many theories to explain the strange evening.

Perhaps one of the parents was a sleepwalker and picked up the children and put them outside while under the influence of some strange dream.

Others with more vivid imaginations suggested that gypsies, known to frequent that neighborhood, broke into the house, snatched the children, and then were scared away, leaving the youngsters to be found on the front doorstep. But that does not explain why the doors and windows were still locked from inside. Or their dry clothing.

For decades after the incident, scores of curious visitors found the old stone house, crumbling and vacant, standing forlornly at the base of the mound. They sometimes paused as they crossed the expansive lawn, perhaps in the shade of one of the towering oaks, and wondered: What really happened on that strange night so very long ago? There did not seem to be a rational explanation.

The Nodolfs have not been forgotten.

A choral composition based on the episode and written by Wisconsin composer Heidi Joosten had its world premiere in Platteville on October 26, 2015. With funding from the Wisconsin Arts Board and the Platteville Community Fund, Joosten was the composer-in-residence for the public schools' sixth through twelfth grade choirs. Over 160 vocalists and musicians performed the composition at school assemblies, and for the general public.

Joosten titled her work "The Strange Night."

Indeed. And not one to be forgotten.

Return of the Hanged Man

Mineral Point

The Walker House in Mineral Point is one of Wisconsin's oldest inns. With exterior stone in its walls dating to the 1830s, the solidly handsome, three-story building, with its newer two-story addition at one end, has a decidedly early American frontier elegance.

Tucked into a hillside that was among those producing the lead ore once mined in the region from the 1820s, the Walker House could have been a nobleman's hunting lodge transplanted to Wisconsin. Inside, massive stone fireplaces and heavy, rough-hewn beams, with tree bark still on them, gave character to the original ceilings of the main-floor rooms. A massive bar and walls adorned with hunting trophies dominate an upstairs tavern.

From its very earliest years, the Walker House did a brisk business. Wisconsin's territorial officers were sworn in at Mineral Point, and the little village teemed with politicians traveling between the state's temporary capital at nearby Belmont and their home communities. Cornish miners, frontiersmen, and speculators poured into town, eager for the riches that the lead and zinc deposits promised. At night, the men crowded into the village bars and lodgings, including the Walker House, jostling one another for drink, food, and perhaps a bed for the night.

But on the morning of November 1, 1842, a "customer" of a different kind patronized the Walker House. He was a murderer who would hang later that day from a scaffold erected in front of the inn. His name was William Caffee and he had been convicted of shooting and killing a man during an argument in the community of Gratiot several months before.

A crowd some estimated at over four thousand turned out for the execution. Men crowded the narrow streets and mothers with children and picnic baskets camped on the hills ringing the town, all jostling for a view of the condemned man swinging from a rope. That was not usual "entertainment" on the rough American frontier.

The execution was a macabre affair from some reports. Caffee sat astride his casket and beat out the rhythm of a funeral march with two empty beer bottles. Such a carefree and contemptuous attitude toward his own death brought him a sort of posthumous fame, even in this rough and tumble mining region. No one who witnessed his execution would ever forget him.

Just to make sure his memory would be preserved in this place where he so nonchalantly met death, Caffee is alleged by some to have settled into the Walker House as a ghost. If true, the Walker House would be one of the oldest haunted buildings in the United States.

The ghostly appearances attributed to William Caffee became widely known to the public sometime after 1964. In that year, Ted Landon and several partners bought the old inn. It had closed its doors and stood vacant for seven years, ruined by neglect and vandalism. Landon, an Iowa County social worker and local artist, could not bear to witness further destruction of the historic building. He and his associates wanted to transform and restore the Walker House into a restaurant and perhaps a bed and breakfast.

Landon's restoration was extensive. He hired crews of young people to dig out dead trees, replace some eight hundred window panes, and build a massive fireplace of native stone in what they called the Pub. Oak planks from an abandoned barn became the Pub's walls. It took several years, but in time one dining room had been refurbished, and the Walker House opened for business, serving Cornish-style luncheons and dinners to honor the region's original settlers from Cornwall. The next year, another dining room was opened, and in 1974, a second-floor tavern was ready for guests.

In 1978 Landon and his partners sold the Walker House to David F. Ruf, a medical doctor from Darlington, Wisconsin.

At the time Ruf took over, a student from Madison was living in a second-floor apartment at one end of the building, above the office.

What happened to him may have been the first incidence of a possible haunting.

The student complained the doorknob would turn this way and that at night. He heard other unidentifiable noises that did not seem "natural." After countless sleepless nights, he moved out.

Walker Calvert understood the student's fear. Calvert, a distant relative of the inn's early owner, had been hired by Ruf as a manager and chef, and almost immediately he began to witness curious incidents.

In the main dining room, adjoining the office, a small wooden door covered a rectangular, floor-level opening concealing water pipes. When it was removed, one could peer inside straight up to the second floor. One day Calvert said he saw the door slide along the wall and drop down a few inches to the floor. He said it was just like someone had taken it in hand and slid it across the floor, out of the way. He saw that happen several times, as did a few of the waitresses on staff.

The main dining room presented its own head-scratching incidents.

On three different occasions, Calvert said he found himself talking to someone only to find that no one was there.

"I didn't know I wasn't talking to a real person," said Calvert.

In the kitchen, the banging and clanking of pots and pans sometimes created a din, except that no pans were being used at the time.

One of the older staff members became so frightened she refused to work alone in the kitchen. Calvert understood.

"When I was in there, I thought someone was following me around," he said.

Several of the waitresses told Calvert they would fix drinks, turn around, and seem to bump into something solid, like a person, but no one was ever there. At other times a sort of white haze floated in the air across the room.

One waitress had been particularly outspoken in her disbelief of the ghost stories. Soon after, while she was in the kitchen, something grabbed her ponytail and pulled it straight up into the air.

"Get away!" she screamed.

Her ponytail remained upright a moment, dropped limply to her back, then suddenly shot straight up again.

Other female customers also related that they felt their hair being lifted or stroked when no one else was around.

The ghost was always acting up, Calvert said. It was as if he tried to prove to everyone that he was there.

Things like heavy breathing and footsteps scared a number of employees. On one occasion, a bartender cleaning in a secondfloor barroom stooped to check his supply of glasses in a lower cupboard. Hearing heavy breathing, he froze. He thought he knew who it was.

"Leave me alone!" he yelled.

As he straightened up, gripping the edge of the counter, the breathing become shallower, and then the bartender heard what seemed to be someone walking away across the squeaky floorboards.

On a December morning just before the place closed for the winter season, Calvert was working alone in his office. He heard someone walking across the hardwood floors outside his open office door. The footfalls stopped at the doorway. He turned to see who it was.

"All I heard was a deep groan. I ran out [because] it scared me to death."

Calvert said whenever he was alone in the restaurant it was like the ghost wanted to let him know it was there, too. But then once he reacted, the ghost would leave him alone.

The ghost of William Caffee—if that is indeed who was responsible for these oddities—developed quite an affinity for doors and locks. Several times, either in early morning or late at night, someone might hear keys jiggling in the front-door lock. Or a door that was unlocked would suddenly be found locked.

Calvert said sometimes when he or the waitresses were ready to leave for the night, they found the outside door locked—from the inside. That particular door used a deadbolt locking system with a key that only Calvert possessed.

The ghost did his best to scare people away, Calvert believed. It was as if he resented crowds of people. Considering William Caffee was executed in front of a crowd of thousands, it might be understandable if he resented large gatherings.

Walker Calvert and his wife and comanager, Linda, were inside one spring day preparing to open for the season. One of the entrances has outside and inside doors, creating a small airlock vestibule between them. The outside door was seldom used and always kept locked. The interior one had been sealed in plastic to keep out drafts. When Calvert removed the plastic and Linda opened the door, a voice called out, "Hello!" Linda jumped back, startled.

Curiously, Calvert did not see an actual *something* that could have been the ghost until several years after he started working there.

Just before sunset on a crisp October evening, Calvert went upstairs to check the door that opened from the far end of a second-story bar onto a wide porch. The porch contained an L-shaped wooden bench and an attractive tree that grew up through a hole in the floor. An exterior wooden stairway led up to the porch from ground level.

As Calvert opened the door to the porch, he noticed what looked to be a person sitting on the porch bench barely two feet away, attired in a gray miner's jacket and denim pants. But Calvert says he knew immediately the man was not real—because he had no head. A black felt hat rested directly on his shoulders.

Calvert said the clothes were old, rumpled, and dusty, but not ill-fitting. His body was turned to face Calvert.

"I didn't reach out to try and touch him," said Calvert. "I didn't want to get that close!"

He put the key in the lock and closed the door. When he looked back at the bench, it was empty.

Surprisingly, Calvert was not in the least upset by this encounter. "I'd had so many connections with him that I didn't think much of it," he said.

He had been told the ghosts of hanging victims might appear as headless apparitions. He assumed the ghost was that of William Caffee.

The same week that Calvert saw the man on the porch, a waitress saw the ghost of a younger man in the second-floor barroom, adjacent to the porch. This one had a head. He stood by the bar for a moment, then vanished.

To Walker Calvert's knowledge, the ghost of William Caffee never harmed anyone, nor was he a threat to the Walker House. He did not smash dishes or try to set fire to the place. The ghost did get irritated, however, by those large crowds. Caffee's last earthly sight, of course, was the raucous throng pushing against the scaffold, eager to see him swing. Caffee had been brandishing beer bottles just before he mounted the scaffold for his early afternoon hanging. Could that account for the beer bottles that sometimes flew into the air and crashed to the floor during busy lunch hours at the restaurant? Calvert wondered about that.

Caffee's ghost was certainly prankish, and, at times, downright frightening to someone startled by his sudden presence. Yet perhaps he was only trying to be "helpful," rattling pans in the kitchen, checking out the bar, and helping to lock up at night. The ghost may have wanted to do nothing more than to look over the books on the morning the ghost surprised Calvert in the office. It is not always possible to predict a ghost's wishes.

Before he went to work at the Walker House, Calvert scoffed at the supernatural.

"Now it's all possible."

Current owners of the Walker House acknowledge that the paranormal is a part of the history of the building but term the stories isolated "anecdotes." They say that over the years numerous psychics, ghost hunters, and researchers have searched for evidence of the paranormal but with little or no success. Video and audio equipment have not detected anything that could be identified as a "presence." People who have lived for several years in the Walker House say they have never encountered William Caffee or any other ghostly being.

A Mother's Plea

Southwestern Wisconsin

The bond between a mother and her child is often beyond comprehension — a slight, unexpected stirring from the baby's nursery can awaken her from deepest slumber, a kind of sixth sense warning her of imminent danger to her child. But does that sense of peril end at what is taken by most of us to be death?

In the nineteenth and early twentieth centuries, cholera was a terrifying disease, a nearly always fatal intestinal infection that swept across various regions of the United States, leaving thousands dead in its wake. No one was exempt. Not until well into the twentieth century were cholera epidemics brought under control; even today the word "cholera" evokes images of slow, agonizing death, sometimes coming within hours of a diagnosis if it is left untreated.

The story of little five-year-old Maxie Hoffman's reprieve from "the yellow death," as it was called, is one of the most amazing such tales to have emerged during this time, albeit one that is nearly impossible to verify.

Maxie lived with his parents, brothers, and sisters on a small Wisconsin farm in the mid-nineteenth century. Shortly after his fifth birthday, he contracted cholera. The doctor looked in on him, but he knew little about the disease and even less about its treatment. All he could do was make the child comfortable and offer his sympathies to the family. And, he added, pray that no one else in the family contracted the disease.

Maxie died three days later. The doctor ordered that the child be buried immediately to help prevent the cholera from spreading any further.

His small body was placed in a simple pine coffin. His father used part of the family's savings to buy silver handles for the casket. Maxie was buried in the country cemetery.

On the night following his death, Mrs. Hoffman awoke wild-eyed, screaming in panic. Her husband reached out to console her as she sobbed out the nightmarish scene that had been more vivid than life.

"It was Maxie . . . in his coffin. But dear God, he was alive!"

She collapsed in her husband's arms.

"He . . . he was trying to get out. I saw him. His hands were under his right cheek. He was twisted. Oh! He's alive . . . I know it! We must go to him!"

Mr. Hoffman said he understood. The agony had been great for both of them. As the "baby" in the family, Maxie held a special place in their hearts.

Mrs. Hoffman's dream reappeared the next night.

The details were the same as the night before. Maxie lay twisted in his coffin, one tiny hand clenched tightly under his head.

This time, Mr. Hoffman acquiesced, reluctantly agreeing to her pleadings. He sent his eldest child to a neighbor's house for help. Together the men would exhume Maxie's body. Mr. Hoffman believed this was the only way to persuade his wife that her son had indeed passed away, as horrifying as the experience would be.

It was well past one o'clock in the morning when the Hoffmans' neighbor held the lantern high as they raised Maxie's coffin from the freshly dug earth. Mrs. Hoffman huddled close with two of the older children as her husband pried off the top.

A gasp arose nearly simultaneously from everyone's lips.

Maxie's body was twisted onto his right side, a hand clenched under his cheek.

Just as his mother had dreamed.

Although the child showed no outward signs of life, Mr. Hoffman scooped up the boy's still form, placed it gently into the buckboard, and drove through the night to the same doctor who had pronounced Maxie dead only days earlier.

After answering the pounding at his door, the physician drew back quickly from Mr. Hoffman when he saw Maxie cradled in his arms. Reluctantly, but at the family's insistence, the doctor tried to revive the child, if only to please the distraught mother. He detected something, an unnatural warmth in the frail body, perhaps, that caused him to continue his efforts.

The minutes passed. At last, nearly an hour after the doctor first began, Maxie's eyelids fluttered open. Everyone huddled around, almost afraid to hope, while the doctor coaxed some brandy down the child's throat, then placed heated salt bags under Maxie's arms, a common restorative in those days.

Within the week, Maxie Hoffman, healthy and normal as ever, played cheerily with his brothers and sisters. He would remember nothing of his own premature "death."

Is there an explanation? We can only guess that Maxie was one of those rare medical cases in which an individual showing no apparent signs of life has been pronounced dead only to revive later. In the nineteenth century, the technology for assessing the presence of life was limited to the doctor's stethoscope or intuition. The child was fortunate indeed. His mother's dream saved him from death after burial.

Maxie Hoffman lived a long life until his death at the age of eighty-five in Clinton, Iowa. The silver handles from his first coffin always held a place of prominence on the fireplace mantel in his home.

The Psychic Detective

Milwaukee

There is no reliable evidence, of course, that the fictional Sherlock Holmes, the master of Victorian detection, ever visited America, let alone Milwaukee. More's the pity, for Holmes, and his creator, Arthur Conan Doyle, missed the opportunity to meet a man of that city whose abilities to solve seemingly impenetrable crimes were said to have nearly matched Holmes's own.

Or did they?

Arthur Price Roberts, known as "Doc" or "The Professor" to his friends, was a psychic detective. Like Holmes, Doc Roberts was called on by authorities and private clients to help unravel intricate crimes or to find lost possessions. But unlike Holmes, who solved his puzzling cases through the powers of observation and deduction, Roberts claimed to use his own mysterious "psychic powers."

Doc Roberts was born in Denbigh, Wales, in 1866. He immigrated to this country as a young boy, settling first with an uncle in Fox Lake, Wisconsin. As a teenager, he headed for Blanchard, North Dakota, and took a job herding cattle. There, he once said, he first became aware of his psychic powers. Roberts claimed that a man named Wild lost some money and Roberts found it. He said that he "saw" a picture in his mind's eye of its hiding place.

Incredibly, Roberts remained nearly illiterate all his life. He feared an education would destroy his psychic abilities.

Doc Roberts rose to fame in the late nineteenth century and continued his celebrated career for over forty years. Most of his psychic puzzlesolving took place in Wisconsin, although he occasionally was called upon to solve cases elsewhere in the United States.

Roberts did possess one of Sherlock Holmes's more startling traits—the ability to correctly surmise a person's background, current difficulties, and other personal information through mere observation. In 1905, for instance, he took on the case of Duncan McGregor, a Peshtigo, Wisconsin, man who had been missing for a number of months. His distraught wife sought Roberts out when authorities reached a dead end in their investigation.

Mrs. McGregor said later that when she visited Roberts, he met her at the door to his home and proceeded to accurately identify her and the cause of her distress. There is no evidence that Roberts either knew of the case or had ever seen the woman before.

He concluded that first, brief meeting by saying that he could not help her at that moment. But, he added, she should come back in a few hours after he had some time to concentrate on the case.

Roberts took an unusual step for him and went into a sort of trance. Normally, when asked to put his abilities to work, he received a mental picture immediately.

The trance apparently worked.

Mrs. McGregor returned early that evening. Gently, Roberts revealed that her husband had been murdered, but he could not identify the individuals responsible.

"The testimony I could give would not be admissible in court," he apologized. He told her that the body of her husband was in the Menomonee River near Milwaukee, snarled in some sunken logs that prevented it from rising to the surface.

Mrs. McGregor alerted police, who dragged the river at the location Roberts specified. They found McGregor's body. His clothing had become entangled in sunken logs on the river bottom.

Geography did not constrain Doc Roberts's psychic senses.

In one of his more dramatic cases, he found the body of a missing man in Arizona without ever leaving his Milwaukee home.

In this case, wealthy Chicago financier J. D. Leroy sought out Roberts after his brother vanished on a trip to the American Southwest six months earlier. The police did not have a clue as to the man's whereabouts.

Doc Roberts disclosed that the man had been murdered and his body dumped in a place called Devil's Canyon in Arizona. He then described for J. D. Leroy the area in which his brother's remains would be found.

A few weeks later, Roberts received a letter from Leroy. Police had found his brother's corpse in Devil's Canyon, only a few hundred feet from the very scene Roberts described. The body bore signs of foul play.

In yet another case, Roberts allegedly tracked a murder suspect to Canada without leaving his home state. He was visiting Fond du Lac when police in that city approached him for help on an old, unsolved murder case. Their search for a suspect had been stymied.

Roberts listened carefully to their story, then held up his hand for silence. He proceeded to describe the murder victim in detail. Although the police were amazed, the cynics still were not satisfied. They claimed Roberts really had not revealed anything that could not have been obtained from published accounts of the crime.

But what happened the next morning surprised everyone. Doc walked into police headquarters and asked to look through their mug shots of known criminals. He sat for several hours scanning the faces as he slowly turned the pages. At last he called detectives over and placed his finger on the picture of one man, known to officers as a petty criminal.

"That's your killer, gentlemen!" he exclaimed. He said police could find him in Canada—working for the Royal Canadian Mounted Police.

Fond du Lac police notified their Canadian brethren of the man's name and description and said he was wanted for murder. Sure enough, the Canadians found him, working for the Mounties. He confessed to the Fond du Lac murder.

In another dramatic case, Doc Roberts claimed to have saved a man from the electric chair. The family of Chicagoan Ignatz Potz asked Doc for help while Potz was awaiting execution after being convicted of first degree murder. He claimed that, although he was present at the killing, he took no part in it.

Roberts went to work and uncovered evidence supporting Potz's claims. The death sentence was commuted to life imprisonment.

Roberts made more headlines in the mid-1920s in two separate crime investigations.

He was consulted by Northwestern National Bank officials following a bank robbery. Based on a séance Roberts held, a suspect was identified and arrested. However, the man was later acquitted for lack of admissible evidence.

One of Wisconsin's most famous murder mysteries also involved Roberts. The body of Clara Olson was found in a shallow grave near Mt. Sterling, in Crawford County, on December 2, 1926. After her husband, Erdman Olson, became the prime suspect in the murder, he dropped out of sight. Doc Roberts predicted that Erdman would never be found alive. He was not and the case remains unsolved. Roberts apparently was not able to "picture" the culprit.

Roberts's crowning achievement came in the months of October and November 1935 when Milwaukee was rocked by a series of terrorist bombings that held the city in their grip for over a week. Roberts allegedly predicted not only the bombings but the final horrific blast, which proved to be an accidental detonation caused by the bomb makers.

The extraordinary episode began on October 18, 1935, a Friday afternoon. Roberts told a group of acquaintances that the city would experience several bombings in the very near future. His audience wanted desperately not to believe this awful prediction, but they were too familiar with Roberts's uncanny accuracy to dismiss his words. It is not clear if anyone considered informing the police.

On Saturday night, October 26, the Shorewood Village Hall was dynamited at 7:23 p.m. The estimated five sticks of dynamite ripped a hole in the building's foundation and splintered a tall, white column. The explosion was felt for blocks around with windows blown out in scores of homes and offices. The resulting fire consumed what remained of the village offices at 3930 North Murray Avenue.

Less than twenty-four hours later, investigators had no more than just begun their investigation when two more explosions shook the city. This time the targets of dynamite bombs were two branch offices of the First Wisconsin National Bank. At 6:40 p.m., October 27, a hole was blown in the rear wall of the bank branch offices at 3602 North Villard. Damage was limited to the back wall and many shattered windows.

Forty minutes later, the east side office of the First Wisconsin National Bank at North Farwell and East North Avenue was targeted.

There was no major damage to the bank, although eight cars in a parking lot were demolished. In both of the bank explosions, witnesses saw the suspects flee in a small, gray motor car.

By this time, Milwaukee realized a reign of terror might have been set loose on the city. Dozens of federal, state, and local investigators converged on the explosion sites.

So far, there had been no serious injuries, but officials feared that in the next bombing they might not be so fortunate.

Guards were posted at all governmental and bank buildings since these seemed to be the chosen targets. Investigators theorized that the bombers may have mistaken the Shorewood City Hall for a bank building.

The city was fearful and on edge as the following week passed uneventfully. Police determined that the dynamite in the early explosions had been stolen from a Works Project Administration work site several weeks earlier. One hundred and fifty pounds of explosives had been taken, along with four hundred fifty fuse caps and two hundred feet of fuse. Authorities were now even more concerned. That much dynamite could cause massive destruction.

The terrorists struck again on Thursday, hitting two police substations. Once again, good fortune limited the damage to the buildings with no personal injuries.

So far, Arthur Price Roberts had been proven correct. Police knew that and, in desperation, turned to him for "advice." He told them the last explosion would come on Sunday, November 3, somewhere south of the Menomonee River.

Could he identify the criminals?

No.

Did he know precisely where the explosion would occur?

No.

Regretfully, that was all the information he could "see."

That Sunday an army of police officers flooded the city south of the river. Sharpshooters kept watch from rooftops. Every officer was told to shoot first and ask questions later. As the countdown to Roberts's predicted catastrophe began, all suspicious persons were stopped and questioned and abandoned buildings searched.

Somehow the police missed the old shed behind a house at 2121 West Mitchell Street.

Inside, two young men with long petty-crime records hunched over a potentially deadly arrangement of dynamite and fuse caps. They were concocting their "final surprise" for Milwaukee.

Then something went terribly wrong for them.

Whether the youthful bombers incorrectly set a timing device or just grew careless no one knows for certain. But at 2:40 p.m. on Sunday, November 3, 1935, an estimated forty sticks of dynamite exploded in that shed, leaving only a gaping hole in the earth, charred rubble, and smoking timbers.

The two men inside were Isador Rutkowski, twenty, and Paul Chovenee, sixteen. They were blown to bits. Tragically, there was the first innocent human casualty in this final blast. Little nine-year-old Patricia Mylanarek, of 2117-B West Mitchell, was playing in her second-story bedroom, overlooking the makeshift bomb factory, when it exploded. The blast collapsed her bedroom walls on top of her.

At least ten other persons were injured, the fronts of buildings were blown out for a hundred yards around the shed, and windows were knocked out of houses for several more blocks around. One witness said the area looked like a war zone.

Rutkowski, the apparent ringleader, was an unemployed auto mechanic with a police record. He was identified when cops found his head leaning against a garage thirty feet away. A later investigation showed he had some imagined grievances against bankers.

Chovenee's death was not discovered until the next day when his father reported him missing, saying he had last seen him with Rutkowski. His father identified swatches of his son's hair and scalp, along with the remnants of a blue jacket. Police surmised Chovenee was likely an easily duped sycophant, merely following the older boy's criminal plan.

An additional two boxes of dynamite were found intact in the building rubble, miraculously surviving the massive destruction. Police said that had they exploded, the results would have been even more catastrophic.

The deaths of Rutkowski and Chovenee ended the bombing terror in Milwaukee. Investigators were unanimous in their opinion that Rutkowski and Chovenee had been preparing another bomb when it accidentally exploded. Doc Roberts's premonition was accurate, even down to the final accidental bombing that would end the fear gripping the city.

Doc Roberts was probably frightened on occasion by the future he "saw." Would that have extended to his own intimations of mortality?

It is said—but lightly documented—that a small dinner party was given in his honor in November 1939. He told the gathering how very pleased he was with the tribute and proceeded to reminisce about his own incredible life-solving mysteries. He was elderly now and though he seemed to be in good health, his psychic senses told him otherwise. Or perhaps he had a terminal illness that only he knew about.

As the group planned for their next dinner together after the New Year, Roberts expressed his regrets. "I won't be with you beyond January 2, 1940," he confided with a tinge of sorrow.

Less than two months later, on the morning of Tuesday, January 2, 1940, Arthur Price Roberts died peacefully in his sleep at the age of seventy-three. His *Milwaukee Journal* obituary noted that he had been ill for two months. He is buried in Milwaukee's Wanderers Rest Cemetery. The secrets of his psychic ability—if indeed that is what he used to "solve" the cases— were buried with him.

Selected Bibliography

Illinois

Books

Allen, John W. *Legends and Lore of Southern Illinois.* Carbondale: Southern Illinois University Press, 1963.

Brandon, Jim. *Weird America.* New York: E. P. Dutton, 1978.

Bruce, H. Addington. *Historic Ghosts and Ghost Hunters.* New York: Moffat, Yard, & Co., 1908.

Dorson, Richard M. *Buying the Wind: Regional Folklore in the United States.* Chicago: University of Chicago Press, 1964.

Drake, S. A. *Myths and Fables of To-day.* Boston: Lee and Shepard, 1900.

Gaddis, Vincent H. *Mysterious Fires and Lights.* New York: David McKay, 1967.

Hintze, Naomi A., and J. Gaither Pratt. *The Psychic Realm: What Can You Believe?* New York: Random House, 1975.

Holzer, Hans. *Psychic Investigator.* New York: Hawthorn Books, 1968.

Illinois: A Descriptive and Historical Guide. American Guide Series. Chicago: A. C. McClurg and Co., 1939.

Lamon, Ward Hill. *Recollections of Abraham Lincoln, 1847–1865.* Chicago: A. C. McClurg and Co., 1895.

Lindley, Charles, Viscount Halifax. *Lord Halifax's Ghost Book.* New York: Didier, 1944.

Murphy, Gardner, and Robert O. Ballou, compilers and eds. *William James on Psychical Research.* New York: Viking Press, 1960.

Rogo, D. Scott. *The Poltergeist Experience.* New York: Penguin Books, 1979.

Sibley, Mulford Q. *Life after Death?* Minneapolis: Dillon Press, 1975.

Smith, Susy. *The Enigma of Out-of-Body Travel.* New York: Helix Press, 1965.

Smith, Warren. *Strange Hexes*. New York: Popular Library, 1970.

Strange Stories, Amazing Facts: Stories That Are Bizarre, Unusual, Odd, Astonishing, and Often Incredible. Pleasantville, NY: Reader's Digest Association, 1976.

Tyrrell, G. H. M. *Apparitions*. Rev. Ed. New York: Collier Books, 1963.

Walker, Danton. *I Believe in Ghosts*. New York: Taplinger, 1969.

Winer, Richard. *Houses of Horror*. New York: Bantam Books, 1983.

Winer, Richard, and Nancy Osborn. *Haunted Houses*. New York: Bantam Books, 1979.

Winer, Richard, and Nancy Osborn Ishmael. *More Haunted Houses*. New York: Bantam Books, 1981.

Periodicals

Biederman, Pat. "Spirit Abounds in Town of Mediums." *USA Today*, June 2, 1983.

Burkholder, Alex A. "April's Hand of Death." *Firehouse* magazine, April 1983.

Geist, Bill. "Resurrection Mary." *U.S. Catholic*, August 1979.

"Groans, Forms Haunt Slave House's Attic." *Rockford Register Star*, October 9, 1977.

Hahn, Andrew. "Report Challenges 'Old Slave House' Legend." *Southern Illinois University News*, July 30, 2015. http://news.siu.edu/2015/07/073015amh15084.php.

Harris, Jesse, and Julia Neely. "Southern Illinois Phantoms and Bogies." *Midwest Folklore* 1, no. 3 (Fall 1951): 171–78.

"'Haunted' House Conquered by TV Announcer." *Commercial Appeal* (Memphis, TN), November 1, 1978.

Holleran, Scott. "Lake Forest: A History." *Daily North Shore*, November 22, 2015.

Hudson Star-Times (Hudson, WI), February 18, 1870.

Kellman, John. "Death, Darkness and Lies." *Chicago Tribune*, October 28, 2010.

———. "Nearly a Century after Girl's Death, Questions—and Maybe a Ghost—Haunt Lake Forest." *Chicago Tribune*, October 27, 2010.

———. "A Verdict, But Not the End." *Chicago Tribune*, October 31, 2010.

Lawton, Mark. "A Century Later, Lake Forest Murder Trial Still Fascinates." *Lake Forester*, July 13, 2016.

Parker, Molly. "Future of Crenshaw House, or Old Slave House, in Question." *Southern Illinoisan*, February 21, 2016.

Patton, Florence. "Girl in Orpet Case Called 'Ophelia.'" *Los Angeles Herald*, July 1, 1916.

"Peculiar Experiences Connected with Noted Persons (Apparition of the Dead Two Years before the Death of the Percipient)." *Journal of the American Society for Psychical Research* 15 (1921).

Swarbrick, Fran. "He Spent Night, But Was He Alone?" *Rockford Register Star*, November 1, 1978.

Taylor, Troy. "The Girl in the Snow: The Haunting Story of Marion Lambert." *American Hauntings* (blog), February 10, 2013. http://troytaylorbooks.blog spot.com/2013/02/the-girl-in-snow.html.

Unpublished Works

Federal Writers' Project Manuscripts for the Works Progress Administration for the State of Illinois.

Indiana University Folklore Archives, Bloomington.

Indiana

Books

Anderson, Jean. *The Haunting of America*. Boston: Houghton Mifflin, 1973.

Brandon, Jim. *Weird America*. New York: E. P. Dutton, 1978.

Edwards, Frank. *Strangest of All*. New York: Citadel Press, 1956.

Edwards, Janet Zenke. *Diana of the Dunes: The True Story of Alice Gray*. Charleston, SC: History Press, 2010.

Ellis, Edward S. *The History of Our Country from the Discovery of America to the Present Time*. Vol. 3. Cincinnati: Jones Brothers, 1918.

Gaddis, Vincent H. *Mysterious Fires and Lights*. New York: David McKay, 1967.

Historical Hannah House. Undated brochure, no publisher given.

Indiana: A Guide to the Hoosier State. New York: Oxford University Press, 1941.

Keel, John A. *Our Haunted Planet*. Greenwich, CT: Fawcett Publications, 1971.

Norman, Michael, and Beth Scott. *Haunted Heritage*. New York: Tor, 2002.

Scott, Beth, and Michael Norman. *Haunted America*. New York: Tor, 1994.

Smith, Susy. *Life Is Forever*. New York: G. P. Putnam's Sons, 1974.

Smith, Warren. *Strange Hexes*. New York: Popular Library, 1970.

Stuart, Rory, ed. *The Strange World of Frank Edwards*. Secaucus, NJ: Lyle Stuart, 1977.

Winer, Richard, and Nancy Osborn Ishmael. *More Haunted Houses*. New York: Bantam Books, 1981.

Periodicals

Benzkofer, Stephan. "Quirkier by the Lake." *Chicago Tribune*, July 6, 2014.

Boudreau, George, ed. "Haunted Andrew House?" *Oldletter* (LaPorte County Historical Society) 12 (October 1982).

Clements, William M., and William E. Lightfoot. "The Legend of Stepp Cemetery." *Indiana Folklore* 5, no. 1 (1972): 92–141.

Coffeen, Bob. "Up and Down Town with the Town Crier." *LaPorte Town Crier*, November 6, 1975.

"'Diana of the Dunes' Dies of Privation." *New York Times*, February 10, 1925.

Dits, Joseph. "Learn More about Diana of the Dunes." *South Bend Tribune*, October 25, 2014.

Hall, Steve. "Horrors Haunt Hannah House?" *Indianapolis News*, October 27, 1981.

Heady, Linda. "Forum: The Reader's Corner." *Indianapolis Star*, September 5, 1976.

"Historic Hannah House for Sale." *Indianapolis Star*, February 22, 1981.

Johansen, Marguerite Bell. "Dunes Woman." *Dunes Country Magazine* (Winter 1982).

O'Dell, Vicki L. "The Haunted Bridge." *Indiana History Bulletin* 41 (1965).

Sander, David. "Diana of the Dunes: The Real Story." *Dunes Country Magazine* (Summer 1981).

Spiers, Al. "Diana of the Dunes—Michigan's Original Streaker?" *NewsDispatch* (Michigan City, IN), March 13, 1974.

Unpublished Works

Indiana University Folklore Archives, Bloomington.

Marshall, Lyn. "The Andrew House." LaPorte, Indiana, n.d.

Shelby, Tom. "The Legend of the Francesville Light." Indiana University Folklore Archives, September 23, 1977.

Iowa

Books

Baule, John A. *The Ham House and the Life of Its Builder.* Dubuque County Historical Society, n.d.

Ebon, Martin, ed. *Exorcism: Fact Not Fiction.* New York: New American Library, 1974.

Norman, Michael, and Beth Scott. *Haunted Heritage.* New York: Tor, 2002.

———. *Historic Haunted America.* New York: Tor, 1995.

Periodicals

"The Ghost of Simpson College." *Des Moines Register*, November 8, 1979.

Grant, Donald. "Strange Knocking From Table; Family Prays, Calls Spiritualist." *Des Moines Register*, September 11, 1940.

"A Haunted House." *Weekly Gate City* (Keokuk, IA), August 17, 1899.

Hopson, Julie. "Tales to Make Your Blood Run Cold." *Des Moines Register*, October 31, 1976.

Lackey, Patrick. "Stuart, the Friendly Iowa Ghost." *Des Moines Register*, April 22, 1977.

"Mildred Hedges: The Spirit of College Hall." YouTube video, 8:06. Posted by Simpson College, July 31, 2012. https://www.youtube.com/watch?v=i4mPlNK jxqo.

Monson, Val. "Simpson College Ghost Story." *Des Moines Tribune*, October 30, 1980.

Ryder, T. J. "Spending the Night with 'Spirits.'" *Des Moines Register*, October 31, 1978.

Shanley, Mary Kay. "They Didn't Believe in Ghosts Either." *Des Moines Register*, October 28, 1973.

Worrel, Elaine V. "The Ghost Was a Stranger." *Fate*, April 1972.

Unpublished Works

Conaway, Minnie. "The Great Mystery." Federal Writers' Project manuscript, Decatur, IL, 1936.

Kansas

Books

Harter, Walter. *The Phantom Hand and Other American Hauntings*. Englewood Cliffs, NJ: Prentice-Hall, 1976.

Hollenberg Pony Express Station. Topeka: Kansas State Historical Society, n.d.

Kansas: A Guide to the Sunflower State. American Guide Series. New York: Viking, 1939.

Montgomery, Ruth. *A Search for the Truth*. New York: William Morrow, 1967.

Norman, Michael, and Beth Scott. *Haunted Homeland*. New York: Tor, 2006.

Reid, Chick. "Legend of White Woman Creek." Condensed by Daniel Brown. In *History of Early Greeley County*, vol. 1, *A Story of Its Tracks, Trails, and Tribulations*, 96–97. Tribune, KS: Greeley County Historical Book Committee, 1981.

Smith, Warren. *Strange Hexes*. New York: Popular Library, 1970.

Periodicals

Elmer, Timothy R. "Ghostly Deeds Haunt Ancient Topeka Home." *Topeka Capital-Journal*, October 31, 1981.

Findley, Rowe. "The Pony Express." *National Geographic*, July 1980.

"Franc Shor, 60, Dies; Geographic Editor." *New York Times*, July 16, 1974.

Maxwell, Bob. "Ellis County's Own Ghost (1867–1919–1967?)." *Heritage of Kansas* 3, no. 1 (1975).

"This Ghost Enjoys Tickling Sleepers' Feet." *Des Moines Register*, March 25, 1940.

Unpublished Works

William E. Koch Folklore Collection. Kansas State University, Manhattan.

Michigan

Books

Anderson, Jean. *The Haunting of America*. Boston: Houghton Mifflin, 1973.

Dorson, Richard M. *American Folklore*. Chicago: University of Chicago Press, 1959.

———. *Bloodstoppers and Bearwalkers*. Cambridge, MA: Harvard University Press, 1952.

Hamlin, Marie Caroline Watson. *Legends of Le Detroit*. Detroit: Thorndike Nourse, 1884.

Skinner, Charles M. *Myths and Legends of Our Own Land*. Vol. 2. Philadelphia: J. B. Lippincott, 1896.

Steiger, Brad. *Real Ghosts, Restless Spirits and Haunted Minds*. New York: Award Books, 1968.

Stuart, Rory, ed. *The Strange World of Frank Edwards*. Secaucus, NJ: Lyle Stuart, 1977.

Walker, Danton. *I Believe in Ghosts: True Stories of Some Haunted Celebrities and Their Celebrated Haunts*. New York: Taplinger Publishing, 1969.

Periodicals

Chari, C. T. K. "To the Editor of the Journal" (correspondence). *Journal of the American Society for Psychical Research* 57 (1963): 163–67.

Donahue, James. "Great Lakes Ghost Story." *The Mind of James Donahue* (blog), n.d. http://perdurabo10.tripod.com/ships/id133.html.

Johnston, Nina E. "The Haunted Camp." *Saginaw Daily Courier*, March 6, 1889.

"A Lake Huron Ghost Story." *Sun* (New York), August 20, 1883.

Lewis, Walter. *Maritime History of the Great Lakes* (online archive). http://www.maritimehistoryofthegreatlakes.ca. (Photocopied material from various newspapers and one scrapbook; no headlines; first words cited here. *Buffalo Commercial Appeal*: "The following is taken from the protest . . . ," August 3, 1874; "The wrecking steamer Magnet . . . ," August 5, 1874; "The Coast Wrecking Co. has entered . . . ," August 24, 1874; "The underwriters . . . ," March 16, 1875; "Henry A. Haywood dies in Cleveland," April 4 1906. *Chicago Inter-Ocean*:

"Schooner *Board of Trade* . . . ," December 25, 1874. *Toronto Daily Globe*: "Captain Thomas Fountain is wanted by the underwriters . . . ," August 18, 1875; "About seven o'clock Monday evening . . . ," August 20, 1875; "Captain A. R. Manning of Cleveland . . . ," August 21, 1875; "The barque Chicago Board of Trade . . . ," August 31, 1875; "The J.W. Hall Great Lakes Marine Scrapbook," August 31, 1875; "It was sworn by the defence [*sic*] in the Bark Board of Trade," June 1877.)

Volgenau, Gerald. "Of Things That Go Bump in the Night . . ." *Des Moines Register*, March 4, 1979.

Unpublished Works

Wayne State University Archives, Detroit.

Minnesota

Books

Barnouw, Erik. *The Magician and the Cinema*. New York: Oxford University Press, 1981.

Lamont-Brown, Raymond. *Phantoms of the Theater*. New York: Thomas Nelson, 1977.

Minnesota: A State Guide. American Guide Series. New York: Viking Press, 1938.

Norman, Michael. *The Nearly Departed: Minnesota Ghost Stories and Legends*. St. Paul: Minnesota Historical Society Press, 2009.

Potter, Merle. *101 Best Stories of Minnesota*. Minneapolis: Harrison and Smith, 1931.

Smith, Susy. *The Enigma of Out-of-Body Travel*. New York: Helix Press, 1965.

Periodicals

Gendler, Neal. "A Ghost May Be a Projection of a Living Person Through Telepathy." *Minneapolis Tribune*, October 30, 1977.

Giese, Don, and Bill Farmer. "Elusive Phantom 'Haunts' St. Mary's." *Pioneer Press*, February 24, 1969.

———. "Newsmen Spend Sleepless Night." *Pioneer Press*, February 27, 1969.

———. "What Haunts Summit Avenue Mansion?" *Pioneer Press*, February 6, 1969.

"The Haunting of St. Mary's: Fables and Facts." *Nexus* (St. Mary's College, Winona, MN), October 1967.

Hudson Star-Times (Hudson, WI), March 28, 1873.

Minneapolis Journal, February 6, 1924; February 7, 1924.

Minneapolis Morning Tribune, February 6, 1924; February 7, 1924.

Mulvaney, Maureen. "Legendary Spectre Still Skeleton in SMC Closet." *St. Mary's Cardinal*, October 31, 1979.

"Who's Haunting Our House? Albert Lea Family Wonders." *Minneapolis Tribune*, October 30, 1977.

Unpublished Works

Nelson, Jake. "Forty Years in the Roseau Valley." Roseau County Historical Museum and Interpretive Center, Roseau, MN.

Oral History Tapes. Iron Range Research Center, a division of the Department of Iron Range Resources and Rehabilitation, Chisholm, MN.

Missouri

Books

Anderson, Jean. *The Haunting of America*. Boston: Houghton Mifflin, 1973.

Basler, Lucille. *A Tour of Old Ste. Genevieve*. Ste. Genevieve: Lucille Basler & Wehmeyer Printing Co., 1975.

Brandon, Jim. *Weird America*. New York: E. P. Dutton, 1978.

Collins, Earl A. *Folk Tales of Missouri*. Boston: Christopher Publishing House, 1935.

———. *Legends and Lore of Missouri*. San Antonio: Naylor, 1951.

Fornell, Earl Wesley. *The Unhappy Medium: Spiritualism and the Life of Margaret Fox*. Austin: University of Texas Press, 1964.

Gaddis, Vincent H. *Mysterious Fires and Lights*. New York: David McKay, 1967.

Greenhouse, Herbert B. *In Defense of Ghosts*. New York: Simon and Schuster, 1970.

Heywood, Rosalind. *Beyond the Reach of Sense An Inquiry Into Extra-Sensory Perception*. New York: E. P. Dutton, 1961.

Hintze, Naomi A., and J. Gaither Pratt. *The Psychic Realm: What Can You Believe?* New York: Random House, 1975.

The Hornet Ghost Light: One of Nature's Unexplained Mysteries. Neosho, MO: Neosho Chamber of Commerce, n.d.

Moore, Tom. *Mysterious Tales and Legends of the Ozarks*. Philadelphia: Dorrence & Co., 1938.

Neider, Charles, ed. *The Autobiography of Mark Twain*. New York: Perennial, 1959.

Norman, Michael, and Beth Scott. *Haunted America*. New York: Tor, 1994.

Randolph, Vance. *Ozark Magic and Folklore*. New York: Dover Publications, 1964.

Rayburn, Otto Ernest. *Ozark Country*. New York: Duell, Sloan and Pearce, 1941.

Schurmacher, Emile. *More Strange Unsolved Mysteries*. New York: Paperback Library, 1969.

Sibley, Mulford Q. *Life After Death?* Minneapolis: Dillon Press, 1975.

Skinner, Charles M. *American Myths and Legends*. Philadelphia: J. B. Lippincott, 1903.

Visit Historic Ste. Genevieve. Ste. Genevieve, MO: Tourist Information Center, n.d.

Periodicals

Gannon, Robert. "Balls O'Fire!" *Popular Mechanics*, September 1965.

Goodavage, Joseph F. "Skyquakes, Earthlights, and E.M. Fields." *Analog Science Fiction, Science Fact*, September 1978.

Herbert, Amanda. "Ghostly Alumna Haunts Senior Hall, Seeks Lost Lover Every Year, Story Says." *Stephens Life* (Stephens College, Columbia, MO), October 27, 1977.

Peterson, Charles E. "Rediscovering Old Ste. Genevieve." *Gone West Magazine* 3, no. 2 (Spring 1985).

Rand, Willard C. "Spook Light." *Kansas City Star*, October 21, 1973.

Republican (Springfield, MO), January 5, 1896.

"Ste. Genevieve, a French Legacy in Middle America." *Country Home Magazine*, August 1985.

Unpublished Works

Interview with Kristine Basler, April 1987.

LaZebnick, Jack. *The Ghost of Senior Hall*. An original play written in 1983 to commemorate the sesquicentennial of Stephens College, Columbia, MO.

William E. Koch Folklore Collection. Kansas State University, Manhattan.

Nebraska

Books

Kettelkamp, Larry. *Haunted Houses*. New York: William Morrow & Co., 1969.

Norman, Michael, and Beth Scott. *Haunted Heritage*. New York: Tor, 2002.

Rogo, D. Scott. *Parapsychology: A Century of Inquiry*. New York: Taplinger Publishing, 1975.

Scott, Beth, and Michael Norman. *Haunted America*. New York: Tor, 1994.

Steiger, Brad. *Real Ghosts, Restless Spirits, and Haunted Minds*. New York: Award Books, 1968.

Welsch, Roger L., ed. *A Treasury of Nebraska Pioneer Folklore*. Lincoln: University of Nebraska Press, 1939.

Periodicals

"Ghost Failed to Scream, Upsetting Old Tradition." *New York Times*, October 22, 1933.

Selected Bibliography

Unpublished Works

Federal Writers' Project, Works Projects Administration Collection for the State of Nebraska. Nebraska State Historical Society, Lincoln.

Nelson, Burton. "Account of 'Miss Anna.'" Tape-recorded interview, February 28, 1988, in possession of the author.

Ohio

Books

Anderson, Jean. *The Haunting of America*. Boston: Houghton Mifflin, 1973.

Dorson, Richard M., ed. *Negro Folktales in Michigan*. Cambridge, MA: Harvard University Press, 1956.

Fort, Charles. *The Complete Books of Charles Fort*. New York: Dover Publications, 1974.

Holzer, Hans. *Psychic Investigator*. New York: Hawthorn Books, 1968.

Reynolds, James. *Ghosts in American Houses*. New York: Farrar, Straus, and Cudahy, 1955.

Webb, David K. *Ohio Valley Folk Research Project*. Chillicothe, OH: Ross County Historical Society, n.d.

Winer, Richard, and Nancy Osborn Ishmael. *More Haunted Houses*. New York: Bantam Books, 1981.

Periodicals

Abel, Mary Bilderback. "Ghostly Guests Linger at an Inn in Granville." *Columbus Dispatch Magazine*, June 24, 1979.

Condon, George E. "Ghastly Labor and Ghostly." *Plain Dealer* (Cleveland), September 3, 1963.

"Coroner Checks Bone Discovery." *Plain Dealer* (Cleveland), January 20, 1975.

"Ghost Hunt Yields Bodies." *Plain Dealer* (Cleveland), September 16, 1963.

Dawson, Carol A. "Death Calls for Grandpa." *Fate*, April 1972.

Dolgan, Robert. "Priest Sets Bail Benefit in Castle." *Plain Dealer* (Cleveland), April 13, 1975.

Dorn, Clyde, Susan Marie Berg, and Dave Stephenson. "Beyond Incredible." *Ohio Magazine*, November 1980.

Dreimiller, Barbara. "Franklin Castle's Fright-seeing Tour." *Plain Dealer* (Cleveland), February 28, 1975.

"Ghosts Drive Family from Home." *Leader-Telegram* (Eau Claire, WI), March 10, 1984.

330

"A Ghost Story: An Uneasy Grocer of Cleveland Leaves His Grave and Returns to His Home." *Hudson Star-Times* (Hudson, WI), August 19, 1870.

Henkle, Rae D. "A Native Ghost." *Ohio Magazine* 4 (1908).

"His Home Is His Castle." *Plain Dealer* (Cleveland), June 6, 1978.

"Incidents." *Journal of the American Society for Psychical Research* 2 (1908): 113–17.

Inglis, Beth. "Current Ohio Folklore." *Journal of the Ohio Folklore Society* 1, no. 3 (1972): 46–52.

"Judge Refuses to Order News Source Revealed." *Plain Dealer* (Cleveland), July 23, 1975.

Kaib, Tom. "A Tale for Halloween." *Plain Dealer* (Cleveland), October 28, 1973.

Kay, Leslie. "Old Castle's Present, Past Riddled with Fiction, Fact." *Plain Dealer* (Cleveland), May 11, 1975.

Schwanz, Donald M. "Ghost's Work on Film, Photographer Says." *St. Paul Dispatch*, March 7, 1984.

"Strange Things Happen to Family When Daughter Is in the House." *St. Paul Pioneer Press*, March 9, 1984.

Sweet, Fred. "The House the Ghost Built." *Alumni Bulletin* (Denison University, Granville, OH) 23, no. 9 (May 1932).

Wisconsin

Books

Collections of the Minnesota Historical Society. Vol. 1. St. Paul: Minnesota Historical Society, 1902.

Fiedler, George. *Mineral Point: A History.* Madison: State Historical Society of Wisconsin, 1973.

Skinner, Charles M. *American Myths and Legends.* Philadelphia: J. B. Lippincott, 1903.

Stewart, Jim, and Shirley Stewart. *Easy Going: A Comprehensive Guide to Grant, Iowa, and Lafayette Counties.* Madison: Tamarack Press, 1976.

The Story of Mineral Point, 1827–1941. Compiled by the Workers of the Writers' Program of the Work Projects Administration in the State of Wisconsin, 1941. Mineral Point, WI: Mineral Point Historical Society, 1979.

Stuart, Rory, ed. *The Strange World of Frank Edwards.* Secaucus, NJ: Lyle Stuart, 1977.

Periodicals

"A. P. Roberts, Medium, Dies: 'Psychic Detective' Offered Aid in Crime Investigations; Had Many Clients." *Milwaukee Journal*, January 2, 1940.

Brennwald, James. "Ghost Story Adds Dash of Color to Big Foot Beach." *Beloit News*, April 15, 1981.

"The Ghost of Rosslyne Manse." *Journal of the American Society for Psychical Research* 8 (1924).

"House Haunted in 1830's Still Stands near Mound." *Platteville Journal*, 1974.

Kluever, Michael H. "Ghostly Guest Plagues Owners of Modern Ranch." *Milwaukee Sentinel*, November 1, 1978.

"Platteville Schools' 'The Strange Night' Premieres Monday." *SWNews4U.com*, October 21, 2015. http://www.swnews4u.com/archives/28995/.

———. "Shy Shorewood Ghost." *Milwaukee Journal*, September 11, 1980.

———. "Stepfamily—Who Was That Mysterious Guest?" *Milwaukee Journal*, July 29, 1982.

Unpublished Works

Rohde, Roswell B. Letter to Robert Gard, March 27, 1955. State Historical Society of Wisconsin, Madison. Van Antwerp Folklore Collection. Wisconsin Mss. QW.